THE SECOND BOOK

Concerning
THE THREE PRINCIPLES
OF
THE DIVINE ESSENCE

Of the Eternal, Dark, Light, and Temporary World. Showing What the Soul, the Image and the Spirit of the Soul are; and also what Angels, Heaven, and Paradise are. How *Adam* was before the Fall, in the Fall, and after the Fall.

And

What the Wrath of God, Sin, Death, the Devils and Hell are. How all things have been, now are, and how they shall be at the Last.

TRANSLATED BY
JOHN SPARROW

Jacob Boehme

Volume 1

PREFATORY NOTE

THE kind reception accorded by the public to my recent issue of the *Threefold Life of Man* has enabled me to proceed further with the proposed reprint of the complete works of Jacob Boehme, and I trust the present volume will be received with equal favour. If such be the case, I propose to issue next the *Forty Questions of the Soul*, together with the *Clavis*. For the prospectus giving a list of these questions, and stating the subscription price of the volume, etc., applications should be sent to the undersigned, or to the publisher.

A complete list of Boehme's writings will be found in the *Threefold Life*, Appendix A. I regret to say that, in correcting the proofs of that Appendix, I inadvertently allowed it to appear that the *Three Principles* was written in the same year as the *Aurora*. The former belongs to 1618–19, the latter to 1612.

The Introduction to this volume is a translation, by my friend Mrs D. S. Hehner, of the paper on *Jacob Boehme: His Life and Philosophy*, by Professor Deussen, who has kindly allowed me to use it in the present work. To both author and translator I desire to offer my most cordial thanks.

C. J. BARKER.

HILL CROFT, RUSSELL HILL,
  PURLEY, SURREY,
    January 1910.

The Second Book.

CONCERNING

The Three Principles

OF

The Divine Eſſence

Of the Eternal, Dark, Light,
and Temporary World.

SHEWING

What the Soul, the Image and the
Spirit of the Soul are; as alſo what Angels,
Heaven, and Paradise are.

How *Adam* was before the Fall, in the Fall,
and after the Fall.

AND

What the Wrath of God, Sin, Death, the Devils
and Hell are; How all things have been, now are,
and how they shall be at the Last.

Written in the German Language
by
Jacob Behmen;
Alias Teutonicus Philoſophus

LONDON;
Printed by *M.S.* for *H. Blunden* at the Castle
in *Cornhill.* 1 6 4 8.

TO THE READER

SINCE the publishing of this author's *Forty Questions* in English, the minds of several persons have had divers thoughts concerning his writings, and yet have been of searching apprehensions. I would they were well acquainted with his writings, and then they would not only be able to find out the truth in their own thoughts, but also in the written words of him and others, as in the Articles and Confessions of Faith, or any other writings. And it may be, these thoughts they have, though they be true, if rightly understood, yet if they may perhaps be misapprehended, they may hinder themselves of inestimable eternal benefit.

Some have complained of the hardness to understand his writings, and therefore I have endeavoured the Englishing of this book of the *Three Principles*, which, the author saith, is the *A, B, C* to all his writings; and if they read it carefully, they will find it, though hard at first, easy at last, and then all his other books easy, and full of deep understanding. A man cannot conceive the wonderful knowledge before he hath read this book throughly and diligently, which he will find to be contained in it, when he is weighing and deliberating upon the matter as he readeth, and that without hard study, for it will rise in the mind of itself, with a ravishing sweetness and content. And he will find that the *Threefold Life* is tenfold deeper than this, and the *Forty Questions* to be tenfold deeper than that, and that to be as deep as a spirit is in itself, as the author saith ; than which there can be no greater depth, for God himself is a spirit.

And accordingly there appear some glimpses of the most deep, mystical, oriental learning here and there, which is not discovered in any books, and therefore some of the learned men of *Europe* think it may be past their reach, but they may find that ground in him which will make such things easy to be understood ; for the time of disclosing those grounds so plainly was not till now, that the Mysteries which have been hid since the world began should be revealed. Those that had the spiritual understanding of the natural Mysteries, were called Wisemen ; and they that understood the divine Mysteries, were called [1] holy men, and they were Prophets, Preachers, Apostles, Evangelists, and Believers. The wise men of all nations did write darkly of their Mysteries, not to be understood but by such as were lovers of those things : And so the very Scriptures themselves, which contain all things in them, cannot be understood but by such as love to follow, practise, and endeavour

[1] saints.

to do those things which in them they find ought
to be done. And those that led their lives in such
a way, came to understand those Mysteries from
which they were written. And in several nations
their wisdom hath had several names, which hath
caused our age to take all the names of the several
parts of wisdom, and sort them into arts: Among
which the *Magia* and *Cabala* are accounted the
most mystical; the *Magia* consisting in the knowing how things have come to be; and the *Cabala*,
in knowing how the words and forms of things
express the reality of the inward Mystery: But he
that knoweth the Mystery, knoweth both these,
and all the branches of the tree of wisdom, in all
real arts and sciences, and the true signification of
every *Idea* in every thought, and thing, and sound,
and letter, in every language. And therefore this
author, having the true knowledge, could well
expound the letters of the names of God, and other
words and syllables, the signification of which he
saith is well understood in the language of nature.
And as one jot or tittle of the word of God shall
not pass away till all be fulfilled, so there is no
tittle of any [1] letter, that is proceeded from that
eternal essential Word, as all things are, but hath
its weighty signification, in the deep understanding,
in that word from whence it came, even in the
voices of all men, and sounds of all other creatures:
also the letters and syllables of a word, of some
language, do express something of the Mystery

[1] As in the *Revelations*; *I am A and Ω, the Beginning and the End.*

more exquisitely than of another, and therefore I conceive the author useth sometimes to expound words borrowed from the Hebrew and Greek, and some Latin words, and other words of art, as well as German words, and not always words of his own native language only, according to their signification in the language of nature: For that language doth shew, in every one's mother tongue, the greatest mysteries that have ever been in the nature of any thing, in the letters of that word by which it is expressed; therefore let every one esteem those expositions of his according to their high worth: for the knowledge of that language is only taught by the spirit of the letter.

Some think it is unnecessary to know such Mysteries; indeed every one's nature is not fitted with a capacity for the highest depths, therefore they need not search so far, nor trouble themselves to look for the understanding of that they desire not to know; but that they may see how necessary his writings are, let them read the author's own Preface to this book, and there they may find the necessity of [1] knowing themselves, for else they can never know God, and then they cannot know the way to God, though they read it never so plainly set down in the Scriptures. And besides, the way to God is, in his writings, more easy to be understood by those of our age, than in the Scripture, because that hath been so veiled by doubtful interpretations, expositions, inferences

[1] Γνῶθ Σεαυτόν.

and conclusions; and therefore it must needs be highly necessary that such a foundation be laid as may assure us of the true meaning of the Scriptures, which teach that which is so absolutely necessary to salvation. Moreover, his grounds will teach us the way to get such understanding, that we shall know and feel, as well as they to whom the Apostle *John* wrote, that we shall not need any man to teach us anything, for we shall know and get that unction, which teacheth all things, and leadeth into all truth; though it is thought people cannot have that now, by such as know not what is in man, for want of examining what is in themselves. Yet they may well perceive, that the ground of what hath ever been lieth in man; for whatsoever any man hath been, or can be, must needs be in that man that attaineth to it, as the ground of the most excellent flower is in the root from whence it groweth. And then sure the ground of all that was in *Adam*, or any that have been since, or shall be, is in any one of us; for whatsoever ground lay in God, the same lieth in Christ, and in him it lieth in us, because he is in us all. There is nothing but may be understood, if we do but consider how everything that ever was, or shall be known truly, is feelingly understood, by and in him that knoweth it as he ought. And he that thus knoweth God within him, cannot but know the Father, Son, and Holy Ghost, angels, men, and all other creatures, even the devils, and may well be able to speak the word of God infallibly, as the holy men that penned the Scriptures, and others also. And he that can understand these things in himself, may well know who speaketh by the spirit of God, and who speaketh his own fancies and delusions; as our Saviour said, *He that doth the will of my Father which is in heaven, shall know of my words whether they be of God.* But if that will of his Father in heaven had not been in them from the beginning of their life, in their conception in their mother's womb, how could they, to whom he said this, have done that will, whereby they might know whence his words proceeded? And according to this rule may any discern the words and writings of all. Therefore such things as these are necessary to be known.

There are some who have desired his writings might be epitomized, for ease of those that have not leisure to read so large treatises. Truly the spare time they spend in any other outward thing, may be spent with more benefit a thousandfold in this; and where he hath written at large it would not be understood if it were contracted more in brief; and all his books, as large as they are, are but a small spark of the Great Mystery; and where he hath written more in brief it is so obscure to some that they think it impossible to be understood. He wrote both so briefly and obscurely, as I conceive, that none but such as would be diligent in the practice of that which he hath written plainly and at large should be able to understand it.

It is intended that the book of the *Threefold Life* (which with the *Three Principles* and *Forty Questions* are a complete contence[1] of all the Mysteries) should be published in English with the soonest conveniency ; and in the meantime, for a taste of the spirit of prophecy which the author had, there is a little treatise of some prophecies concerning these latter times collected out of his writings by a lover of the Teutonic philosophy, and entitled *Mercurius Teutonicus*.

In turning the German into English I retain in some places the propriety of the German language, because the author should be rendered as near as might be in his own expression, that those excellent notions which he layeth down might not be slipped over as men do common current English, but that the strangeness of the words may make them a little stay, and consider what the meaning may be, having some difference from the vulgar English phrase. Also, where it is somewhat hard at first sight to know what some of the words mean, I have set the synonyms in the margin, and sometimes the English rendering between two semiquadrates [ ].[2]

In the Preface to the lovers of wisdom set before the *Forty Questions* in English, there are some of

---

[1] *Obs.* = Table of contents.

[2] *Note.*—The side-notes and all words within square brackets in the text are *additions* by the translator. Marks of parenthesis are usually equivalent to commas, the enclosed words being translations from the German.—C. J. B.

the many benefits mentioned that would arise from
the studying this author's writings, which may
there be read. Among the rest there is a hint
about reforming the laws, by degrees, in every
nation; and there is no doubt, but if those in
whose hands it is to make laws did but consider
what the spirit of God is, and may be stirred up
in them, they would stir him up and make a
reformation according to that spirit of love, the
Holy Ghost. And then they would be God's true
vicegerents; they would be the fathers of their
country, and deal with every obstinate rebellious
member in the kingdom as a father would do with
a disobedient child. First tell him lovingly and
shew him his faults; if that will not do, he will
inquire the reason, and study some course to
remedy the cause that hindereth his amendment.
But if he should go beyond the bounds of reason
and be beside himself, he would take care of his
safety, livelihood and cure. God taketh such care
for us all, though we be most obstinate enemies
against him; and we should do so for all our
brethren, the sons of Adam; though they be our
enemies, we should examine their wants in all
things, and supply them, that necessity may not
compel them to be our enemies still, and offend
God, that they may but live. If they will not be
quiet when they have their wants supplied, and
their wrongs redressed, but will turn murderers,
and so deserve to live no longer, in mercy let them

be provided for as other more friendly children of the Commonwealth, and removed to live by themselves, in some remote uninhabited country, where they may have no occasion to do hurt among those whom they would not suffer to live quietly. But let them not there want that which may give them honest subsistence, as others who are willing to transplant themselves. And for those that desire to live quietly and peaceably at home, let all their earthly things be so ordered that they may easily understand what right and wrong are, by having most brief, plain and easy laws to be governed by, and have their wants considered and supplied. Then all hearts will bless the hands of such reformers, and love will cover all the ends of the earth, and the God of love will give us his blessing of peace all the world over, and then the King of Glory will dwell with men, and all the kingdoms of the earth will be his. Who would not desire such a thing, with me, *The unworthiest of the children of men?*

J. S.

THE AUTHOR'S PREFACE
TO THIS BOOK

1. MAN can undertake nothing from the beginning of his youth, nor in the whole course of his time in this world, that is more profitable and necessary for him, than to learn to know himself; what he is, out of what, from whence, and for what he is created, and what his [1] office is. In such a serious consideration he will presently find, that he, and all the creatures that are, come all from God; he will also find, among all the creatures, that he is the most noble creature of them all; from whence he will very well perceive how God's intent is towards him, in that he hath made him lord over all the creatures of this world, and hath endued him with [2] mind, reason, and understanding, above all the rest of the creatures, especially with speech or language, so that he can distinguish everything that soundeth, stirreth, moveth, or groweth, and judge of everything's virtue, effect, and original; and that all is put under his hand, so that he can bend them, use, and manage them, according to his will, as pleaseth him.

[1] duty, employment, or business is.

[2] Or sense.

2. Moreover, God hath given him higher and greater knowledge than this, in that he can penetrate into the heart of everything, and discern what essence, virtue, and property it hath, both in the creatures, in earth, stones, trees, herbs, in all moveable and immoveable things; also in the stars and elements, so that he knoweth what substance and virtue they have, and that in their virtue, all natural sensibility, [1] vegetation, [2] multiplication, and life, doth consist.

[1] growing.
[2] propagation or increase.

3. Above all this, God hath given him the understanding and perception to know God his Creator; what and whence man is, how he is, and where he is, and out of what he proceeded, or was created; and how he is the image, [3] substance, [4] propriety, and child of the eternal, uncreated, and infinite God, and how he is created out of the substance of God, in which God hath his own substance and propriety, in whom he liveth and governeth with his spirit, by which God manageth his own work, and loveth him dearly as his own heart and substance; for whose sake he created this world, with all the creatures that are therein, which for the most part, without the reason and government of man, could not live in such a [5] condition [as they do].

[3] Or being.
[4] inheritance or possession.

[5] Or qualification, or manner of life.

4. The divine wisdom itself standeth in such a high consideration, and hath neither number nor end; and therein is the love of God towards man known, in that man knoweth what his Creator is,

and what he would have him do, and leave undone. And it is the most profitable thing for man in this world that he can search for, and seek after; for herein he learneth to know himself, what matter and substance he is of; also from whence his understanding [cogitation, perceptibility] and sensibility are stirred, and how he is created out of the [1]substance of God. And as a mother bringeth forth a child out of her own substance, and nourisheth it therewith, and leaveth all her goods to it for its own, and maketh it the possessor of them, so doth God also with man, his child; he hath created him, and preserved him, and made him heir to all his eternal goods. In and by this consideration the divine knowledge buddeth and groweth in man, and the love towards God, as of a child to its parents, so that man loveth God his Father, for that he knoweth that he is his Father, in whom he liveth, is, and hath his being, who nourisheth him, preserveth him, and provideth for him; for thus saith Christ our Brother, (who is begotten of the Father, to be a Saviour, and sent into this world), *This is the eternal life, that they know thee to be the only true God, and whom thou hast sent, Jesus Christ.*

[1] essence or being.

5. Now seeing we ourselves know that we are created out of God's own substance, and made his image, substance, and peculiar inheritance, it is therefore right that we should live in obedience to him, and follow him, seeing he leadeth us as a

father doth his children. And we have also his promise, that if we follow him, we shall obtain the light of the eternal life. Without such a considera- tion as this, we are altogether blind, and have no knowledge of God ; but we run on as dumb beasts, and we look upon ourselves and upon God's creation as heifers look upon a [1] new door made to their stalls, and set ourselves against God and his will, and so live in opposition and enmity, to the perdition of body and soul, and of God's noble creatures. We fall into this terrible and abomin- able darkness, because we will not learn to know ourselves, what we are, of what [2] substance, what we shall be, whether we are eternal, or whether we are wholly transitory, as the body is ; or whether also we must give an account of our [3] matters and doings, seeing we are made lords of all creatures, and of the whole creation, and have all this in our power to manage.

6. Even as we see, know, and find undeniably, that God will require an account of all our doings, how we have kept house with his [4] works, and that when we fall from him and his commandments, he will punish us terribly, of which we have fearful examples, from the beginning of the world, and among the Jews, Heathen, and Christians, espe- cially the example of the Flood, and in Sodom and Gomorrah ; also in *Pharaoh*, and the Children of *Israel* in the Wilderness, and ever since till this very time. Therefore it is indeed most necessary

[1] Which, being strange, they start back at it, and are afraid to go into their own lodging.

[2] Or matter.

[3] substance.

[4] Or creation.

that we learn wisdom, and learn to know ourselves, how great vice and wickedness we carry about us, how horrible wolves are amongst us, which strive against God and his will.

7. For there is none that can excuse himself, and plead ignorance, because the will of God is put into, and written in our minds, so that we very well know what we should do ; and all the creatures bear witness against us. Moreover, we have God's Law and Commandments, so that there is no excuse, but only our drowsy, lazy negligence and carelessness, and so we are found to be slothful, unprofitable servants in the Lord's vineyard.

8. Lastly, it is in the highest measure most needful for us to learn to know ourselves, because the devil dwelleth with us in this world, who is both God's enemy and ours, and daily misleadeth us, and entrappeth us, as he hath done from the beginning, that we might fall away from our God and Father, that so he might enlarge his kingdom, and bereave us of our eternal salvation ; as it is written, *He goeth about as a roaring lion, and seeketh whom he may devour.*

9. Seeing therefore we are in such horrible danger in this world, that we are environed with enemies on every side, and have a very unsafe pilgrimage or journey to walk; and above all, we carry our worst enemy within us, which we ourselves hide, and desire not to learn to know it,

[1] Viz. our evil and corrupt nature and will, which is inclined to all evil.

though [1] it be the most horrible guest of all, which casteth us headlong into the anger of God ; yea itself is the very anger of God, which throweth us into the eternal fire of wrath, into the eternal, unquenchable torment ; therefore it is most needful for us to learn to know this enemy, what he is, who he is, and whence he is ; how he cometh into us, and what in us is his proper own ; also what right the devil hath to us, and what access of entrance into us; how he is allied with our own enemy that dwelleth in us, how they favour and help one another, how both of them are God's enemies, and continually lay wait for us to murder us, and bring us to perdition.

10. Further, we must consider the great reasons why it is very necessary to learn to know ourselves, because we see and know that we must die and perish for our enemy's sake, which is God's enemy and ours, which dwelleth in us, and is the very half of man. And if he groweth so strong in us, that he get the upper hand, and be [2] predominant, then he throweth us into the abyss to all devils, to dwell there with them eternally, in an eternal, unquenchable pain and torment, into an eternal darkness, into a loathsome house, and into an eternal forgetting of all good, yea into God's contending will, where our God and all the creatures are our enemies for ever.

[2] the chief ruling part.

11. We have yet greater reasons to learn to know ourselves, because we are in good and evil and have the promise of eternal life, that (if we overcome our own enemy and the devil) we shall

be the children of God, and live in his kingdom,
with and in him, among his holy angels, in eternal
joy, [1] brightness, glory, and welfare, in meekness   [1] clarity.
and favour with him, without any touch of evil,
and without any knowledge of it, in God eternally.
Besides, we have the promise, that if we overcome
and bury our enemy in the earth, we shall rise
again at the Last Day in a new body, which shall
be without evil and pain, and live with God in
perfect joy, loveliness, and bliss.

12. Also we know and apprehend, that we have
in us a reasonable soul, [2] which is in God's love,   [2] Or which
and is immortal; and that if it be not vanquished   God hath a
love to.
by its adversary, but fighteth as a spiritual champion
against its enemy, God will assist it with his Holy
Spirit, and will enlighten and make it powerful,
and able to overcome all its enemies; he will fight
for it, and at the overcoming of the evil, will glorify
it as a faithful champion, and crown it with the
[3] brightest crown of heaven.   [3] Or fairest.

13. Now seeing man knoweth that he is such
a twofold man, in the [4] capacity of good and evil,   [4] Or potenti-
and that they are both his own, and that he him-   ality of being
good or evil.
self is that only man which is both good and evil,
and that he shall have the reward of either of them,
and to which of them he inclineth in this life, to
that his soul goeth when he dieth; and that he
shall arise at the Last Day in power, in his labour
[and works] which he exercised here, and live
therein eternally, and also be glorified therein;

[1] source or sustenance.

and that shall be his eternal food and [1] subsistence; therefore it is very necessary for him to learn to know himself, how it is with him, and whence the impulsion to good and evil cometh, and what indeed the good and evil merely are in himself, and whence they are stirred, what properly is the original of all the good, and of all the evil, from whence, and by what [means] evil is come to be in the devils, and in men, and in all creatures; seeing the devil was a holy angel, and man also created good, and that also such [2] untowardness is found to be in all creatures, biting, tearing, worrying, and hurting one another, and such enmity, strife, and hatred in all creatures; and that every [3] thing is so at odds with itself, as we see it to be, not only in the living creatures, but also in the stars, elements, earth, stones, metals, in wood, leaves, and grass; there is a poison and malignity in all things; and it is found that it must be so, or else there would be no life, nor mobility, nor would there be any colour or virtue, neither thickness nor thinness, nor any perceptibility or sensibility, but all would be as nothing.

[2] Or evil disposition.

[3] *Corpus*, or body, or natural substance.

14. In this high consideration it is found that all is through and from [4] God himself, and that it is his own substance, which is himself, and he hath created it out of himself; and that the evil belongeth to the [5] forming and mobility; and the good to the love; and the austere, severe, or contrary will belongeth to the joy; so far as the

[4] Viz. through and from God's wrath and love.

[5] imaging, fashioning, framing.

creature is in the light of God, so far the wrathful and contrary will maketh the rising, eternal joy; but if the light of God be extinguished, it maketh the rising, painful torment, and the hellish fire.

15. That it may be understood how all this is, I will describe the *Three Divine Principles*, that therein all may be declared, what God is, what nature is, what the creatures are; what the love and meekness of God is, what God's desiring or will is, what the wrath of God and the devil is, and in [1] conclusion, what joy and sorrow are; and how all took a beginning, and endureth eternally, with the true difference between the eternal and transitory creatures, especially of man, and of his soul, what it is, and how it is an eternal creature: And what heaven is, wherein God and the holy angels and holy men dwell; and what hell is, wherein the devils dwell; and how all things originally were created, and had their being. In sum, what the [2] Essence of all essences is.

16. Seeing the love of God hath favoured me with this knowledge, I will set it down in writing for a Memorial or remembrance to myself, because we live in this world in so great danger between heaven and hell, and must continually wrestle with the [3] devil, if perhaps through weakness I might fall into the anger of God, and thereby the light of my knowledge might be withdrawn from me, that it may serve me to recall it to memory, and raise it up again; for God willeth that all men

[1] in brief, or in sum.

[2] Being of all beings, or Substance of all substances; not the pure Deity, as Aristotle hath supposed, but the eternal nature, God's love and wrath.

[3] all evil affections or practices of the devil in the anger of God.

should be helped, and willeth not the death of a sinner, but that he return, come to him, and live in him eternally; for whose sake he hath suffered his own Heart, that is, his Son, to become man, that we might cleave to him, and rise again in him, and [departing] from our sins and enmity, or contrary will, be new-born in him.

17. Therefore there is nothing more profitable to man in this world, while he dwelleth in this miserable, corrupted house of flesh, than to learn to know himself: Now when he knoweth himself aright, he knoweth also his Creator, and all the creatures too: Also he knoweth how God intendeth towards him, and this knowledge is the most acceptable and pleasant to me that ever I found.

18. But if it should happen, that these writings should come to be read; and perhaps the Sodomitish world, and the fatted swine thereof, may light upon them, and root in my garden of pleasure, who cannot know or understand anything, but to scorn, scandalize, reproach, and [1]cavil in a proud haughty way, and so know neither themselves, nor God, much less his children; I intend not my writing for them, but I shut and lock up my book with a strong bolt or bar, from such idiots and wild heifers of the devil, who lie over head and ears in the devil's murdering den, and know not themselves. They do the same which their [2]teacher the devil doth, and remain children of the severe

[1] Or dispute; always arguing, without looking after the salvation of their souls.

[2] Or schoolmaster.

anger of God. But I will here write plainly and clearly enough for the children of God. The world and the devil may roar and rage till they come into the abyss; for their hour-glass is set up, when every one shall reap what he hath sown: and the hellish fire will sting many a one sufficiently for his proud, spiteful, and despising haughtiness, which he had no belief of while he was here in this life.

19. Besides, I cannot well neglect to set this down in writing, because God will require an account of every one's gifts, how they have employed them; for he will demand the talent which he hath bestowed, with the increase or use, and give it to him that hath gained much: But seeing I can do no more in it, I commit it to his will, and so go on to write according to my knowledge.

20. As to the children of God, they shall perceive and comprehend this my writing, what it is, for it hath a very convincing testimony, it may be proved by all the creatures, yea in all things, especially in man, who is an image and similitude of God: But it continueth hidden and obscure to the children of malignity or iniquity, and there is a fast [1] seal before it; and though the devil disrelish the smell and savour, and raise a storm from the east to the north, yet there will then, in the wrathful or crabbed sour tree, grow a lily with a root as broad as the tree spreadeth with

[1] A seal that can be opened by no academic, university, or scholastic learning; but by earnest repentance, fasting, watching, praying, knocking, and seeking in the sufferings of Jesus Christ by the Holy Ghost.

its branches, and bring its scent and smell even into paradise.

21. There is a wonderful time coming. But because it beginneth in the [1] night, there are many that shall not see it, by reason of their sleep and great drunkenness; yet the sun will shine to the [2] children at midnight. Thus I commit the reader to the [3] meek love of God. *Amen.*

[1] Or great darkness, or blindness.

[2] children of *Sophia*, or divine wisdom.

[3] Or sweet.

CONTENTS

c

INTRODUCTION [1]

*" My knowledge is not, as yours, the outcome of fancy or opinion ; but
I have living knowledge through vision and experience."*—JACOB BOEHME
(*contra Tylcken*, ii. 53).

IT has been affirmed by Goethe, in a well-known
passage of his writings, that the main theme of
the world's and of mankind's history is the struggle
between faith and infidelity. But what is faith, and
what is infidelity? Has not the infidelity of one age,
after meeting with revilings and provoking persecutions,
yet often become later the faith of another age? Therefore, we would reinterpret or rectify Goethe's statement
by suggesting that the main and essential theme of
history consists in the struggle of the living with the
dead. Again and again we observe the same world's
drama unfolding itself. When a great truth arises that
opposes time-consecrated traditions, how few, beside the
very noblest minds of the day, are able to seize upon
it, and to become its martyrs, until it wins at last, after
long strife, and becomes the common possession of mankind! Then again we see how, in the grasp of the
multitude, that which was living becomes dead; how
that which was deeply thought and felt, turns into
empty forms and meaningless words; how that which
was originally treasured for its own sake is degraded

---

[1] *Jacob Boehme: His Life and Philosophy.* An Address delivered at
Kiel, 8th May 1897, by Dr Paul Deussen, Professor of Philosophy in the
University of Kiel. Enlarged and published in aid of a fund for the
raising of a Memorial-monument to Jacob Boehme. Kiel, 1897. Translated
by Mrs D. S. Hehner, and here printed by the author's special permission.
[The references are to the English editions of J. B.'s works.]

into a mere tool for personal purposes; thus the once persecuted becomes persecutor; the old and moribund opposes the new and living, until, defeated and ousted, it lingers behind as a powerless shadow and survives but as a ghost in the world's history.

Numerous are the illustrations that might be given in support of these facts; and the same observations apply also, if, taking our standpoint in the Indian mind-world, we confine our outlook and considerations to Western development.

There was a time when the Mosaic law was the highest word of the day. Sacrifices were offered, and they were offered from the living impulse of the heart; for, in the sacrifice, man offered himself and his own will to the Divine; until later, in the custody of a priesthood that made out of sacrificial rites a lucrative business, the idea perished, and the dead form survived, against which the new and living arose in the preaching of the prophets: "I desired mercy and not sacrifice." But the word of the prophets also perished, and soon law and prophets were but a dead letter. Then came among the dead a mighty living One, the same who commanded the would-be disciple to follow and let the dead bury their dead; the same who, when asked what punishment should be meted unto the adulterous woman, stooped down and wrote on the ground—wrote nothing else, we believe, but the word of the law which condemned the woman to die. There it stood, the holy word of the law, written in the dust, a dead letter! But He had come to bring new life unto men; He hung upon the Cross for it; yet the mustard-seed of His teaching, full of life-power, grew into a tree, in the shade of which the nations were to dwell. Not with fire and sword, but with the sap of its inner life, Christianity conquered the world. And then, scarce had its victory been won, when again life gave way to death. The living word of Jesus hardened into fixed and authoritative dogma. Even as Jesus had deplored the fact that "the Scribes and the

Pharisees sit in Moses' seat," so also history repeated itself under another form, and in the seat of Jesus sat the Popes of the Middle Ages.

Neoplatonism and mediæval Mysticism vainly sought with a fresh impetus to break through the crust of orthodoxy; but the storm of the Reformation burst at last, swept away the crystallized traditions and breathed a new life into moribund Christianity. But a short time later, this also fell under the common law of all religious development. The reformers had gone back to the Bible as the source of mediæval traditions; the way was clear before them; the indications pointed to a further going back, without halt or hesitation, beyond and behind the letter of the Bible, right into the very fountain-head whence all revelations, including the Bible, have ever flowed forth, right into the divine powers that slumber in the abysmal depths of every human mind. These living powers were, as before in Jesus and in Paul, awake in Luther, and had given him inspiration: but the well he had begun to sink was soon choked through endless religious strife; and a hundred years after Luther, there arose, almost as domineering and intolerant as Popery itself, the letter-bound Lutheran orthodoxy.

In such times lived Jacob Boehme, who, as a religious and philosophical genius, has not often had his equal in the world's history, and might have been the very man fitted to finish Luther's half-done work of Church-reformation, and bring about a reconciliation between science and faith, such as we are still lacking in our days. But unfavourable circumstances hindered his endeavours, both outwardly and inwardly; and while his life was consumed in a continual struggle with the fanatical, letter-ridden orthodoxy, he succeeded but imperfectly, limited as he was by the literal sense of the Bible, in bringing into expression the truly free and truly devout spirit that inwardly animated him.

Both the life and the teaching of the man are well worthy of deep consideration; and both offer over again the same peculiar drama of life wrestling with death, yet unable to overcome altogether.

In Oberlausitz, Silesia, two hours south from Görlitz, and quite near the Bohemian frontier, lies the little town of Seidenberg, and close by, the village Alt-Seidenberg. Here our philosopher was born in the year 1575 (the day is not known), the son of simple but respectable peasants. As, though healthy, he was not of robust constitution, his parents decided to let him learn a trade, and he became a shoemaker; which sedentary occupation afforded his mind opportunity for absorption in deep interior thought; while his physical development remained somewhat backward. "His external appearance," writes his friend and biographer, Abraham von Frankenberg, "was worn and " very plain; he was of short stature; he had a low fore-" head, but broad temples, a somewhat aquiline nose, a " thin and short beard; greyish eyes, lighting up into " heavenly blue, and sparkling even as the windows of " Solomon's Temple (1 Kings vi. 4); his voice was feeble, " but his conversation full of kindness and sweetness; he " was gentle in manner, modest in his words, humble in " conduct, patient in suffering, and meek of heart."

In his fourteenth year Jacob Boehme was apprenticed to a master in Seidenberg; three years later he started on his travels [Wanderjahre]. How far he wandered and where, nobody knows; but he at last reached Görlitz, where in 1599 he won his "Mastership," and married the same year.

His wife, the daughter of a butcher, bore him four sons and probably also two daughters, and stood faithfully by him during five-and-twenty years, in fact, till his death. In 1610 he became proprietor of a house situate near the Neisse (now Breslauerstrasse 45). In 1613 he sold his workshop, and took to trading in woollen gloves and similar articles, visiting Prague very often to sell his goods; for his own shoemaking had suffered greatly during the latter part of his life, owing to his activities and continual industry as an author. And so he lived, meek and humble, a good citizen, a good husband and father, minding his work, bringing up his children in the fear of God, in modest but well-regulated circumstances; a peaceful, unassuming, and truly devout life.

But this quiet life was shaken interiorly by mighty storms, fearful wrestlings and glorious victories, in comparison with which the deeds of a world's conqueror, viewed from the standpoint of eternal things, seems mean and insignificant.

Already, as a boy, he had had wonderful visions, that to his excited fancy took the form of external occurrences. Of this kind is the incident that took place in his childhood. He was minding cattle on the "Land's Crown," when he discovered, in a strange open vault, a vessel full of money, upon which he looked with a feeling of horror, and ran away in great alarm. Again, during his apprenticeship, he once sold a pair of shoes to a stranger, who called him by his name, and prophesied his future greatness, as well as future troubles and persecutions. These experiences may have been of a subjective character—a turning of the mind from all desire for earthly goods, a premonition of his great calling and a forewarning of the enmity and opposition he would have to bear; but, coupled with, and supported by, chance external circumstances, they built themselves into external images, and were unconsciously accepted as objective, though they were really not so. Apart from such visions, Jacob Boehme sometimes fell into ecstasies. Thus, for instance, as he told a friend in confidence, during his years of travel, and whilst engaged in his daily work, he was once for seven days surrounded by glorious heavenly light, and lifted interiorly into a state of open vision and divine peace and joy.

Such spiritual experiences were repeated again and again in his life; and only those can fail to gauge their meaning and importance, who, devoid of understanding, overlook similar occurrences in the lives of St Paul, of Plotinus, and of many an Indian philosopher.

The inward strife and yearning of soul that filled the years of his youth are well illustrated by a highly instructive part of his book *Aurora,* viz., Chapter 19, from which we will quote the following words: " When I plainly found out that good and evil are in all " things, as well in the elements as in creatures; and " that in this world the God-fearing fare no better than " the Godless, I fell into depression and sadness, and not " even the Scriptures, which were well known to me, " could give me any comfort. The devil must surely " have rejoiced at this, and often impressed my mind " with heathenish thoughts, whereof I will make no " mention here." (Namely, the pantheistic thought that since the world is God's, all things therein must also be good.). . . . "But as, in my awakened zeal and eager- " ness, I stormed violently against God and all the Gates " of Hell, ... my spirit at last broke through into the " innermost Birth of the Divinity and was caught up in " Love, as a Bridegroom embraces his dear Bride. The " triumph in my soul cannot be told or described; I can " liken it only to the birth of life through death, and com- " pare it to a resurrection from the dead" [pars. 8–12].

This " breaking through into the innermost birth of the Divinity " took place, according to another state- ment, twelve years before he began to write the *Aurora* (1600), and the same year it happened that, as his glance met the bright reflection of the sun's rays upon a pewter vessel, he suddenly was ". . . . introduced into the innermost essence or centre of occult nature." The sun—so he may have mused—is the only source of light here, and yet this light could not be manifest, were it not for the dark pewter which throws it back and makes it visible. Indeed in this one thought lies the very kernel of his whole later system, and in his 2nd *Epistle* [Ellistone, 1649] the philosopher himself sets forth the development of this idea.

"In this my most earnest seeking and desire, ...
" a gate was opened unto me, so that in a quarter of an
" hour, I saw and learnt more than if I had studied
" many years in some university; . . . . for I perceived
" and recognized the Being of all beings, the Byss and
" the Abyss; also the birth of the Holy Trinity, the
" descent and origin of this world and of all creatures,
" through the Divine Wisdom. I discovered also within
" myself the three worlds, namely: (1) the divine,
" angelical or paradisical; then (2) the dark world, as
" the original of nature to the fire; and of (3) this
" external visible world, as a procreation or external
" birth, or as a substance manifested forth out of both
" inner and spiritual worlds. I saw and understood the
" whole nature of good and of evil, their origin and
" mutual relation, and what constitutes the womb of the
" genetrix; so that I not only wondered greatly, but
" also rejoiced.

"And it was powerfully borne upon my mind to write
" down these things as a Memorial, however difficult they
" might be of apprehension to my outer self, and of ex-
" pression through my pen. I felt compelled to begin at
" once like a child going to school, to work upon this very
" great Mystery. Interiorly I saw it all well enough, as
" in a great depth; for I looked through as into a chaos
" wherein all things lie [latent, undifferentiated]; but
" the unravelling thereof proved impossible.

"From time to time, however, an opening took place
" within me, as of a growth. I kept this to myself for
" twelve years (1600–1612), being full of it, and experi-
" enced a vehement impulse, before I could bring it out
" into expression; but at last it overwhelmed me like a
" cloud-burst; what it smites, it smites indeed. And so
" it went with me: whatsoever I could grasp sufficiently
" to bring it out, that I wrote down."

This book, which saw the light in 1612, and which the
author meant to write only for himself, was entitled
Morning Redness; later, a friend gave it the title *Aurora*.

The MS. of the unfinished (and never-to-be finished) work having been entrusted as a loan to a follower of Schwenkfeld, a nobleman named Karl von Ender, he caused a number of copies to be taken and further circulated. In this wise the book came under the notice of the Pastor Primarius, or chief pastor of Görlitz, Gregorius Richter, an orthodox and fanatical Lutheran, who took great offence thereat, and resolved to make of Jacob Boehme an example to frighten the many sectaries of the time; all the more as he had to deal with a simple workman, of whom moreover he had no very pleasant remembrance, owing to an incident that had taken place presumably some time previously. The story is so characteristic of both the men concerned, that we cannot afford to overlook it. True enough, we must not forget that the report comes from one of Boehme's friends (Dr Wiesner of Breslau), and cannot claim to be an original or direct statement of facts; yet, discounting all possible exaggeration or distortion, enough is left to be of interest.[1]

It would seem that a young baker, a relative of Boehme, being short of money, had borrowed one thaler from the chief pastor in order to buy wheatmeal for Christmas cakes. He made one of these fairly large, and presented it as a sort of thank-offering. Soon after the holidays he returned the money, hoping that the reverend gentleman would require no interest, since the loan had been only for a fortnight. The reverend gentleman, however, meant nothing of the sort. He threatened the young man with God's anger and terrible curse, and frightened him to such an extent that for several days afterwards the poor simple fellow went about in great despondency, and in fear for his soul's eternal welfare, sighing deeply and speaking to no one. His wife at last implored the intervention of her cousin, Jacob Boehme; and the latter, having inquired into the whole matter, spoke kindly to the troubled young man,

---

[1] See Dr C. Wiesner's Epistle Narrative, in *The Remainder of the Books of Jacob Boehme*. Sparrow, 1662.

comforted him and bade him be at rest; moreover, he went fearlessly to the angry parson, and begged him in the friendliest possible manner to forgive the young fellow, promising himself to find and pay down the interest on the borrowed thaler; the young man, he added, had done his best, and he thought he had done enough; yet, if the reverend gentleman were not satisfied, let him say what he required and it should be paid. Thereupon the parson, who, while Jacob stood, was himself seated in a comfortable chair, assumed an arrogant and pompous attitude, and flew into a violent rage. Why did the busybody come to him? What had he to do with the matter? Let him mind his own business and take himself off. Jacob, however, earnestly went on pleading for pardon and for permission to settle the debt, till the parson, plainly ashamed, yet unwilling to say how much he wanted, shewed him the door: and as the simple, humble and gentle intercessor turned on the door-step with a kindly parting word, "God bless your Reverence," the enraged parson, angrier than ever, seized one of his slippers and threw it at him, exclaiming: "How dare you wish me good-night or anything else, you Godless villain! Do I ask for your blessings?" and so on. The excellent man, unmoved, picked up the slipper, placed it quietly at the parson's feet, and answered: "Do not be angry, sir! I am doing you no harm. May God protect you!" And he then left him.

It was no doubt shortly after this that a copy of the *Aurora* fell into the hands of the proud and naturally irritable cleric. Boehme had written at the close of his work: "Should Peter or Paul (seem to) have written " otherwise, then look to the essence, to the heart [to the " interior meaning]. If you lay hold of the heart, you " will find the essence well enough " [xxvi. 152]. And these words were quite sufficient to mark him as a heretic. The priest certainly determined openly to brand him as such.

On Sunday, 21st July 1613 (according to Wiesner's

account), the preacher, speaking from the pulpit, violently denounced the meek and gentle man of God, indulging in startling and shocking fulminations; threatening the town with downfall, unless this agitating, mischievous, heretical disturber of the peace were promptly removed; and calling upon the members of the Town Council to use their powers against him for resisting ecclesiastical authority, annoying preachers in their own houses, and writing heretical books. He further declared that unless the offender were punished, the anger of God would fall upon them all, and the town would be swallowed up by the earth, as happened to Korah, Dathan and Abiram, after they resisted Moses, the man of God.

Jacob Boehme, who was a regular church-goer, heard all this from his usual seat facing the pulpit, and after the service waited in the churchyard for the parson, approached him, and quietly asked what he had done to offend; if he only knew of his fault, he would gladly make amends. The parson, instead of answering, looked at him as if he meant to kill him with his glance; then broke out into fearful abuse and curses. "Get thee " behind me, Satan! Go back to thy hell and leave me " alone! Seest thou not that I am a priest, and go " about my office?" — "Yes indeed, Reverend Sir," answered sadly the deeply-injured man, "I do see it, " and therefore have I listened to you in church, as is " meet and proper; and now I come to ask you, as a " priest, to tell me what I have done to you." Turning then to the chaplain, Boehme begged for his help, that he might entreat the preacher to explain the cause of his wrath. Exasperated at this insistence, the priest, beside himself with rage, would there and then have had Boehme arrested and sent to prison, had not the chaplain's counsels prevailed, so that Jacob was after all allowed to return home.

The next day (here Wiesner's account is inaccurate), Boehme was called before the Town Council in order to justify himself. The chief pastor was also invited, but begged to be excused. He would have nothing to do with Town Council or Court of Justice, and declared that he had said from the pulpit all that was needed; the Council had only to act up to it, and banish the insolent heretic, so that the holy clerical dignity might no longer be offended, and that the town might escape the divine vengeance.

The magistrates, disturbed by these threats, anxious perhaps to avoid any possible popular excitement with its consequences, had the book *Aurora* brought to the town-hall and placed under lock and key. In the meantime, Boehme, who was under arrest, was served with an order to leave the town: even his wish to take leave of his family and set in order a few private matters was disregarded. Boehme only said: "Since this must be, dear sirs, I am content." And he left the town.

During the night, the Councillors seem to have come to their senses and regretted their haste; for they assembled again early in the morning and resolved to bring back again the man they had banished the day before. After a great deal of searching, he was found in the neighbourhood and led home in triumph. This account of Wiesner is, he himself admits, by no means a first-hand one, and therefore probably much embellished. Certain it is that the fragments preserved out of the diary of Bartholomew Scultetus, then mayor of Görlitz, shew nothing that refers to an actual banishment, but chronicle the following facts only (Ueberfeld's ed., 1730):—"That on Friday, 26th July 1613, Jacob " Boehme, a shoemaker, domiciled between the town-gates, " behind the hospital smithy, had been summoned to the " town-hall and questioned regarding his enthusiastic " beliefs, and thereupon placed under arrest, while the " book in quarto-folio which he had written was fetched " from his house: that later, he had been set at liberty " with a caution to leave such things alone.

"Also, that on Tuesday, 30th July, Jacob Boehme, a " shoemaker, had been summoned before the clergy of

" Görlitz, assembled in the house of the Primarius, in
" order to be carefully examined regarding his faith.

" Also, that two days previously, on Sunday, 28th July,
" the Primarius Gregorius Richter, preaching on false
" prophets, had in his sermon sharply rebuked the shoe-
" maker Jacob Boehme."

These notes probably state all the facts which form
the basis of Wiesner's account. It is easy to detect in
the story the elements of popular romance that joined
into one three separate incidents, and exaggerated a
mere threat into an actual banishment: yet, though the
story is not actually correct, it furnishes a decidedly
graphic representation of human character.

Concerning the examination that took place before
the assembled clergy, 30th July 1613, as mentioned in
Scultetus's diary, Boehme himself states the following,
in a document of the 3rd April 1624, written as an
answer to the Council:—" When I appeared before him
" [Gregorius Richter] to defend myself and indicate my
" stand-point, the Rev. Primarius exacted from me a
" promise to give up writing, and to this I assented,
" since I did not yet see clearly the divine way, nor did
" I understand what God would later do with me. On
" the other hand, the Rev. Primarius, together with the
" other preachers, agreed to say nothing more about the
" matter from the pulpit. He, however, did not keep his
" word, but, on the contrary, never ceased slandering me
" and spreading shameful accusations against me, mis-
" leading the whole town thereby, and disgracing me in
" the eyes of all; so that I, with my wife and children,
" was made a spectacle, and must have been as a clown
" and a fool among them. Moreover, by his order, I
" gave up for many years (1613–1618) all writing or
" speaking about my knowledge of Divine things, hoping
" vainly that the evil reports would at last come to an
" end, instead of which they only grew worse and more
" malignant."

As a natural result of these prolonged persecutions,

the attention of a large number of learned men was drawn to the workman-philosopher. Many who were, like Schwenkfeld and Weigel, highly dissatisfied with the current orthodoxy and inclined to secede, naturalists and physicians, customs officials and noblemen, both in Görlitz and in the neighbouring towns, became his friends and patrons, and represented to him that he should not bury the talent he had received; that he ought to obey God rather than men, and so on. At the same time, the increasing pressure of his own interior impulse compelled him to give a form at last to that which was fermenting within him; and, after a silence of five years, he again took up his pen, and during the next six years of his life wrote a number of his more considerable works: *The Three Principles, The Threefold Life of Man*, the *Signatura Rerum*, the *Mysterium Magnum*, and many others. As long as only MS. copies of his books were circulated among his friends, objectors heard little of them, and no opposition was raised. But towards the end of the year 1623, three little devotional works, *Of True Repentance, Of True Resignation*, and *Of the Supersensual Life*, were printed together under the title *Way to Christ* and published by Sigismund von Schweinitz; and then the storm broke afresh. To the slanders he uttered from the pulpit, the Primarius now added poetical effusions in the shape of Latin verses of an abusive character, some of which (7th, 26th and 27th March 1624) were later printed and circulated. The beginning of one of these productions runs thus :—

> " Quot continentur lineæ, blasphemiæ
> Tot continentur in libro sutorio,
> Qui nil nisi picem redolet sutoriam,
> Atrum et colorem, quem vocant sutorium,
> Pfuy ! Pfuy ! teter sit fœtor a nobis procul !"

(The shoemaker's book contains as many blasphemies as lines. They have a dreadful odour of shoemakers' pitch and blacking, etc.)

The clergy of Liegnitz, spurred into opposition by

Richter, also lodged a complaint about the heretic before the Town Council of Görlitz, and on the 26th of March 1624 Boehme was summoned again to the town-hall. The memorable record of this sitting is still preserved; it runs as follows :—

" Jacob Boehme, the shoemaker and rabid enthusiast, " declares that he has written his book *To Eternal Life*, " but did not cause the same to be printed. A nobleman, " Sigismund von Schweinitz, did that. The Council gave " him warning to leave the town; otherwise the Prince " Elector would be apprised of the facts. He thereupon " promised that he would shortly take himself off."

The chief pastor's triumph was now complete, as is shewn in his verses of the 27th March :—

" Gorlicium tandem te sutor pellit ab urbe,
  Et jubet ire illuc, quo tua scripta valent."

(At last, O shoemaker, the town of Görlitz drives thee forth; get thee now where they will know thy worth, etc.)

But Boehme did not mean to give way. He well knew that in Dresden, then capital of the province, he would find supporters, who would receive his book gladly. He writes (15th March 1624) " . . . I was asked to speak " before a number of high personages at the Court of " the Prince Elector, and have consented to do so at the " end of the Leipzig fair." [33rd *Epistle*, Ellistone, 1649.]

He wrote an answer and protest—still preserved—to the Town Council of Görlitz, against the calumnies and falsehoods spread by the Primarius. This the magistrates declined to consider, because the parson forbade them to do so, and, moreover, continued to storm and rave. Boehme writes on the 2nd of April 1624 :—" I must tell " you, sir, that yesterday the pharisaical devil was let " loose, cursed me and my little book, and condemned the " book to the fire. He charged me with shocking vices ; " with being a scorner of both Church and Sacraments, " and with getting drunk daily on brandy, wine, and

" beer; all of which is untrue; while he himself is a
" drunken man."

On the 9th of May, Boehme left for Dresden, where
he spent two months as the guest of the Court physician,
Dr Hinkelmann, and where he found among the nobility
and high clergy a most friendly welcome, while the strife
still raged in Görlitz. "My wife," writes Boehme from
Dresden on the 13th of June, "need not have any
" window-shutters put up. If they wish to break them
" (the windows), they may; it will only shew the fruits
" of the high-priest's influence. . . . If the high-priest
" means to storm the house, let him do so; it will only
" make evident to the whole country that he is an
" agitator, and that will be great honour indeed for him
" and his. He also deserves commendation before the
" Prince Elector for having, through his servants, laid
" violent hands on my house and broken the windows."

Towards the end of Boehme's stay in Dresden, the
Prince Elector appointed three Professors of Theology,
and several other learned doctors, to examine his
opinions. The report which the Prince expected from
them turned out to be a mere request that " His Highness
" would please to have a little patience, and allow the
" man sufficient time for a clearer exposition of his ideas.
" They failed as yet to understand him, but hoped that
" he would after a while become more intelligible; then
" only would they give a judgment, not before."

Wiesner, in whose presence two other professors,
Gerhard and Meissner, exchanged opinions, relates that
Gerhard said: "I would not for the whole world be
" party to the man's condemnation."—"Neither would
" I, brother," replied Meissner; "who knows what lies
" behind it all? We cannot judge that which we have
" not understood, nor are able to understand, whether it
" be right, or black or white."

When Boehme was allowed to "go in peace," and left
Dresden apparently in favour with the Prince Elector
himself, he returned home, but soon accepted an invita-

tion from Herr von Schweinitz, at whose country-seat he began the writing of his last work, the 177 *Theosophic Questions.*

In the meantime, our philosopher's old opponent, Gregorius Richter, died on the 14th of August. Boehme himself was to survive him only by a few months. While he still was with Herr von Schweinitz, he was seized with a fatal bowel complaint. He returned home very ill on the 7th of November, and his friends and his family doctor were unable to give him any hope of recovery. He expressed a desire for the Sacrament, which was granted only after he had answered satisfactorily a long list of questions. During the night of the 17th November, he spoke of hearing most beautiful music, and asked to have the door opened in order to listen. Towards morning, he took leave of his wife and sons, blessed them, and said: "Now I go hence into Paradise." Then he asked his son to turn him over on his other side, sighed deeply, and fell asleep, leaving this world easily and peacefully.

The clergy refused to give him a Church funeral, until a special order from the Governor of Lausitz compelled the second Pastor of Görlitz to perform the burial service. The latter began his sermon by declaring that he would rather have walked twenty miles than have officiated at the funeral of such a man. He also rejected the text that had been submitted to him, and chose the words: "And as it is appointed unto men once to die, but after this the judgment." The cross upon Boehme's grave was pulled down by the mob. Now, a block of porphyry marks the resting-place of the "Philosophus Teutonicus," and soon, we hope, the monument raised to his memory will prove that a grateful posterity is at pains to atone for the sins of his contemporaries.

As we now turn from the personality of our philosopher to his works, the newest edition of which (Schiebler, Leipzig, 1830–47) consists of seven fairly bulky volumes, we are struck at once and not a little delighted with the highly original treatment of first principles that we discover therein. Everywhere Boehme appears as an independent, bold and profoundly penetrating thinker, who laboriously endeavours to bring into intelligible expression his deep interior perceptions. If he does but imperfectly succeed, if he again and again returns to the same idea, yet without achieving a perfectly clear and consistent presentation throughout, that is due to his complete lack of a suitable education. The invaluable advantage of a study of the classics was denied him. He knew nothing of the art of connectedly considering and preparing, clearly linking and grouping in order, the vast array of his conceptions. For the rest, he had assimilated much of the knowledge of his time. He was thoroughly conversant with the Bible, and he states himself (*Aurora*, x. 45) that he read "the writings of many great masters," but had found therein "only a half-dead spirit." By these words he refers principally to works of the school of Paracelsus, wherefrom he took his idea of the threefold nature of man; namely, a body formed out of the elements, a spirit originating from the stars, and a soul inbreathed from God. From the same sources he also borrowed many technical, philosophical and alchemical terms, some of which, however, he had partly misunderstood. Yet all this applies only to the external side of his teaching, the shell, as it were, which encloses the kernel of his own peculiar and deep knowledge of essential truth. This same knowledge he claims, and rightly enough, to have obtained through revelation; for he drew from the same fountain-head as all teachers of religion and philosophy before him; from the same source that is also open to us, if we are but willing to plunge and sink into the mysterious depths of our own innermost Spirit, and therein reach the very Heart of God.

We shall now endeavour to present and bring out distinctly, and into clear light, the eternal truths that are to be found in his system, quite apart from the quaint and variegated forms of half-understood or mis-understood traditions wherewith he clothed his thoughts.

The fundamental conception of Jacob Boehme's philosophy might be characterized as Pantheo-dualistic; that is to say, he attempts to harmonize the undeniable claim of Pantheism that God is not to be known out of and apart from Nature, but in it and through it; with the equally undeniable fact of dualism, *i.e.* the evident opposition in this divine world of good and evil. Let us try to elucidate these ideas.

Pantheism is—here the very word points out the explanation—the counterpart of Theism, and, as can readily be shewn, the unavoidable result of the same. By the term Theism we understand the belief—well known to us from our youth—in a personal anthropomorphic God, who, at a definite period of time, has created the world out of nothing, by a special act of His will. Such a conception was possible and bearable in the dark Middle Ages, which followed after scholastic subtleties, but were blind to the facts of nature. Here below, so they reasoned, is the earth upon which man has his being, and up above in the blue heavens, behind the clouds, lives the Good Lord. Then came Copernicus, who proved that what we call heaven is nothing else but the infinite space which surrounds us on every side, wherein nothing is to be found beyond fixed stars like our sun, and planets like our earth, with all that they contain. In doing away with the old idea of Heaven, Copernicus had, without knowing or wishing it, taken away God. In the new astronomical system, there was no room left for Him. In the same way, a creation of the world out of nothing was no longer admissible after natural research had begun, and when it became more and more clearly recognized that, since matter does not vanish into nothingness, neither can it originate from nothingness, but must have been from all eternity.

If, in such circumstances, the idea of God was to be

held fast, there was nothing to do but shift from the
Theistic theory to the Pantheistic; remove God into
nature itself, since there was no room for Him without,
and consider the universe as His Self-manifestation.
Following up the various stages of development of the
new philosophy, we observe how, in the conceptions of
thinkers, God melts away more and more into the
universe; how the Theism of Descartes is gradually
modified by Geuliner and Malebranche, until, in the com-
pletely Pantheistic system of Spinoza, it reaches its last
unavoidable consequence. This identification of nature
and God, or God and nature (which comes to the very
same thing), is expressed in the well known words of
Goethe :—

> " Was wär' ein Gott, der nur von aussen stiesse,
> Im Kreis das All am Finger laufen liesse !
> Ihm ziemt's, die Welt im Innern zu bewegen,
> Natur in Sich, Sich in Natur zu hegen,
> So dass, was in Ihm lebt und webt und ist,
> Nie Seine Kraft, nie Seinen Geist vermisst."

> What were a God, who did, but from without,
> Upon its course, the Universe impel !
> Him it behoves within His world to move,
> Nature in Him, He in Nature to dwell :
> So that in Him, what lives and moves and is,
> May never miss His Spirit nor His Power.

Our Jacob Boehme was filled with this great knowledge of Pantheism long before Goethe, indeed long before
Descartes and Spinoza. In *Aurora*, ch. xxiii., he
writes :—

" Many will say, what were a God whose body, sub-
" stance and virtue consisted of Fire, Air, Water and
" Earth ? But see, thou unbelieving man, I will shew
" thee the true essence of the Godhead. Inasmuch as
" this whole substance is not God, thou art not God's
" Image; wheresoever there be a strange God, thou hast
" no part in Him. For thou art created out of God, and
" livest in Him, and He ever gives thee, out of Himself,
" power, blessing, food and drink; thy knowledge also is
" all from Him, and, when thou diest, thou wilt be buried

" in Him. . . . See; that is the true and only God, out of
" whom thou art created, and in whom thou livest.
" When thou lookest upon the deep, and upon the stars,
" and the earth, thou seest thy God, and in Him thou art
" and livest, and this same God governs thee also, and
" from the same God hast thou [received] thy senses, and
" thou art a creature in Him and from Him; otherwise
" wert thou nothing.　Now thou wilt say that what I
" write is heathenish.　But hear and see and mark the
" difference, how it all is; for what I write is not
" heathenish, but philosophical.　I am no heathen; but
" I have the deep and true knowledge of the one great
" God who is the All " (pars. 3, 4, 9, 10).

　　" Therefore we cannot say that God's being is some-
" thing afar, that possesses or occupies any particular spot
" or place; for the Abyss of nature and creature is God
" Himself " (*Divine Contemplation*, iii. 21).

　　But, decidedly as Boehme declares himself in these
words on the side of Pantheism, he is yet very far from
accepting it as all-sufficient.　" Since it is the truth, I
" must affirm that God is all.　But what shall I do with
" such a statement? for it is no religion.　Such a
" religion did the devil accept, and wanted to be manifest
" in all things and mighty in all " (*Apol. II. contra
Tylcken*, 140).　By declaring Pantheism insufficient, and
describing it as the devil's religion, our philosopher
means doubtless that Pantheism must take account of
all that is in the world, and look not only upon good,
but also upon evil, as God's Self-manifestation; and that
therefore the pantheistic god is not only God, but, as
first originator of evil, also the devil.　While ordinary
Pantheism makes light of the fact of evil, and explains
it away as merely negative, as the unavoidable shadow
to the light, and so on, Jacob Boehme, on the contrary,
deeply filled with the consciousness of this same fact
of evil, considers it in all its magnitude, and earnestly
strives to find an answer to the question, Whence is evil?
A question over which all pantheistic and theistic

theories alike come to grief. For Pantheism, considering the universe as God Himself, cannot admit evil as such; and Theism is unable adequately to explain it even by falling back upon the doctrine of free-will, since it allows that free-will is divinely created, and therefore ultimately, though indirectly, God must be regarded as the originator of evil.

There is another solution of these difficulties; but it lies very deep and becomes only possible by looking upon the human soul not—according to Pantheism—as a mode of the divine substance; nor, according to Theism, as the work of the Creator; but rather as absolutely self-existent. In other words, it is to be considered that good and evil, God and the devil, heaven and hell are opposed possibilities within the soul, in relation to which the soul possesses perfect liberty of choice, and full independence from any external influence and from any predetermined inherent condition; for even this is the deep meaning of the word free-will.

This solution of endless difficulties was, it is true, not perceived quite fully or clearly by Jacob Boehme; but, in his best moments, he comes nearer to it than any other philosopher before him, and expresses it occasionally as distinctly as was possible to him under the influence of Biblical theistic tradition. Let us compare such quotations as the following: " For each man is free, " and as a god to himself; he may transform himself in " this life, in the wrath or in the light" (*Aurora*, xviii. 43). "Since man has free-will, God is not Almighty " over him, to do with him what He wills. The free- " will has neither beginning nor cause; it is neither " limited, nor formed by anything. It is its own Self's " origin, out of the Word's divine virtue, out of God's " love and anger. It forms for itself in its own will a " centre to its own seat; it begets itself in the first " Principle to the fire and to the light. Its true origin " is from the no-thing, when the no-thing . . . . intro- " duces itself into a liking for contemplation [perception,

" vision], and the liking introduces itself into a will, and
" the will into a desire, and the desire into a substance "
(*Mysterium Magnum*, xxvi. 53). " So he lives in two
" Principles, both of which draw him and desire to have
" him, (1) in the source of the fierceness, whose origin is
" the darkness of the abyss, and (2) in the divine virtue,
" whose source is the light and the divine joy in the
" broken [burst] gates of heaven. . . . Thus is man
" attracted to both and held by both; but in him stands
" the centre, which holds the balance between the two
" wills " (*Three Principles*, xxi. 19, 20). "Thus we
" should take heed and beget that which is good out of
" ourselves. If we make an angel of ourselves, we are
" that; if we make a devil of ourselves, we are that
" also " (*Incarnation*, II., ix. 12–14). " Therefore let
" each (one) heed what he does. Each man is his own
" God and also his own devil; as he inclines to, or gives
" himself unto, either of these Principles, the same impels
" and leads him, and becomes his master " (*Incarnation*,
I., v. 133).

Summing up these thoughts, and freeing them as
much as possible from all obscurity, we obtain as the
fundamental essence of Boehme's philosophy the following
propositions :—The Principle of all things, the Godhead,
must be regarded as a Being in whom the contraries
good and evil are already contained, yet not as good
or evil; but as an equilibrium of mutually opposed,
yet complementary and harmoniously working, forces.
They are already good and evil, but only in possibility,
not in reality ;(not yet " kindled " as Boehme has it; not
made actual, as we should express it. This possible
good and evil which is latent in God becomes actual
only when the soul in its own primordial freedom
chooses the one or the other. The soul is not a being
different from God, but, on the contrary, is fundamentally
the divine substance itself, inasmuch as it brings into a
reality the possible opposition between good and evil.
In Boehme's own words: " The inner essence of the soul

" is the divine nature . . . . and is neither evil nor good,
" but . . . . in the kindled life of the soul the same will
" divides itself; . . . . it is itself its own cause to good
" and evil; for it is the centre of God, where God's love
" and anger are latent and undeveloped in one essence"
(*Election*, viii. 275–278). "Therefore the soul is God's
own substance" (*Three Principles*, iv. 20).

And therefore also our re-birth and salvation through
the Christ within us are but a return to our own primordial divine being. Boehme writes: "Nothing can
" rest in itself; it must return to that whence it came.
" The mind has turned away from unity in a desire for
" perception [experience], to try the qualities in separa-
" tion [as apart from one another], and therefore the
" separation [division, contrary will, evil] arose in it,
" which now governs the mind. Neither can it be set
" free, until it forsakes itself in the desire for the
" qualities, and lifts itself again into perfect stillness,
" silencing its own will, so that the will may penetrate
" [merge again] beyond all sense and form, into the
" eternal will of the Abyss whence it originated; willing
" nothing of itself, but only what God wills through it"
(*Mysterium Magnum, Abstract* 7).

We have tried in the above to extract from Boehme's
teaching that kernel which lies embedded therein, of
first principles and essential truths drawn from nature,
and therefore irrefutable. We will now briefly consider
the shell of myth and symbolism which encloses the
same. / Boehme himself is well aware of the inadequacy
of his exposition, inasmuch as he unceasingly impresses
upon his readers that, on account of human weakness,
he describes as a time-process that which is eternal, and
sets side by side things which are inter-dependent and
joined with one another in a perfect unity. Having
pointed this out, he describes how originally God only is
the Abyss out of which all "Byss" issues; the primordial condition of all being, and therefore Himself

without substance, nature or qualities; the eternal silence, the All and the No-thing; neither darkness nor light; manifest to none, not even to Himself. In the portraying of this eternal One, Boehme links the Christian tradition of the Trinity with the Neoplatonic division of the One in subject and object, by placing Son and Spirit between the Father (subject) and the "wisdom" wherein He mirrors His being (world of ideas). "The first only will, without a beginning, begets "in itself a comprehensible will which is Son to the "Abyssal Will, when the Nothing makes itself within "itself into a Something . . . . wherein the Abyss "conceives [forms] itself into a Byss, and the issue of "the Abyssal Will through the conceived Son is called "Spirit; and that which is issued is the delight wherein "the Father ever finds and beholds Son and Spirit; and "it is called God's Wisdom, or Contemplation" (*Election*, i. 10–17). "Therein lie all things as a divine Imagina- "tion, wherein all ideas of angels and souls are seen "eternally in divine likeness, not as creatures, but as a "reflection; as when a man beholds himself in a mirror" (*Clavis*, par. 43). This constructive blending of Christian and Neoplatonic traditions, on account of which Boehme was reproached with teaching a "Quaternary" ('quartitatem' instead of 'quantitatem' is anyhow used in Richter's abusive verses), is entirely in contradiction to his fundamental idea, because it assumes opposites to be already in God; while the very lack of contraries and the necessity for the same is made the motive for further developments, as the following shews :—

"The reader must know that all things consist in "Yes or No, whether Godly, devilish, earthly, or whatso- "ever it may be called. The One, as the Yes, is pure "power [virtue] and life, and is the truth of God, or "God Himself. But God would be unknowable to "Himself, and would have in Himself no joy, perception "or exaltation without the No. The No is the opposite "[antithesis] to the Yes or the truth. In order that the

" truth may be manifest as a Something, there must be
" a contrary therein" (*Theosoph. Quest.* iii. 2. 4).   As the
light of the sun is made visible by the dark pewter
vessel, so can God manifest Himself only through con-
trariety in Himself.   Boehme construes this con-
trariety or opposition by taking as starting-point the
two fundamental attributes of Divine Being, as revealed
in Holy Scripture, namely, the Wrath and the Love.
These further branch out into the seven throne Spirits
(*Revel.* i. 4; iv. 5), the first three of which represent God's
wrath, and the last three, God's love; while the central
fourth constitutes the pivot-point of both worlds, being
common to the wrath or darkness and to the love or
light.   These seven forms, to which Boehme constantly
refers, and which he describes again and again as being
his fundamental idea, are however not the basic powers
of actual nature; but constitute what our philosopher
calls "the eternal nature in God."   Now he had of
course to borrow the colours wherewith he pictures this
eternal nature, from the world of our experience, and
the difficulty to understand him arises from his ever
renewed endeavours to describe each of these properties
or forms and their inter-relation and operation; whereby
the picture becomes so overdone, so complex and
variegated, that it is scarcely possible to follow the main
conception.   Indeed, it almost becomes doubtful at times,
owing to the many variations of symbol and imagery,
whether any main idea underlies the whole scheme as a
unifying foundation.   Thus, for instance, he describes
the first form as the astringency, the hardness, the coldness, attraction, desire; the second as motion, perception,
sweetness, the sting, the fleeing; the third arises from
both the others, and is called anguish, wandering, the
wheel of life, etc.   "In these first three forms consists
" the essence of anger, of hell, and of all that is wrath-
" ful."   The fourth form is the fire, the origin of life, the
desire; and is a fire of anger in relation to the first
three, and a love-fire in relation to the last three.   And

these last three forms which constitute God's eternal kingdom of joy are, (5) the light, love, (6) the sound, intelligent life, (7) the (ideal) loveliness, in no corporeal sense, but essential and manifest; the eternal, substantial Wisdom of God; the epitome of all forms, all colours and all beauty.

The first four forms constitute the first Principle, corresponding to the "Father"; the last four (beginning again from the fourth) constitute the second Principle, corresponding to the "Son." By the third Principle, Boehme understands, now the interaction of both Principles, as the Holy Spirit; now the corporeal nature derived from the seven forms.

The motive for this whole teaching of "forms" or "qualities" is, owing to the abundance and variety of imagery, not easy to discern or point out. But we may venture to suppose that the philosopher was guided by his awareness of the presence of good and evil in all things, and that he found the good in the visibility, the audibleness and the form, in the intellectual side, in short of nature, wherefrom he took light, sound and loveliness as the last three forms; while the impression of the "furious madness" of mutually antagonistic elemental forces in lifeless inorganic nature furnished material for his first three forms. Describing the arising of the anguish (3rd form) out of the two first forms, Boehme uses the following words: "The hardness " (1st form) is a holding, and the drawing [or pull] is " afleeing. One wills (to stay) in itself; the other (to " go) out of itself; but as they cannot yield or part, they " become, within one another, as a turning-wheel . . . . " and hence follows a fearful anguish [terror]." Now, on reading the above, everyone will probably be reminded of Attraction and Repulsion, the struggle of which begets, in a body circumscribed in space, limitation, or, as Boehme calls it, "the anguish." Only here, as everywhere, other elements have been brought into this view of the fundamental facts of nature, and distort it so as to make it well-nigh unrecognizable. Yet the under-lying idea ever breaks through, namely, that the peculiar essence of the first three forms, and, through these, of the others, is a hunger, a desire, a will which in the fourth form becomes fire, the origin of life, and that therein also the forms of light and love have their foundation. "The wrath is the root of all things." "And if the will be in darkness, it is then in the "anguish; for it desires (to be) out of the dark-"ness . . . . and excites the root of the fire . . . . and "dwells in the broken [burst] darkness, in the light, in "sweetness and joy in itself" (*Three Principles*, xxi. 13, 16).

The fourth form, the, fire, is the *centrum naturæ*; it is the pivot between the kingdom of light and that of darkness, between love and anger, between good and evil; it is the turning-point whence the will may exercise its sway in either direction, be it backward into the darkness, or forward into the world of light and divine love. "It is free, and has the choice between both of these."

The freedom of the will—Boehme develops this theme in connection with Biblical tradition and through a highly spiritual treatment of the same—leads to the fall, which consists in a breaking away of self-will from the divine will. The fall of Adam is preceded by that of Lucifer. The latter was created the mightiest angel in heaven; but instead of setting his "imagination in the light of God," and to "walk in God," he attempted, on the strength of his free-will, to measure himself against God, "triumph over the divine birth and lift himself above the Heart of God," and thereby "he removed himself out of God's love into God's anger," inclined himself towards "the dark world with the kingdom of phantasy," went out of the light, became limited to the first forms, which without the eternal light, constitute the Abyss, the anger of God and hell. "The foundation of hell is from all eternity, but was not manifest, until awakened." The division between heaven and hell is not in terms of space. "Heaven is in " hell and hell in heaven, and neither manifest to the " other" (*Mysterium Magnum*, viii. 28). In the place of the rejected Lucifer—here Boehme expounds the Mosaic creation story—God created man in His own likeness, more perfect than the Angels, destined to rule over all things. "Heaven, earth, stars and elements, all, as well " as the divine Trinity, are represented in man, and " nothing can be named that is not in man."—"The soul " of Adam was from the eternal will, out of the *centro* " *naturæ*, where light and darkness divide. Understand! " he is no separated spark, as a part from the whole; " for he is no part, but the whole altogether; just as " every point is a whole" (*Threefold Life*, vi. 47, 49).

Man was placed between the kingdoms of light and darkness, free to choose. "The will of the soul is free, " either to sink in itself and heed nothing, but to grow " as a branch on a tree and eat of God's love, or to lift " itself in the fire, in its own will and be an own tree " " (*Forty Quest.*, ii. 2). "But the will of life broke itself " away from the Divine Essence, and went into percep- " tion [experience], out of unity into variety [complexity], " and resisted the unity as the eternal rest and only " good" (*Divine Contemplation*, ii. 7). "The soul's " essence became enamoured with the creation of the " formed word in its freedom of choice, and lifted itself " in longing for freedom" (*Election*, vi. 73). "When the " longing for the spirit of this world became uppermost " in Adam, he sank into sleep."—"The sleep denotes " death and an overcoming."—"But with the sleep, time " became manifest in man; he fell asleep to the angelical " world, and awakened to the external world." The Virgin, the Divine Wisdom, who hitherto had dwelt in him, now fled from him, and in her stead, the earthly wife was given him, with whom the fall into sin was consummated and extended to the whole of mankind; " for the souls of men are altogether as if they were one "soul" (*Threefold Life*, xvi. 13). But redemption also remained, hidden as a germ in humanity (Boehme conveys this through allegories of the deepest meaning, by following up the idea throughout the Old Testament), until it was born, as the Saviour from Mary, into whom had also passed [entered] the eternal Virgin, the Divine Wisdom.

But "the historical belief in Christ is a mere spark (of " the fire) that must first be set alight."—"None is a " Christian, unless Christ lives and works in him."— " When Christ arises, then Adam dies with his serpent- " substance; when the sun rises, the night is swallowed " up in the day and there is no more night."—"Whoso- " ever has Christ in himself is a Christian, is crucified " and dead with Christ, and lives in His resurrection."— " Zion is not born first outwardly, but interiorly; we " must seek and find ourselves within ourselves."—"No " one need run anywhere . . . . but in himself is the gate " to the Divinity. . . . Whither shall the soul lift itself, " since it is itself the source of Eternity?"

A newer theologian (Harless, *J. Boehme and the Alchemists*) affirms, on account of these statements, that Boehme has wiped out Christ for us, and left only Christ in us. We would remark in answer that, if those who possess Him yet miss anything, then must their conception of Christ in us be very inadequate.

As regards the question: Where does the soul go after death? Boehme writes in his little book, *Of the Supersensual Life*: "It has no need to go; it has heaven and " hell within itself. The kingdom of God is within you."— " Heaven and hell are within one another and are to "one another as a nothing."

"Wheresoever thou dost not dwell according to thy "Selfhood and thine own will, there do the angels dwell " with thee and everywhere; and wheresoever thou " dwellest according to thy Selfhood and thine own will, " there do the devils dwell with thee and everywhere."

And as he expressed in such words the nothingness of

space, so does he also express the nothingness of this
temporal order of life in the verse he used to write in
his friends' albums :—

> "Weme Zeit ist wie Ewigkeit
> Und Ewigkeit wie die Zeit,
> Der ist befreit
> Von allem Streit."

(He is made free from all strife, to whom time is as
Eternity and Eternity as time.)

THE FIRST CHAPTER

Of the first Principle of the Divine ¹ Essence.

¹ Being or Substance.

1. SEEING we are now to speak of God, what he is, and where he is, we must say, that God himself is the essence of all essences; for all is generated or born, created and proceeded from him, and all things take their first beginning out of God; as the Scripture witnesseth, saying, *Through him, and in him are all things.* Also, *The heaven and the heaven of heavens are not able to contain him:* Also, *Heaven is my throne, and the earth is my footstool:* And in *Our Father* is mentioned, *Thine is the kingdom and the power;* understand all power.

2. But there is yet this difference [to be observed], that evil neither is, nor is called God; this is understood in the first Principle, where it is the earnest fountain of the wrathfulness, according to which, God calleth himself an angry, wrathful, and zealous God. For the original of life, and of all mobility, consisteth in the wrathfulness; yet if the [tartness] be kindled with the light of God, it is then no more tartness, but the severe wrathfulness is changed into great joy.

1

[1] Or materials, materia.

[2] essence, or substance.

[3] Or Scorching.

[4] begetteth, beareth, or bringeth forth.

[5] astringency, or attracting.

[6] infecteth, impregnateth, or mixeth seed in itself.

3. Now when God was to create the world, and all things therein, he had no other [1] matter to make it of, but his own [2] being, out of himself. But now, God is a spirit that is incomprehensible, which hath neither beginning nor end, and his greatness and depth is all. Yet a spirit doth nothing but ascend, flow, move, and continually generate itself, and in itself hath chiefly a threefold manner of form in its generating or birth, *viz.* Bitterness, Harshness, and [3] Heat, and these three manners of forms are none of them the first, second, nor third; for all these three are but one, and each of them [4] generateth the second and third. For between [5] harshness and bitterness, fire is generated : and the wrath of the fire is the bitterness or sting itself, and the harshness is the stock or father of both these, and yet is generated of them both; for a spirit is like a will, sense [or thought], which riseth up, and in its rising beholdeth, [6] perfecteth, and generateth itself.

4. Now this cannot be expressed or described, nor brought to the understanding by the tongue of man; for God hath no beginning. But I will set it down so as if he had a beginning, that it might be understood what is in the first Principle, whereby the difference between the first and second Principles may be understood, and what God or spirit is. Indeed there is no difference in God, only when it is enquired from whence evil and good proceed, it is to be known, what is the first and original fountain of anger, and also of love, since they both proceed

from one and the same original, out of one mother, and are one thing. Thus we must speak after a creaturely manner, as if it took a beginning, that it might be brought to be understood.

5. For it cannot be said that fire, bitterness, or harshness, is in God, much less that air, water, or earth is in him; only it is plain that all things have proceeded out of that [original]. Neither can it be said, that death, hell-fire, or sorrowfulness is in God, but it is known that these things have come out of that [original]. For God hath made no devil out of himself, but angels to live in joy, to their comfort and rejoicing; yet it is seen that devils came to be, and that they became God's enemies. Therefore the source or fountain of the cause must be sought, *viz.* What is the *prima materia*, or first matter of evil, and that in the originalness of God as well as in the creatures; for it is all but one only thing in originalness: All is out of God, made out of his [1] essence, according to the Trinity, as he is one in essence and threefold in Persons.

[1] being or substance.

6. Behold, there are especially three things in the originalness, out of which all things are, both spirit and life, motion and comprehensibility, viz. [2] *Sulphur*, [3] *Mercurius*, and [4] *Sal*. But you will say that these are in nature, and not in God; which indeed is so, but nature hath its ground in God, according to the first Principle of the Father, for God calleth himself also an angry zealous God; which is not so to be understood, that God is angry

[2] Wherein the kindling consisteth.

[3] The spirit of a substance.

[4] Salt, body, or substantiality.

in himself, but in the spirit of the [creation or] creature which kindleth itself; and then God burneth in the first Principle therein, and the spirit of the [creation or] creature suffereth pain, and not God.

7. Now to speak in a creaturely way, *Sulphur*, *Mercurius*, and *Sal*, are understood to be thus. *S U L* is the soul or the spirit that is risen up, or in a similitude [it is] God: *P H U R* is the *prima materia*, or first matter out of which the spirit is generated, but especially the [1]harshness: *Mercurius* hath a fourfold form in it, *viz.* harshness, bitterness, fire, and water: *Sal* is the child that is generated from these four, and is harsh, eager, and a cause of the comprehensibility.

8. [2]Understand aright now what I declare to you: Harshness, bitterness, and fire, are in the originalness, in the first Principle: The water-source is generated therein: And God is not called God according to the first Principle; but according to that he is called wrathfulness, angriness, the earnest [severe or tart] source, from which evil, and also the woeful tormenting, trembling, and burning, have their original.

9. This is as was mentioned before; the harshness is the *prima materia*, or first matter, which is strong, and very eagerly and earnestly attractive, that is *Sal*: The bitterness is [3]in the strong attracting, for the spirit sharpeneth itself in the strong attracting, so that it becometh wholly aching

[1] astringency or attraction.

[2] Observe or consider.

[3] generated.

[anxious or vexed]. For example, in man, when he is enraged, how his spirit attracteth itself, which maketh him bitter [or sour] and trembling ; and if it be not suddenly withstood and quenched, we see that the fire of anger kindleth in him so, that he burneth in malice, and then presently a [1] substance or whole essence cometh to be in the spirit and mind, to be revenged.

[1] an essential, real imagination, or purpose.

10. Which is a similitude of that which is in the original of the generating of nature : Yet it must be set down more intelligibly [and plainly]. Mark what *Mercurius* is, it is harshness, bitterness, fire, and brimstone-water, the most horrible [2] essence ; yet you must understand hereby no *materia*, matter, or comprehensible thing; but all no other than spirit, and the source of the original nature. Harshness is the first essence, which attracteth itself; but it being a hard cold virtue or power, the spirit is altogether prickly [stinging] and sharp. Now the sting and sharpness cannot endure attracting, but moveth and resisteth [or opposeth] and is a contrary will, an enemy to the harshness, and from that [3] stirring cometh the first mobility, which is the third form. Thus the harshness continually attracteth harder and harder, and so it becometh hard and tart [strong or fierce], so that the virtue or power is as hard as the hardest stone, which the bitterness [that is, the harshness' own sting or prickle] cannot endure ; and then there is great anguish in it, like the horrible brimstone spirit,

[2] being, substance, or thing.

[3] Or wriggling.

and the sting of the bitterness, which rubbeth itself so hard, that in the anguish there cometh to be a twinkling flash, which flieth up terribly, and breaketh the [1] harshness : But it finding no rest, and being so continually generated from beneath, it is as a turning wheel, which turneth anxiously and terribly with the twinkling flash [2] furiously, and so the flash is changed into a pricking [stinging] fire, which yet is no burning fire, but like the fire in a stone.

11. But seeing there is no rest there, and that the turning wheel runneth as fast as a swift thought, for the prickle driveth it so fast, the prickle kindleth itself so much, that the flash (which is generated between the astringency and bitterness) becometh horribly fiery, and flieth up like a horrible fire, from whence the whole *materia* or matter is terrified, and falleth back as dead, or overcome, and doth not attract so [3] strongly to itself any more, but each yieldeth itself to go out one from another, and so it becometh thin. For the fire-flash is now predominant, and the *materia*, or matter, which was so very harsh [astringent or attracting] in the originalness, is now feeble, and as it were dead, and the fire-flash henceforth getteth strength therein, for it is its mother; and the bitterness goeth forth up in the flash together with the harshness, and kindleth the flash, for it is the father of the flash, or fire, and the turning wheel henceforth standeth in the fire-flash, and the harsh-

[1] Or astringent attraction.

[2] Or senselessly and madly.

[3] Or eagerly.

ness remaineth overcome and feeble, which is now the water-spirit; and the *materia*, or matter of the harshness, henceforth is like the brimstone-spirit, very thin, raw, aching, vanquished, and the sting in it is trembling; and it drieth and sharpeneth itself in the flash; and being so very dry in the flash, it becometh continually more horrible and fiery, whereby the harshness or astringency is still more overcome, and the water-spirit continually greater. And so it continually refresheth itself in the water-spirit, and continually bringeth more matter to the fire-flash, whereby it is the more kindled; for (in a similitude) that is the [1] fuel of [1] Or wood. the flash or fire-spirit.

12. [2] Understand aright the manner of the [2] Or consider seriously, observe, or mark. existence of this *Mercurius*. The word M E R, is first the strong, tart, harsh attraction; for in that word (or syllable *Mer*) expressed by the tongue, you understand that it jarreth [proceeding] from the harshness, and you understand also, that the bitter sting or prickle is in it; for the word M E R is harsh and trembling, and every word [or syllable] is formed or framed from its power or virtue, [and expresseth] whatsoever the power or virtue doth or suffereth. You [may] understand that the word [or syllable] C U, is [or signifieth] the rubbing or unquietness of the sting or prickle, which maketh that the harshness is not at peace, but [3] heaveth [3] Or boileth. and riseth up; for that syllable [thrusteth itself or] presseth forth with the virtue [or breath] from the

heart, out of the mouth. It is done thus also in the virtue or power of the *prima materia* [or first matter] in the spirit, but the syllable C U having so strong a pressure from the heart, and yet is so presently snatched up by the syllable R I, and the whole understanding [sense or meaning] is changed into it; this signifieth and is the bitter prickly ^1 Or geniture. wheel in the ¹generating, which vexeth and whirleth itself as swiftly as a thought : The syllable U S is [or signifieth] the swift fire-flash, that the *materia*, or matter, kindleth in the fierce whirling between the harshness and the bitterness in the swift wheel; where you may very plainly understand [or observe] in the word, how the harshness is terrified, and how the power or virtue in the word sinketh down, or falleth back again upon the heart, and becometh very feeble and thin : Yet the sting or prickle with the whirling wheel, continueth in the flash, and goeth forth through the teeth out of the mouth; where then the spirit hisseth like a fire a-kindling, and returning back again strengtheneth itself in the word.

13. These four forms are in the originalness of nature, and from thence the mobility doth exist, as also the life in the seed, and in all the creatures, hath its original from thence; and there is no comprehensibility in the originalness, but such a virtue or power and spirit. For it is a poisonous ² being, es- or venomous, hostile or inimicitious ²thing: And sence, or it must be so, or else there would be no mobility,
substance.

but all [would be as] nothing, and the source of wrath or anger is the first [1] original of nature.

[1] originalness or originality.

14. Yet here I do not altogether [mean or] understand the *Mercurius* [mercury or quicksilver] which is in the third Principle [2] of this created world, which the apothecaries use (although that hath the same virtue or power, and is of the same essence), but I speak [of that] in the first Principle, *viz.* of the originalness of the essence of all essences, of God, and of the eternal beginningless nature, from whence the nature of this world is generated. Although in the originalness of both of them there is no separation; but only the outward and third Principle, the sidereal and elementary kingdom [region or dominion] is generated out of the first Principle by the Word and spirit of God out of the eternal Father, out of the holy heaven.

[2] or.

THE SECOND CHAPTER

Of the first and second Principles, what God and the Divine Nature are; wherein is set down a further description of the Sulphur and Mercurius.

1. BECAUSE there belongeth a divine light to the knowledge and apprehension of this, and that without the divine light there is no comprehensibility at all of the divine essence, therefore I will a little represent the high hidden secret in a creaturely manner, that thereby the Reader may come into the depth. For the divine essence cannot be wholly expressed by the tongue; the *spiraculum vitae* (that is, the spirit of the soul which looketh into the light) only comprehendeth it. For every creature seeth and understandeth no further nor deeper than its mother is, out of which it is come originally.

2. The soul which hath its original out of God's first Principle, and was breathed from God into man, [1]into the third Principle, (that is, into the sidereal and elementary [2]birth) that seeth further into the first Principle of God, out of, in and from,

[1] Or in.

[2] generating of the stars.

10

the essence and property of which it is proceeded. And this is not marvellous, for it doth but behold itself only in the rising of its birth; and thus it seeth the whole depth of the Father in the first Principle.

3. This the devils also see and know; for they also are out of the first Principle of God, which is the source of God's original nature. They wish also that they might not see nor feel it; but it is their own fault that the second Principle is shut up to them, which is called and is God, one in essence, and threefold in personal distinction, as shall be mentioned hereafter.

4. But the soul of man, which is enlightened with the Holy Spirit of God, (which in the second Principle proceedeth from the Father and the Son in the holy heaven, that is, in the true divine nature [1] which is called God), this soul seeth even into the light of God, into the same second Principle of the holy divine [2] birth, into the heavenly essence: But the [3] sidereal spirit wherewith the soul is clothed, and also the elementary [spirit] which [4] ruleth the source, or springing and impulsion of the blood, they see no further than into their mother, whence they are, and wherein they live.

[1] Viz. The Holy Ghost.

[2] Or working.

[3] astral, or starry spirit.

[4] Or hath.

5. Therefore if I should speak and write that which is purely heavenly, and altogether of the clear Deity, I should be as dumb to the Reader, who hath not the knowledge and the gift [to understand it]. Yet I will so write in a divine,

and also in a creaturely way, that I might stir up any one to desire and long after the consideration of the high things : And if any shall perceive that they cannot do it, that at least they might seek and knock in their desire, and pray to God for his Holy Spirit, that the door of the second Principle might be opened to them ; for Christ biddeth us to pray, seek, and knock, and then it shall be opened unto us. For he saith, All that you shall ask the Father in my name, he will give it you : Ask and you shall receive ; seek, and you shall find ; knock, and it shall be opened unto you.

6. Seeing then that my knowledge hath been received by seeking and knocking, I therefore write it down for a Memorial, that I might occasion a desire in any to seek after them, and thereby my talent might be improved, and not be hidden in the earth.   But I have not written this for those that are wise aforehand, that know all things, and yet know and comprehend nothing, for they are [1] fully satisfied already, and rich ; but I have written it for the simple, as I am, that I may be refreshed with those that are like myself.

[1] That is, wise in their own conceit, and in their blindness think they see well enough.

Further of the Sulphur, Mercurius, and Sal.

7. The word [or syllable] S U L, signifieth and is the soul of a thing ; for in the word it is the oil or light that is generated out of the syllable P H U R ; and it is the beauty or the [2] welfare of a thing, that which is lovely and dearest in it : In a creature it

[2] well-doing, or flourishing, or beneficialness.

is the light by which the creature seeth [or per-
ceiveth]: and therein reason and the senses consist,
and it is the spirit which is generated out of the
PHUR. The word or syllable PHUR, is the
prima materia [or first matter], and containeth in
itself in the third Principle the [1] *macrocosm,* from [1] Or great
which the elementary dominion, or region, or essence world.
is generated: But in the first Principle it is the
essence of the most inward birth, out of which
God generateth or begetteth his Son from eternity,
and thereout the Holy Ghost proceedeth; understand out of the SUL and out of the PHUR.
And in man also it is the light which is generated
out of the sidereal spirit, in the [2] second centre of [2] Or second
the *microcosm*; but in the *spiraculum* and spirit of ground of the
the soul, in the most inward centre, it is the light little world.
of God, which that soul only hath which is in the
love of God, for it is only kindled and blown up
from the Holy Ghost.

8. Observe now the depth of the divine [3] birth; [3] Or of the
there is no Sulphur in God, but it is generated from eternal divine
him, and there is such a virtue or power in him. working.
For the syllable PHUR is [or signifieth] the most
inward virtue or power of the original source or
spring of the anger of the fierce tartness, or of the
mobility, as is mentioned in the first chapter, and
that syllable PHUR hath a fourfold form [property
or power] in it, as first, harshness [or astringency],
and then bitterness, fire, and water: the harshness
is attractive, and is rough, cold and sharp, and

maketh all hard, hungry, and full of anguish; and that attracting is a bitter sting or prickle, very terrible, and the first swelling or boiling up existeth in the anguish; yet because it cannot rise higher from its seat, but is thus continually generated from beneath, therefore it falleth into a turning or wheeling, as swift as a thought, in great anguish, and therein it falleth to be a twinkling flash, as if a steel and flint, or stone, were strongly struck together, and rubbed one against another.

9. For the harshness is as hard as a stone [or flint], and the bitterness rusheth and rageth like a [1] breaking wheel, which breaketh the hardness, and stirreth up the fire, so that all falleth to be a terrible [2] crack of fire, and flieth up; and the harshness or astringency breaketh in pieces, whereby the dark tartness is terrified and sinketh back, and becometh as it were feeble or weak, or as if it were killed and dead, and runneth out, and becometh thin, and yieldeth itself to be overcome: But when the strong flash of fire [3] shineth back again upon or into the tartness, and is mingled therein, and findeth the harshness so thin and overcome, then it is much more terrified; for it is as if water were thrown upon the fire, which maketh a crack: Yet when the crack or terror is thus made in the overcome harshness, thereby it getteth another source [condition or property], and a [4] crack, or noise of great joy, proceedeth out of the wrathful fierceness, and riseth up in fierce strength, as a kindled

[1] as the wheel in a fire-lock striketh fire by turning round.

[2] rumbling, or thunderclap.

[3] Or reflecteth.

[4] Or shriek.

light: For the crack, in the twinkling of an eye, becometh white, clear, and light; for thus the kindling of the light cometh in that very moment, as soon as the light (that is, the new crack of the fire) is infected or [1] impregnated with the harshness, [1] Or filled. the tartness or astringency kindleth, and shrieketh, or is affrighted by the great light that cometh into it in the twinkling of an eye, as if it did awake from death, and becometh soft or [2] meek, lively and [2] Or lovely. joyful; it presently loseth its dark, rough, harsh, and cold virtue, and leapeth or springeth up for joy, and rejoiceth in the light; and its sting or prickle, which is the bitterness, that triumpheth in the turning wheel for great joy.

10. Here observe, the shriek or crack of the fire is kindled in the anguish in the brimstone-spirit, and then the shriek flieth up triumphantly; and the aching, or anxious harshness, or brimstone-spirit, is made thin and sweet by the light. For as the light or the flash becometh clearer or brighter from the crack of the fire in the vanquished harsh tartness, and loseth its wrathful fierce [3] property, so [3] dominion, or jurisdiction. the tartness loseth its authority by the infection or mixture of the light, and is made thin or transparent and sweet by the white light: For in the original the harshness or astringency was altogether dark, and aching with anguish, by reason of its hardness and attracting; but now it is wholly light, and thereupon it loseth its own quality or property, and out of the wrathful harshness there cometh to

¹ Or springing substance.

be an ¹essence that is sharp, and the light maketh the sharpness altogether sweet.

The ² Gates of God.

² The divine everlasting Gates or Doors, by which we have entrance to the Deity.

11. Behold now, when the bitterness, or the bitter sting [or prickle] (which in the original was so very bitter, raging and tearing, when it took its original in the harshness) attaineth this clear light, and tasteth now the sweetness in the harshness, which is its mother, then it is so joyful, and cannot rise or swell so any more, but it trembleth and rejoiceth in its mother that bare it, and triumpheth like a joyful wheel in the birth. And in this triumph the birth attaineth the fifth form, and then the fifth source springeth up, *viz.* the ³ friendly

³ Or loving-favour.

love; and so when the bitter spirit tasteth the sweet water, it rejoiceth in its mother [the sour tart harshness], and so refresheth and strengtheneth

⁴ with, or for.

itself therein, and maketh its mother stirring ⁴in great joy; where then there springeth up in the sweet water-spirit a very sweet pleasant source or fountain: For the fire-spirit (which is the root of the light, which was a strong [fierce rumbling shriek, crack, or] terror in the beginning) that now riseth up very lovely, pleasantly and joyfully.

12. And here is nothing but the kiss of love, and wooing, and here the bridegroom embraceth his beloved bride, and is no otherwise than when the pleasing life is born or generated in the sour, tart, or harsh death; and the birth of life is thus,

in a creature. For from this [1] stirring, moving, or wheeling of the bitterness in the essence of the harsh astringent tartness of the water-spirit, the birth attaineth the sixth [2] form, *viz.* the sound or noise of the motion. And this sixth [2] form is rightly called *Mercurius*; for it taketh its form, virtue, and beginning, in the aching or anxious harshness, by the raging of the bitterness; for in the rising it taketh the virtue of its mother (that is, the [3] essence of the sweet harshness) along with it, and bringeth it into the fire-flash, from whence the light kindleth. And here the trial [or experience] beginneth, one virtue beholding the other in the fire-flash, one [virtue] feeleth the other by the rising up, by the stirring they one hear another, in the essence they one taste another, and by the pleasant, lovely [source, spring, or] fountain, they one smell another, from whence the sweetness of the light springeth up out of the essence of the sweet and harsh spirit, which from henceforth is the water-spirit. And out of these six forms, now in the birth, or generating, cometh a sixfold self-subsisting essence, which is inseparable; where they one continually generate another, and the one is not without the other, nor can be, and without this birth or substance there could be nothing; for the six forms have each of them now the essences of all their sixfold virtue in it, and it is as it were one only thing, and no more; only each form hath its own condition.

[1] Or wriggling.

[2] property, virtue, or power.

[3] The substance that springeth or buddeth out of the tartness.

2

13. For observe it, although now in the harshness there be bitterness, fire, sound, water, and that out of the springing vein of the water there floweth love (or oil) from whence the light ariseth and shineth; yet the [1]harshness retaineth its first property, and the bitterness its property, the fire its property, the sound or the stirring its property, and the overcoming the first harsh or tart anguish (*viz.* the returning down back again) or the water-spirit, its property, and the springing fountain, the pleasant love, which is kindled by the light in the tart or sour bitterness, (which now is the sweet [source or] springing vein of water) its property; and yet this is no separable essence parted asunder, but all one whole essence or substance in one another. And each form or birth taketh its own form, virtue, working and springing up from all the forms; and the whole birth now retaineth chiefly but these four forms in its generating or bringing forth; *viz.* the rising up, the falling down, and then through the turning [of the wheel in the sour, harsh] tart essence, the putting forth on this side, and on that side, on both sides like a cross; or, as I may so say, the going forth from the point [or centre] towards the east, the west, the north and the south: For from the stirring, moving, and ascending of the bitterness in the fire-flash, there existeth a cross birth. For the fire goeth forth upward, the water downward, and the essences of the harshness sideways.

[1] Or astringent attraction.

THE THIRD CHAPTER

Of the endless and numberless manifold engendering [¹ generating] or Birth of the eternal Nature.

The Gates of the great Depth.

1. READER, understand [and consider] my writings aright, we have no power or ability to speak of the birth of God [or the birth of the Deity], for it never had any beginning from all eternity ; but we have power to speak of God our Father, what he is, and how he is, and how the eternal ² geniture is.

2. And though it is not very good for us to know the austere, earnest [strong, fierce, severe] and original birth, into the knowledge, feeling and comprehensibility of which our first parents have brought us, through the ³ infection [instigation] and deceit of the devil, yet we have very great need of this knowledge, that thereby we may learn to know the devil, who dwelleth in the most strong [severe or cruel] birth of all, and [that we may learn to know] our own enemy *Self*, which our first parents ⁴ awakened and purchased for us,

¹ begetting, hatching, bearing, bringing, forth, or propagation.

² nativity, birth, or generation, or working.

³ mixture, poisoning, envenoming, or temptation.

⁴ Or roused up.

which we carry within us, and which we ourselves now are.

3. And although I write now, as if there were a beginning in the eternal birth, yet it is not so; but the eternal nature thus begetteth [or generateth] itself without beginning. My writings must be understood in a creaturely manner, as the birth of man is, who is a similitude of God. Although it be just so in the eternal being [essence or substance], yet that is both without beginning and without end; and my writing is only to this end, that man might learn to know what he is, what he was in the beginning, how he was a very glorious eternal holy man, that should never have known the gate of the strong [or austere] birth in the eternity, if he had not suffered himself to lust after it through the ¹ infection of the devil, and had not eaten of that ² fruit which was forbidden him; whereby he became such a naked and vain man in a bestial form, and lost the heavenly garment of the divine power, and liveth now in the kingdom of the devil in the ³ infected *Salnitre*, and feedeth upon the infected food. Therefore it is necessary for us to learn to know ourselves, what we are, and how we might be redeemed from the anguishing austere birth, and be regenerated or born anew, and live in the new man (which is like the first man before the fall) in Christ our ⁴ Regenerator.

4. For though I should speak or write never so much of the fall, and also of the regeneration in

¹ Or temptation.

² Viz. the fruit of the austere matrix or genetrix.

³ Or poisonous virtue.

⁴ Who bringeth us forth out of the wrath into the love of God.

Christ, and did not come to the root and ground,
what the fall was, and by what it was we came to
perish, and what that property is which God
abhorreth, and how that was effected, contrary to
the command and will of God, what should I understand of the thing? Just nothing! And then
how should I shun or avoid that which I have
no knowledge of? Or how should I endeavour
to come to the new birth, and give myself up
into it, if I knew not how, wherein, nor wherewith
to do it?

5. It is very true, the world is full of books and
sermons of the fall, and of the new birth: But in
the most part of the books of the [1]divines, there [1] theology.
is nothing but the history that such a thing hath
been done, and that we should be regenerated in
Christ. But what do I understand from hence?
Nothing, but only the history, that such a thing
hath been done, and done again, and ought to
be done.

6. Our divines set themselves hand and foot,
with might and main, with their utmost endeavour,
by persecution and reproach, against this, [and say]
that men must not [dare to] search into the deep
grounds what God is; men must not search nor
curiously pry into the Deity. But if I should
speak plainly what this trick of theirs is, it is the
dung and filth wherewith they cover and hide the
devil, and cloak the injected malice and wickedness
of the devil in man, so that neither the devil, nor

¹ Or evil will.

² But remaineth hidden and undiscovered.

the anger of God, nor the ¹ evil beast in man, ² can be discerned.

7. And this is the very reason, because the devil smelleth the matter, and therefore he hindereth it, that his kingdom might not be revealed, but that he might continue to be the great prince [of the world still]. For otherwise, if his kingdom were known, men might fly from him. Where is it more needful for him to oppose, than on that part where his enemy may break in? He therefore covereth the hearts, minds, thoughts, and senses of the divines; he leadeth them into covetousness, pride, and wantonness, so that they stand amazed with fear and horror at the light of God, and therefore they shut it up, for they are naked, nay they grudge the light to those that see it; this is rightly called the service and worship of the devil.

8. But the time is coming, when the Aurora or Day-Spring will break forth, and then the beast, that evil child [or child of perdition] shall stand forth naked and in great shame; for the judgment of the whore of the great beast goeth on. Therefore awake and fly away, ye children of God, that you bring not the mark of the great evil beast upon your forehead with you, before the clear light; or else you will have great shame and confusion of face therewith. It is now high time to awake from sleep, for the bridegroom maketh himself ready to fetch home his bride, and he cometh with a clear shining light; they that shall have oil in

their lamps, their lamps shall be kindled, and they shall be guests; but those that shall have no oil, their lamps shall continue dark, and they shall sleep still, and retain the marks of the beast till the sun rise, and then they shall be horribly affrighted, and stand in eternal shame; for the judgment shall be executed; the children of God shall observe it, but those that sleep shall sleep till day.

Further of the Birth.

9. The birth of the eternal nature is like the [thoughts or] senses in man, as when a [thought or] sense is generated by somewhat, and afterwards propagateth itself into infinite many [thoughts], or as a root of a tree generateth a stock and many buds and branches, as also many roots, buds, and branches from one root, and all of them from that one first root. Therefore observe what is mentioned before, whereas nature consisteth of six forms [or properties] so every form generateth again a form out of itself of the same quality and condition of itself, and this form now hath the quality and condition of all the forms in itself.

10. But [1] observe it well: the first of the six forms generateth but one [2] source like itself, after the similitude of its own fountain-spirit, and not like the first mother the harshness, but as one twig or branch in a tree putteth forth another sprout out of itself. For in every fountain-spirit there is but one centre, wherein the fire-source or fountain

[1] Or understand and consider it aright.

[2] Or budding property.

ariseth, and the light ariseth out of the flash of the fire, and the first sixfold form is in the [1]source or fountain.

[1] Or springing property.

11. But mark the depth, in a similitude which I set down thus: The harsh spring in the original is the mother out of which the other five springs are generated, *viz.* Bitterness, Fire, Love, Sound, and Water. Now these are members of this birth [of their mother], and without them there would be nothing but an anguishing dark vale [or *vacuum*], where there could be no mobility, nor any light or life: But now the life is born in her by the kindling of the light, and then she rejoiceth in her own property, and laboureth in her own tart sour quality to generate again; and in her own quality their riseth a life again, and a centre openeth itself again, and the life cometh to be generated again out of her in a sixfold form, yet not in any such anguish as at the beginning, but in great joy.

12. For the spring of the great anguish, which was in the beginning before the light, in the [tart] harshness, from which the bitter sting or prickle is generated, that is now in the sweet fountain of the love in the light changed from the water-spirit, and from bitterness or prickliness is now become the fountain or spring of the joy in the light. Thus now henceforth the fire-flash is the father of the light, and the light shineth in him, and is now the only cause of the moving birth, and of the birth of the love. That which in the beginning

was the [1]aching source, is now *SUL*, or the oil [1] Or lake of torment
of the lovely pleasant fountain, which presseth
through all the fountains, so that from hence the
light is kindled.

13. And the sound or noise, in the turning
wheel, is now the declarer or pronouncer in all the
fountains, that the beloved child is born; for it
cometh with its sound before all doors, and in all
essences; so that in its awakening, all the virtues
or powers are stirring, and see, feel, have smell,
and taste one another in the light, for the whole
birth nourisheth itself in its first mother, *viz.* the
[2]harsh essence, being now become so thin [or pure], [2] Or sour, tart, springing substantiality.
meek, sweet, and full of joy, and so the whole
birth standeth in very great joy, love, meekness,
and humility, and is nothing else than a mere
pleasing taste, a delighting sight, a sweet smell, a
ravishing sound to the hearing, a soft touch,
beyond that which any tongue can utter or express.
How should there not be joy and love, where, in
the very midst of death, the eternal life is generated,
and where there is no fear of any end, nor can be?

14. Thus in the harshness there is a new birth
again; understand, where the tart [sour astrin-
gency] is predominant in the birth, and where the
fire is not kindled according to the bitter sting or
prickle, or from the beginning of the anguish: But
the rising [or exulting] joy, is now the centre
and kindling of the light, and the tartness [or
astringency] hath now [3]in its own quality the [3] Or for.

SUL, oil, and light of the father: Therefore now the birth out of the twig or branch of the first ¹ tree is qualified altogether according to the ¹ harsh fountain; and the fire therein is a tart [or sour] fire; and the bitterness a tart bitterness; and the sound a tart sound; and the love a tart love; but all in mere perfection, and in a totally glorious love and joy.

¹ Or tart, sour fountain.

15. And thus also the first bitter sting or prickle, or the first bitterness (after the light is kindled, and that the first birth standeth in perfection) generateth again out of its own quality an ² essence, wherein there is a centre, where also a new fountain or source springeth up in a new fire or life, having the condition and property of all the qualities, and yet the bitterness in this new sprout is chiefest among all the qualities; so that there is a bitter bitterness, a bitter tartness, a bitter water-spirit, a bitter sound, a bitter fire, a bitter love, yet all perfectly in the ³ rising up of great joy.

² twig or branch.

³ Or exulting great joy.

16. And the fire generateth now also a fire, according to the property of every quality; in the tart spirit it is tart; in the bitter, bitter; in the love, it is a very hearty yearning, kindling of the love, a total, fervent, or burning kindling, and causeth very vehement desires; in the sound it is a very shrill tanging ⁴ fire, wherein all things are very clearly and properly distinguished, and where the sound in all qualities telleth or expresseth, as it were with the lips or tongue, whatsoever is in

⁴ Or life.

all the fountain-spirits, what joy, virtue, or power, essence, substance, or property [they have], and in the water it is a very drying fire.

17. The propagation of the love is most especially to be observed, for it is the loveliest, pleasantest, and sweetest fountain of all. When the love generateth again a whole birth, with all the fountains of the original essences out of itself, so that the love in all the [1] springing veins in that new birth be predominant and chief, so that a centre ariseth therein, then the first essence, *viz.* the tartness, is wholly desirous or longing, wholly sweet, wholly light, and giveth itself forth to be food to all the qualities, with a hearty affection towards them all, as a loving mother hath towards her children, and here the bitterness may be rightly called joy, for it is the rising or moving [thereof]. What joy there is here, there is no other similitude of it, than when a man is suddenly and unexpectedly delivered out of the pain and torment of hell, and put into the light of the divine joy.

18. So also the sound, where the love is predominant; it bringeth most joyful tidings or news into all the forms of the birth, as also the fire in the love, that kindleth the love rightly in all the fountain-spirits, as is mentioned above; and the love kindleth love in its essence. When the love is predominant in love, it is the sweetest, meekest, humblest, most loving fountain of all that springeth in all the fountains; and it confirmeth and fixeth

[1] Or well-spring.

the heavenly birth, so that it is a holy divine essence or substance.

19. You must also mark the form of the water-spirit; when that generateth its like, so that it is predominant in its regeneration or second birth, and that a centre is awakened in it, (which itself in its own essence doth not awaken, but the other fountain-spirits do it therein), it [the water-spirit] is still and quiet as a meek mother, and suffereth the others to sow their seed into it, and to awaken the centre in it, so that the fire riseth up, from whence the life [1] is moved. In this [form] the fire is not a hot burning [scorching] fire, but cool, mild, soft and sweet; and the bitterness is no bitterness, but cool, mild, budding, and flowing forth, from whence the forming [or figuring and beauteous shape] in the heavenly glory proceedeth, and is a most beautiful substance; for the sound also in this birth floweth forth most pleasantly and harmoniously, all as it were palpably or feelingly; or in a similitude, as a word that cometh to be an essence, or a comprehensible substance. For in this regeneration that is brought to pass in the water-spirit, (that is, in the true mother of the regeneration of all the fountain-spirits), all is as it were comprehensible or substantial; although no comprehensibility must be understood here, but spirit.

[1] Or beginneth to stir.

THE FOURTH CHAPTER

Of the [1] true Eternal Nature, that is, of the

Of the [1] true Eternal Nature, that is, of the
numberless and endless [2] generating of the
Birth of the eternal Essence, which is the
Essence of all Essences; out of which was
generated, born, and at length created, this
World, with the Stars and Elements, and all
whatsoever moveth, stirreth, or liveth therein.

[1] Or right.

[2] begetting, or propagation.

The open Gate of the Great Depth.

1. HERE I must encounter with the proud and seeming conceited wise, who doth but grope in the dark, and knoweth or understandeth nothing of the spirit of God, and must comfort both him and also the desirous longing Reader who loveth God, and must shew them a little door to the heavenly essence; and shew them in what manner they should understand these writings, before I come to the [3] chapter itself.

[3] Or point.

2. I know very well, and my spirit and mind sheweth me as much, that many will be offended at the simplicity and meanness of the author, for offering to write of such high things; and many will think (with themselves) he hath no authority

to do it, and that he doth very sinfully in it, and runneth clean contrary to God and his will, in presuming, being but a man, to go about to speak and say what God is.

3. For it is lamentable, that since the fall of *Adam*, we should be so continually cheated and befooled by the devil, to think that we are not the children of God, nor of his [1] essence. He continually putteth the monstrous shape or form into our thoughts, as he did into our mother *Eve*, which she gazed too much upon, and by her representing it in her imagination, she became a child of this world, wholly naked and vain, and void of understanding: And so he doth to us also still continually; he would bring us into another image, as he did *Eve*, that we might be ashamed to appear in the presence of the light and power of God, as *Adam* and *Eve* were, when they hid themselves behind the trees (that is, behind the monstrous shape or form), when the Lord appeared in the centre of the birth of their lives, and said, Where art thou, *Adam*? And he said, I am naked, and am afraid; which was nothing else, but that his belief [or faith] and knowledge of the holy God was put out; for he beheld the monstrous shape which he had made to himself by his imagination and lust, by the devil's [instigation] representation, and false persuading, to eat of the third Principle wherein [2] corruption was.

4. And now when he saw and knew by that

[1] substance, or offspring.

[2] destruction or perdition.

which God had told him, that he should die and
perish, if he did eat of the knowledge of good and
evil, it made him continually imagine that he was
now no more the child of God, and that he was
not created out of God's own essence or substance,
out of the first Principle. He conceived that he
was now but a mere child of this world, when he
beheld his corruptibility, and also the monstrous
image which he [1] was in; and that the paradisical
[2] understanding, delight and joy were departed
from him, so that his spirit and perfection were
driven out of paradise (that is, out of the second
Principle of God, where the light or the Heart of
God is generated from eternity to eternity, and
where the Holy Ghost proceedeth from the Father
and the Son), and that he now lived no more
merely by the Word of God, but did eat and drink,
viz. the [3] birth of his life henceforward consisted in
the third Principle, that is, in the [region] kingdom,
or dominion of the stars and elements, and he must
now eat of the virtue and fruit thereof, and live
thereby: And thereupon he then supposed, that he
was past recovery, and that the noble image of
God was destroyed. And besides, the devil also
continually represented his corruptibility and
mortality to him, and himself could see nothing
else, being he was gone out of paradise, that is, out
of the incorruptible holy [4] geniture [or operation]
of God; wherein he was God's holy image and
child, in which God created him to continue therein

[1] Or carried about him.

[2] wit, reason or skill.

[3] preservation, or propagation.

[4] preservation, or protection.

for ever. And if the merciful love of God had not appeared to him again in the centre of the birth of his life, and comforted him, he would have thought that he was wholly departed, or quite separated from the eternal divine birth, and that he was no more in God, nor God any more in him, and that he was no more of God's essence.

[1] *unigenitus.*

5. But the favourable love (that is, the [1] only begotten Son of God, or that I may set it down so that it may be understood, the lovely fountain where the light of God is [2] generated) sprang up,

[2] *begotten, or born, or brought forth.*

and grew again in *Adam* in the centre of the birth of his life, in the fifth form of his birth; whereby *Adam* perceived that he was not broken off from the divine root, but that he was still the child of God, and repented him of his first evil lust: And thereupon the Lord shewed him the Treader upon the Serpent, who should destroy his monstrous birth; and so he should from the monstrous birth be regenerated anew, in the shape, form, power and virtue of the Treader upon the Serpent, and be brought with power again into

[3] *Verbum Domini.*

paradise, into the holy birth, and eat of the [3] Word of the Lord again, and live eternally, in spite of

[4] Or power.

all the [4] gates of the wrathfulness, wherein the devil liveth; concerning which there shall be further mention made in its due place.

6. But mark and consider this well, dear Reader, and let not your simplicity deceive you, the author is not greater than others, he knoweth no more,

neither hath he any greater authority than other
children of God. Do but look upon yourself, why
have you earthly thoughts of yourself? ⟨Why will
you be mocked by the devil, and be fooled by the
world, [so as to be led to think] that you are but
a kind of figure like God, and not generated or
begotten of God? ⟩

7. Your monstrous form or shape indeed is
not God, nor of his essence, or substance, but
the hidden man, [1] which is the soul, [2] is the proper
essence of God, forasmuch as the love in the light
of God is sprung up in your own centre, out of
which the Holy Ghost proceedeth, wherein the
second Principle of God consisteth: How then should
you not have power and authority to speak of
God, who is your Father, of whose essence you
are? Behold, is not the world God's? And the
Light of God being in you, it must needs be also
yours, as it is written, *The Father hath given all
things to the Son, and the Son hath given all to
you.* The Father is the eternal power, or virtue,
and the Son is the Heart and light continuing
eternally in the Father, and you continue in the
Father and the Son. ⟨And now, being the Holy
Ghost proceedeth from the Father and the Son,
and that the eternal power or virtue of the Father
is in you, and that the eternal light of the Son
shineth in you, why will you be fooled?⟩ Know
you not what *Paul* said: *That our conversation
is in heaven, from whence we expect our Saviour*

[1] which the
soul is.

[2] Or out of
God's own
essence or
substance, as
a child is the
father's own
substance.

3

Jesus Christ, who will bring us out of this monstrous image, or birth (in the corruption of the third Principle of this world), in the [1]paradisical birth to eat the Word of the Lord?

8. Why will you be fooled by Antichrist, by his laws [precepts] and pratings? Where will you seek God? in the deep above the stars? You will not be able to find him there. Seek him in your heart, [2]in the centre of the birth of your life, and there you shall find him, as our father *Adam* and mother *Eve* did.

9. For it is written, *You must be born anew through the water and the spirit, or else you shall not see the kingdom of God.* This birth must be done within you: The Heart, or the Son of God must arise in the birth of your life; and then the Saviour Christ is your faithful Shepherd, and you are in him, and he in you, and all that he and his Father have is yours, and none shall pluck you out of his hands; and as the Son (*viz.* the Heart of the Father) is one [with the Father], so also the new man is one in the Father and the Son, one virtue or power, one light, one life, one eternal paradise, one eternal heavenly [3]birth, one Father, Son, and Holy Ghost, and thou his child.

10. Doth not the son see plainly what the father doth in his house? And now if the son learn to do the same thereby, what displeasure will the father have towards his son for it? Nay, will not the father be well pleased that his son is

so apt [and forward to learn]? Then why should the heavenly Father be so displeased with his children in this world, which depend upon him, and enquire after him, which would fain learn to know him, fain labour in his works, and do his will? Doth not the Regenerator bid us come to him, and whosoever cometh to him, he will not reject? Why should any [1]resist the spirit of prophecy, which is God's? Look upon Christ's Apostles, did any other teach them than God, who was in them, and they in him?

[1] Or withstand the spirit of the manifestation of the hidden things of God.

11. O dear children of God in Christ, fly away from Antichrist, who hath set up himself over all the coasts of the earth, and who setteth a painted image before you, as the serpent did before our mother *Eve*, and [2]painteth your own image of God [as if it were] far off from God: But consider what is written, *The Word is near thee, yea in thy heart and lips.* And God himself is the Word which is in thy heart and lips.

[2] Or representeth to you.

12. But Antichrist hath never sought anything else but his own pleasure in the third Principle, and to fulfil it in the house of flesh; and therefore he hath detained people with laws of his own inventing, which are neither grounded in nature, nor in the paradise of God, neither are they to be found in the centre of the birth of life.

13. Dear children, consider, how mightily and powerfully, with wonders, miracles, and works, the spirit of God went forth in word and deed in

the times of the Apostles, and after, till Antichrist
and the spirit of self-pride, with his invented laws
and astral wisdom, brake forth, and set himself up
by that worldly and fleshly arm [or by the authority
of the worldly magistrate], merely for his own
pleasure and honour's sake, where the most precious
words of Christ (who gave no laws to man, but
the law of nature and the law of love, which is
his own heart) must be a cloak for him, *viz.* for
Antichrist, who is a prince in the third Principle;
what he ordains must be as the voice to *Moses* out
of the bush: And so the man of pride makes as if
himself had [1] divine power upon earth, and knoweth
not, in his blindness, the Holy Ghost will not be
[2] tied [or bound up to their canons and human
inventions].

[1] divine or
apostolical
authority, or
Jus Divinum.
[2] Or blinded
and mocked
by them.

14. But if any would attain salvation, he must
be born again, through the water in the [3] centre
of the birth of life, which springeth up in the
centre in the light of God; for which end God the
Father hath by his Son commanded Baptism, that
so we might have a law, and a remarkable sign of
remembrance, signifying how a child void of understanding receiveth an outward sign, and the inward
man the power and the new birth in the centre
of the birth of life; and that there ariseth the
confirmation, which the light of God brought into
Adam, when the light of God the Father, in the
centre of the fifth form of the birth of the life of
Adam, brake forth or sprang up.   Thus it is both

[3] In the
ground where
the grain of
mustard seed
is sown and
springeth up.

in the baptism of an infant or child, and also in the repenting convert, that in Christ returneth again to the Father.

15. The Last Supper of Christ with his disciples is just such another covenant as the [Pædobaptism or] baptism of infants. That which is done to the infant in baptism, that is done also to the poor sinner which awakeneth from the sleep of Antichrist, and cometh to the Father in and through Christ; as shall be handled in its place.

16. I have therefore been desirous to warn you, and tell you beforehand, that you must not look upon flesh and blood in these high things, nor upon the worldly wisdom of the universities, or high schools; but that you should consider, that this wisdom is planted and sown by God himself in the first, and last, and in all men: And you need only to return with the prodigal lost son to the Father, and then he will clothe you with a new garment, and put a seal-ring upon the hand of your mind; and in this garment only you have power to speak of the [1] birth of God.

[1] Or divine birth.

17. But if you have not gotten this garment on, and will prattle and talk much of God, then you are a thief and a murderer, and you enter not into the sheepfold of Christ by the door, but you climb over into the sheepfold with Antichrist and the robbers, and you will do nothing but murder and steal, seek your own reputation, esteem, and pleasure, and are far from the kingdom of God.

Your university learning and arts will avail you nothing : it is your poison, that you are promoted by the favour of man to sit in great authority and place, for you sit upon the stool of pestilence; you are but a mere servant or minister of the Antichrist. But if you be new born, and taught by the Holy Ghost, then your place or office is very pleasing and acceptable to God, and your sheep will hear your voice, and you shall feed them and bring them to the chief Shepherd : God will require this at your hands, therefore take heed what you teach and speak of God without the knowledge of his spirit, that you be not found to be a liar.

Now here followeth the Chapter.

[1] Or begetting.

18. The eternal [1] generating is an unbeginning birth, and it hath neither number nor end, and its depth is bottomless, and the band of life [2] incorruptible: [3] The sidereal and elementary spirit cannot discern it, much less comprehend it ; it only feeleth it, and seeth a glimpse of it in the mind; which [mind] is the chariot of the soul, upon which it rideth in the first Principle in its own seat in the Father's eternal generating [or begetting]; for its own substance is altogether [4] crude, without a body, and yet it hath the form of the body in its own spiritual form, understand according to the image; which soul, if it be regenerated in the light of God, it seeth in the light of the Father, (which light is his glance, lustre, or Son),

[2] indissoluble.

[3] astral, starry, or airy spirit of man.

[4] weak, feeble, empty, and dry.

in the eternal birth, wherein it liveth and remaineth eternally.

19. Understand and consider it aright, O man! God the Father made man ; the beginning of whose body is out of the [one] element, or root of the four elements, from whence they proceed, which [one] element is the fifth essence [or quintessence] hid under the four elements, from whence the dark chaos [mist, cloud, or dust] had its being, before the times of the earth ; whose original is the spring of water, and out of which this world with the stars and elements, as also the heaven of the third Principle, were created.

20. But the soul was breathed into man merely out of the original birth of the Father by the moving spirit (understand, the Holy Ghost which goeth forth from the Father out of the light of the Father). Which original birth is before the light of life, which is in the four [1] anguishes, out of which the light of God is kindled, wherein is the original of the name of God ; and therefore the soul is God's own essence or substance.

[1] Or aching properties.

21. And if it elevate itself back into the anguish of the four forms of the original, and will horribly [2] breathe forth out of pride in the original of the fire, knowing itself [shall] so [become] powerful ; it so becometh a devil : For the devils also with their legions had this original, and they out of pride would live in the [3] fierce wrath of the fire, and so they perished, and remained devils.

[2] Or work in continual generating: As the breath goeth in and out continually for the preserving of life.

[3] Or strong.

[1] Or exercise its thoughts and purposes in resignation.

[2] *Verbum Domini.*

[3] laughing for joy.

[4] Or Hallelujahs.

[5] Note, what is possible to be spoken of, and what not.

22. Yet if the soul elevate its [1]imagination forward into the light, in meekness and comeliness or humility, and doth not (as Lucifer did) use the strong power of its fire, in its qualification [or breathing], then it will be fed by the [2]Word of the Lord, and get virtue, power, life, and strength, in the [2]Word of the Lord, which is the Heart of God; and its own original strong [fierce wrathful] source of the birth of the eternal life becometh paradisical, exceeding pleasant, friendly, humble, and sweet, wherein the [3]rejoicing and the fountain of the eternal [4]songs of praise spring up: and in this imagination it is an angel and a child of God, and it beholdeth the eternal generating of the [5]indissoluble band; and thereof it hath ability to speak (for it is its own essence or substance), but [it is] not [able to speak] of the infinite generating, for that hath neither beginning nor end.

23. But if it undertaketh to speak of the unmeasurable space [or infinite geniture], then it becometh full of lies, and is troubled and confounded: For it belieth the unmeasurable Deity; as Antichrist doth, which will have the Deity to be only above the starry heaven, that thereby himself may remain to be God upon earth, riding upon the great beast, which yet must shortly go into the

[6] Or dominion of the anger of God.

original lake of brimstone, into the [6]kingdom of king Lucifer; for the time is come that the beast shall be revealed and spewed out; concerning which we may be well enough understood here by the children

of hope ; but there is a wall and seal before the
servants or ministers of [1] Antichrist, till the wrath
be executed upon her whoredom, and that she
hath received her full wages, and that the [2] crown
of their dominion which they have worn be their
shame, and till the eyes of the blind be opened ;
and then she will sit as a scorned whore, which
every one will adjudge to damnation.

[1] the whore of the beast.

[2] Or ornament of her kingdom.

The very sublime Gate of the Holy Trinity, for the Children of God.

24. If you lift up your thoughts and minds, and
ride upon the chariot of the soul, as is before
mentioned, and look upon yourself, and all creatures,
and consider how the birth of life in you taketh its
original, and the light of your life, whereby you
can behold the shining of the sun ; and also look
with your imagination, without the light of the
sun, into a huge vast space, to which the eyes of
your body cannot reach, and then consider what
the cause might be that you are more rational than
the other creatures, seeing you can search what is
in every thing ; and consider farther, from whence
the elements fire and air take their original, and
how the fire cometh to be in the water, and
generateth itself in the water ; and how the light
of your body generateth itself in the water ; and
then if you be born of God, you attain to what
God and the eternal birth is.

25. For you see, feel, and find, that all these

must yet have a higher root from whence they proceed, which is not visible, but hidden; especially if you look upon the starry heaven which endureth thus unchangeably; therefore you ought to consider from whence it is proceeded, and how it subsisteth thus, and is not corrupted, nor riseth up above, nor falleth down beneath, though indeed there is neither above nor beneath there. Now if you consider what preserveth all thus, and whence it is, then you find the eternal birth that hath no beginning, and you find the original of the eternal Principle, *viz.* the eternal indissoluble band: And then, secondly, you see the separation, in that the material world, with the stars and elements, are out of the first Principle, which containeth the outward and third Principle in it; for you find in the elementary kingdom or dominion, a cause in every thing, wherefore it is, generateth, and moveth as it doth: But you find not the first cause, from whence it is so: There are therefore [1]two several Principles; for you find in the visible things a corruptibility, and perceive that they must have a beginning, because they have an end.

[1] Viz. the first and the third Principles.

26. And thirdly, you find in all things a glorious power and virtue, which is the life, growing and springing of every thing, and you find that therein lieth its beauty and pleasant welfare, from whence it stirreth. Now look upon an herb or plant, and consider it, what is its life which makes it grow? And you shall find in the original, harshness, bitter-

ness, fire, and water, and if you should separate these four things one from another, and put them together again, yet you shall neither see nor find any growing; but if it were severed from its own mother that generated it at the beginning, then it remaineth dead; much less can you bring the pleasant smell or colours into it.

27. Thus you see that there is an eternal root which affordeth this; and if you could bring the colours and vegetation or growing into it, yet you could not bring the smell and virtue into it; and thus you will find in the original of the smell and of the taste there must be another Principle, which the stock itself is not, for that Principle hath its original from the light of nature.

28. Now look upon the human life a little further, you neither see, find, nor apprehend any more by your sight than flesh and blood, wherein you are like other beasts; secondly, you find the elements of air and fire which [1] work in you, and that it is but an animal or bestial life, for every beast hath the same in it, from whence proceedeth the lust to fill themselves, and to propagate themselves, as all plants, herbs, and grass, and yet you find no true understanding to be in all these living creatures; for although the stars or constellations operate in [2] man, and afford him the senses, yet they are only such senses as belong to nourishment and propagation, like other beasts.

[1] Or mingle themselves.

[2] animal or bestial man.

29. For the stars themselves are senseless, and

have no knowledge or perception, yet their soft operation in the water maketh a seething, flowing forth, or boiling up one of another, and in the tincture of the blood, they cause a rising, seeing, feeling, hearing, and tasting. Therefore consider from whence the tincture proceedeth, wherein the noble life springeth up, that thus becometh sweet from harshness, bitterness, and fire, and you shall certainly find no other cause of it than the light: But whence cometh the light, that it can shine [1] in a dark body? If you say it cometh from the light of the sun, then what shineth in the night, and enlighteneth your [2] senses and understanding so, that though your eyes be shut, you perceive and know what you do? Here you will say, the noble mind doth lead you, and it is true. But whence hath the mind its original? You will say, the [3] senses make the mind stirring; and that is also true. But whence come they both? What is their birth or offspring? Why is it not so with the beasts?

30. My dear Reader, if you be able, [4] break open all, and look into the pith, yet you shall not find it, though you should seek in the deep, in the stars, in the elements, in all living creatures, in stones, plants, trees, and in metals; also in heaven and earth, you shall not find it. Now you will say, Where then shall I find it? Dear Reader, I cannot so much as lend you the key that will lead you to it. But I will direct you where you shall find it;

[1] Or upon a dark place.

[2] Inward senses or thoughts.

[3] Or thoughts or inward senses.

[4] Or answer this question.

it lieth in the third chapter of the Evangelist St *John*, in these words : *You must be born anew, by water, and by the Holy Ghost.* This spirit is the key : When you attain it, receive it, and go before the first Principle, out of which this world and all creatures are created, and open the first root, from which such visible and sensible things did spring.

31. But you will say, this is only God, and he is a spirit, and hath created all things out of nothing. 'Tis very true, he is a spirit, and in our sight he is as nothing : And if we had not some knowledge of him by the creation, we should know nothing of him at all. And if he himself had not been from all eternity, there could nothing have ever been.

32. But what do you think there was before the times of the world, out of which the earth and stones proceeded, as also the stars and elements ? That out of which these proceeded was the root. But what is the root of these things ? Look, what do you find in these things ? Nothing else but fire, bitterness, and harshness [or astringent sourness], and these three are but one thing, and hence all things are generated. Now this was but a spirit before the times of the world, and yet you cannot find God in these three forms. The pure Deity is a light which is incomprehensible, and unperceivable, also almighty and all-powerful. Where is it then that men may find God ?

33. Here open your noble mind, see, and search further. Seeing God is only good, from whence

cometh the evil? And seeing also that he alone is the life, and the light, and the holy power, as it is undeniably true, from whence cometh the anger of God? From whence cometh the devil, and his [evil] will? Also hell-fire, from whence hath that its original? Seeing there was nothing before the time of this world, but only God, who was and is a spirit, and continueth so in eternity, from whence then is the first *materia*, or matter of evil? For reason giveth this judgment, that there must needs have been in the spirit of God a will to generate the source or fountain of anger.

34. But now the Scripture saith, *The devil was a holy angel.* And further, it saith, *Thou art not a God that willeth evil.* And in *Ezekiel, As sure as I live, I will not the death of a sinner.* This is testified by God's earnest severe punishing of the devils, and all sinners, that he is not pleased with death.

35. What then moved the devil to be angry, and evil? What is the first matter [of it] in him, seeing he was created out of the original eternal spirit? Or from whence is the original of hell, wherein the devils shall remain for ever, when this world, with the stars, and elements, earth, and stones, shall perish in the end?

36. Beloved Reader, open the eyes of your mind here, and know, that no other [anguish] source will spring up in him [and torment him] than his own ¹quality; for that is his hell out of which he is

¹ Or working property.

created and made; and the light of God is his eternal shame, and therefore he is God's enemy, because he is no more in the light of God.

37. Now you can here produce nothing more, that God should ever use any matter out of which to create the devil, for then the devil might justify himself, that he made him evil, or of evil matter. For God created him out of nothing, but merely out of his own essence or substance, as well as the other angels.   As it is written, *Through him, and in him, are all things* : And his only is the *king-dom*, the *power*, and the *glory* ; and all in him, as the holy Scripture witnesseth.   And if it was not thus, no sin would be [1] imputed to the devil, nor men, if they were not eternal, and both in God, and out of God himself.

[1] Or account-ed sin.

38. For to a beast (which is created out of matter) no sin may be imputed, for its spirit reacheth not the first Principle ; but it hath its original in the third Principle, in the elementary and sidereal kingdom, in the corruptibility, and it reacheth not the Deity, as the devil and the soul of man do.

39. And if you cannot believe this, take the holy Scripture before you, which telleth you, that when man was fallen into sin, God sent him his own Heart, life, or light, out of himself into the flesh, and opened the gate of the birth of his life, wherein he was united with God ; and being broken off in the light [part] (yet continued in the original

of the first Principle) he hath kindled that light, and so united himself to man again.

40. If the soul of a man were not (sprung) out of God the Father out of his first Principle, but out of another matter, he could not have bestowed that highest earnest or pledge of his own heart and light upon him, as himself witnesseth, saying, *I am the Light of the world, and the Life of man*; but he could very well have redeemed or helped him some other way.

41. But what do you think that he brought to man into the flesh when he came? Nothing else but what *Adam* and our mother *Eve* had lost in paradise; the same did the Treader upon the Serpent bring again to the monstrous birth, and delivered man out of that elementary and sidereal house of flesh, and set him again in paradise; of which I will write at large hereafter.

42. If therefore you will speak or think of God, you must consider that he is all; and you must look further into the three Principles, wherein you will find what God is, you will find what the wrath, the devil, hell and sin are; also, what the angels, man and beasts are, and how the separation or variation followed, from whence all things have thus proceeded; you will find the creation of the world.

43. Only (Reader) I admonish you sincerely, if you be not in the way of the prodigal, or lost son, returning to his Father again, that you leave my

book, and read it not, it will do you harm.   For
the [1] great prince will not forbear to deceive you ; [1] Satan.
because he standeth naked in this book before the
children of God, and is exceedingly ashamed, as a
man that is put to open shame before all people
for his misdeeds ; therefore be warned.   And if
you love and favour the tender delicate flesh still,
do not read my book ; but if you will not take
warning, and a mischief befall you, I will be
guiltless, blame nobody but yourself ; for I write
down what I know at present, for a Memorial
to myself ; yet God knoweth well what he will
do [with it], which in some measure is hidden
from me.

44. Seeing now that we can find nothing in all
nature, of which we may say, This is God, or here
is God, from whence we might conclude, that God
might be some strange thing ; and seeing himself
witnesseth, that his is the kingdom and the power
from eternity to eternity ; and that he calleth
himself Father, (and the Son is begotten out of
the loins of his Father), therefore we must seek for
him in the original, [2] in the Principle out of which [2] *In Principio.*
the world was generated and created in the
beginning ; and we can say no otherwise, but that
the first Principle is God the Father himself.

45. Yet there is found in the original the most
horrible and [fierce or] strong birth, *viz.* the harshness, bitterness, and fire ; of which we cannot say,
that it is God ; and yet it is the most inward first
4

¹ well-spring or fountain.

¹source of all that is in God the Father; according to which, he calleth himself, an angry, zealous [or jealous] God. And this source (as you find before in the first three chapters concerning the original of the eternal birth) is the first Principle, and that is God the Father in his originality, out of which this world hath its beginning.

² As before, ver. 37.

³ their being made corporeal, continued in the spiritual substance.
⁴ Or one element.

46. But the angels and the devils, as also the soul of man, are merely and purely ²out of the same spirit. The devils and the angels, in the time of ³their bodifying, continued therein; and the soul of man, in the time of the creating of the body, [is] breathed in from the spirit of God, in the ⁴root of the third Principle, and now continueth therein, in eternity, inseparably and immovably in the eternal substance or essence of God. And as little as the pure eternal birth and the indissoluble band of the Father endeth or vanisheth, so little also will such a spirit have an end.

47. Yet in this Principle there is nothing else but the most horrible begetting, the greatest anguish and hostile quickening, like a brimstone-spirit, and is ever the gate of hell, and the abyss wherein prince Lucifer (at the extinguishing of his light) continued; and wherein (*viz.* in the same abyss of hell) the soul continueth, which is separated from the second Principle, and whose light ([which shineth] from the Heart of God) is extinguished, and for which cause also, at the end of this time, there will be a separation or parting

asunder of the saints of light from the damned, whose [1] source will be without the light of God.

48. Now we have shewn you the first Principle, out of which all things take their beginning ; and must speak so of it, as if there were a place, or a separable essence, where there is such a kind of source ; to the end that the first Principle might be understood, so that the eternity, as also the anger of God, sin, eternal death, the darkness (which is so called in respect of the extinguishment of the light), also hell-fire, and the devil, might be known and understood [what they are].

49. So I will now write of the second Principle, of the clear pure Deity, of the [2] Heart of God.   In the first Principle (as I have mentioned above) is [3] harshness, bitterness, and fire ; and yet they are not three things, but one only thing, and they one generate another.   Harshness is the first father, which is strong [fierce or tart], very sharp and attracting to itself ; and that attracting is the [sting] or prickle, or bitterness, which the harshness cannot endure, and it will not be captivated in death, but riseth and flieth up like a strong fierce substance, and yet cannot remove from off its place : And then there is a horrible anguish, which findeth no rest; and the birth is like a turning wheel, twitching so very hard, and breaking or bruising as it were furiously, which the harshness cannot endure, but attracteth continually more and more, harder and harder ; as when

[1] Or working fountain of their conditions as a boiling springing torment.

[2] That is, the power, glory or lustre of the Father.

[3] The attracting, astringent, sour, tart, smartness.

steel and a flint are struck one against the other, from which the twinkling flash of fire proceedeth; and when the harshness perceiveth [1] it, [2] it starteth and sinketh back, as if it were dead and overcome. And so when the flash of fire cometh into its mother, the harshness, and findeth her thus soft and overcome, then it is much more terrified [than the harshness], and becometh in the twinkling of an eye white and clear. And now when the harsh tartness attaineth the white clear light in itself, it is so very much terrified that it [falleth or] sinketh back, as if it were dead and overcome, and expandeth itself, and becometh very thin and [pliable or] vanquished: For its own source was dark and hard, and now is become [3] light and soft; therefore now it is first rightly become as it were dead, and now is the water-spirit.

50. Thus the birth getteth an essence that hath sharpness from the harshness, and sweetness, thinness, and expansion from the light. And now when the flash of fire cometh into its mother, and findeth her so sweet, thin, and light, then it [4] loseth its own propriety in the qualification, and flieth aloft no more, but continueth in its mother, and loseth its fiery right [or propriety], and trembleth and rejoiceth in its mother.

51. And in this joy, in the water-spring [or source], the pleasant [5] source of the [6] bottomless love riseth up, and all that riseth up there is the second Principle: for the whole begetting or gener-

[1] the flash of fire.
[2] the harshness.

[3] As when the rays of the sun turn the hard cold ice into thin fluid water.

[4] Or can work no more.

[5] Or stream.
[6] unsearchable, unfathomable, or inconceivable.

ating falleth into a glorious love; for the harshness
now loveth the light dearly, because it is so
refreshing, cheerly, and beautiful; for from this
pleasant refreshing it becometh thus sweet, [1]cour-   [1] gentle or
teous, and humble [or lowly]; and the bitterness   friendly.
now loveth the harshness, because it is no more
dark, nor so strongly [eagerly or fiercely] attractive
to itself, but is sweet, mild, pure, and light.

52. And here beginneth the taste, whereby one
continually [trieth, tasteth, and] proveth the other,
and with great desire they mingle one within
another, so that there is nothing but a mere
courteous embracing. Thus the bitterness now
rejoiceth in its mother, and strengtheneth itself
therein, and for great joy riseth up through all
the essences, and declareth to the second Principle,
that the loving child is [2]born; to which then all   [2] begotten.
the essences give heed and rejoice at that dear
child; from whence the hearing ariseth, which is
the sixth form where the wheel of the birth
standeth in triumph. And in this great joy the
birth cannot contain itself [within its bounds], but
expandeth itself, flowing forth very joyfully, and
every essence [or substance] generateth now again
a centre in the second Principle.

53. And there beginneth the unfathomable [or
unsearchable] multiplication; for the flowing and
springing spirit, that proceedeth from the first and
second Principles, confirmeth, fixeth and establisheth all; and in the whole birth it is as a

growing or multiplying in one will; and the birth attaineth here the seventh form, *viz.* the multiplication [1] into an essence of love. And in this form consisteth paradise, or the kingdom of God, or the numberless divine birth, out of one only essence [2] into all essences.

54. Although here the tongue of man cannot utter, declare, express, nor fathom this great depth, where there is neither number nor end, yet we have power to speak thereof as children talk of their father. But to dive into the whole depth, that troubleth us, and disturbeth our souls; for God himself knoweth neither beginning nor end in himself.

55. And now being to speak of the Holy Trinity, we must first say, that there is one God, and he is called the Father and Creator of all things, who is Almighty, and All in All, whose are all things, and in whom and from whom all things proceed, and in whom they remain eternally. And then we say, that he is three in Persons, and hath from eternity generated his Son out of himself, who is his Heart, light, and love; and yet they are not two, but one eternal essence. And further we say, as the holy Scripture telleth us, that there is a Holy Ghost, which proceedeth from the Father and the Son, and that there is but one essence in the Father, Son, and Holy Ghost, which is rightly spoken.

56. For behold, the Father is the original essence of all essences. And if now the second Principle did not break forth and spring up in the

[1] Or in.

[2] Or in all things.

birth of the Son, then the Father would be a dark
[1] valley.   And thus you see, that the Son (who is
the Heart, the love, the brightness and the mild
[2] rejoicing of the Father) [in whom he is well-
pleased] openeth another Principle in his birth,
and maketh the angry and wrathful Father (as I
may say, as to the originality of the first Principle)
reconciled, pleased, loving, and as I may say,
merciful; and he is another [manner of] Person
than the Father; for in his [3] centre there is nothing
else but mere joy, love, and pleasure.   And yet
you may see that the Holy Ghost proceedeth from
the Father and the Son, for when the Heart or
light of God is generated in the Father, then there
springeth up (in the kindling of the light in the
fifth form) out of the [4] water-source in the light,
a very pleasant sweet smelling and sweet tasted
spirit; and this is that spirit which in the original
was the bitter sting or prickle in the harshness [or
tartness], and that maketh now in this water-source
many thousand [5] centres, without number or end;
and all this in the fountain of the water.

57. Now you may well perceive that the birth
of the Son taketh its original in the fire, and
attaineth his personality and name in the kindling
of the soft, white, and clear light, which is himself; and himself maketh the pleasant smell, taste,
and satisfaction [or reconciliation and well-pleasing]
in the Father, and is rightly the Father's Heart,
and another Person; for he openeth and produceth

[1] vacuum, or valley of darkness.

[2] Or satiating.

[3] Or ground.

[4] Or well-spring of water, which is the ground of humility.

[5] centra.

the second Principle in the Father; and his own essence is the power or virtue and the light; and therefore his is rightly called the power or virtue of the Father.

58. But the Holy Ghost is not [1]known in the original of the Father before the light [breaketh forth]; but when the soft fountain springeth up in the light, then he goeth forth as a strong almighty spirit in great joy, from the pleasant source of water, and [from] the light, and he is the power and virtue of the source of water, and of the light; and he maketh now the forming [shaping, figuring] and images [or species]; and he is the centre in all essences; in which [centre] the light of life, in the light of the Son, or Heart of the Father, taketh its original. And the Holy Ghost is a several Person, because he proceedeth (as a living power and virtue) from the Father and the Son, and confirmeth the [2]birth of the Trinity.

59. Now we pray thus, *Our Father* [*which art*] *in heaven, hallowed* (or sanctified) *be thy name.* And in the first of *Genesis* it is written, *God created the heaven out of the midst of the water*; by which is [meant or] understood the heaven of the third Principle: And yet indeed he hath created it out of his own heaven wherein he dwelleth. Thus you may easily find, that the birth of the holy Deity standeth in the source of water, and the powerful spirit is moreover the former, framer, and fashioner [or moulder] therein.

[1] acknowledged or manifest, as the air is not known or breathed forth in the original of the fire before the light is kindled.

[2] begetting, generating, or working.

60. Thus now the heaven in this forming or framing, and the framing and generating out of it *in infinitum*, or endlessly, is the paradise of God, as the highly worthy *Moses* writeth: The spirit of God moved upon the water, in the framing [forming or fashioning] of the world. This is, and continueth so in its eternity, that the spirit of God (in the birth of the Son of God) moveth upon the water; for he is the virtue, or power, and the out-flowing in the Father, out of the kindled [1] light [a] water, out of the water and light of God.

[1] light-water.

61. Thus God is one only undivided essence, and yet threefold in personal distinction, one God, one will, one Heart, one desire, one pleasure, one beauty, one almightiness, one fulness of all things, neither beginning nor ending; for if I should go about to seek for the beginning or ending of a small dot [point, *punctum*], or of a perfect circle, I should miss and be confounded.

62. And although I have written here, as if it took a beginning (writing as it were of the beginning [and first springing] of the second Principle and the [2] birth of the divine essence), yet you must not understand it as having any beginning; for the eternal birth is thus [without beginning or end], and that in the originalness. But I write to the end that man might learn to know himself, what he is, and what God, heaven, angels, devils, and hell are, as also what the wrath of God and

[2] Or continual operation.

hell-fire are. For I am permitted to write as far
as of the originalness.

63. Therefore, O child of man, consider what
thou art in this time; esteem not so slightly or
poorly of thyself, but consider that you remain in
paradise, and put not out the divine light in you;
or else you must hereafter remain in the original
of the source of anger or wrath in the valley of
darkness; and your noble image out of God will
be turned into a serpent and dragon.

64. For you must know, that as soon as the
divine light went out in the devils, they lost their
beauteous form and image, and became like serpents,
dragons, worms, and evil beasts; as may be seen
by *Adam's* serpent; and thus it is also with the
damned souls. For this we know in the original
of the first Principle very well. If you ask, How
so? Read this following:

*A description of a Devil, how he is in his own
proper form, and also how he was in the
Angelical form.*

65. Behold, O child of man! All the angels were
created in the first Principle, and by the [1]flowing
spirit were formed and bodified in a true angelical
and spiritual manner, and enlightened from the
light of God, that they might increase the paradisical joy, and abide [therein] eternally. But
seeing they were to abide eternally, they must be
figured [or formed] out of the indissoluble band,

[1] Or moving,
working.

out of the first Principle, which is an indissoluble
band; and they ought to look upon the Heart of
God, and feed upon the Word of God, and this
food would be their holy preservation, and would
make their image clear and light; as the Heart of
God, in the beginning of the second Principle
enlighteneth the Father (that is, the first Principle); and there the divine power, paradise, and
the kingdom of heaven spring up.

66. Thus it is with those angels that continued
in the kingdom of heaven in the true paradise, they
stand in the first Principle in the indissoluble band,
and their food is the divine power, in their
imagination (or imagining) [in their thoughts and
mind] is the will of the Holy Trinity in the Deity;
the confirmation [or establishing] of their life,
will, and doings, is the power of the Holy Ghost;
whatsoever that doth in the generating of paradise,
the angels rejoice at, and they sing the [1] joyful
songs of paradise, concerning the pleasant saving
fruit, and eternal birth.   All they do is an increasing
of the heavenly joy, and a delight and pleasure
to the Heart of God, a holy sport in paradise, a
[satisfying of the desire or] will of the eternal
Father; to this end their God created them, that
he might be manifested, and rejoice in his creatures,
and the creatures in him, so that there might be
an eternal sport of love, in the centre of the
multiplying (or eternal Nature) in the indissoluble
eternal band.

[1] Or Hallelu-
jahs.

67. This [sport of love] was spoiled by Lucifer himself (who is so called, because of the extinguishment of his light, and of being cast out of his throne), who was a prince and king over many legions, but is become a devil, and hath lost his beautiful [fair, bright] and glorious image. For he, as well as other angels, was created out of the eternal nature, out of the eternal indissoluble band, and [hath also] stood in paradise, also felt and seen the [1] birth of the holy Deity, the birth of the second Principle, of the Heart of God, and the confirmation of the Holy Ghost; his food should have been of the Word of the Lord, and therein he should have continued an angel.

[1] Or working.

68. But he saw that he was a prince, standing in the first Principle, and so despised the birth of the Heart of God, and the soft and very lovely [2] qualification thereof, and meant to be a very potent and terrible lord in the first Principle, and would qualify [or work] in the strength of the fire; he despised the meekness of the Heart of God. He would not set his imagination therein [or his thoughts upon it], and therefore he could not be fed from the Word of the Lord, and so his light went out; whereupon presently he became a loathsomeness in paradise, and was spewed out of his princely throne, with all his legions that stuck to him [or depended on him].

[2] working, or influence.

69. And now when the Heart of God departed from him, the second Principle was shut up to

him, and so he lost God, the kingdom of heaven, and all paradisical knowledge, pleasure and joy; he also presently lost the image of God, and the confirmation of the Holy Ghost, because he despised the second Principle, wherein he was an angel and image of God.   Thus all things departed from him, and he remained in the [1] dark valley, and could no more raise his imagination up into God; but he continued in the four anguishes of the originalness.

[1] Or valley of darkness.

70. And when he raised up his imagination, then he kindled to himself the source or root of the fire, and then when the root of the fire sought for the water (*viz.* the true mother of the eternal nature), it found the stern [or tart astringent] harshness, and the mother in the aching death; and the bitter sting [or prickle] formed the birth to be a fierce raging serpent, very terrible in itself, rising up in the indissoluble band, an eternal enmity, a will striving against itself, an eternal despair of all good; [the bitter sting also formed] the mind to be [as] a breaking striking wheel, having its will continually aspiring to the strength of the fire, and to destroy the Heart of God, and yet could never at all be able to reach it.

71. For he is always shut up in the first Principle (as in the eternal death), and yet he raiseth himself up continually, thinking to reach the Heart of God, and to domineer over it; for his bitter sting in the birth climbeth up thus eternally in the [2] source of the fire, and affordeth him a proud will to have all

[2] Or root.

[at his pleasure], but he attaineth nothing; his food is the [1]source of water, *viz.* the brimstone-spirit, which is the most aching mother, from which the indissoluble band is fed and nourished; his refreshing is the eternal [2]fire, and eternal freezing in the harsh mother, and eternal hunger in the bitterness, an eternal thirst in the source of the fire; his climbing up is his fall, the more he climbeth up in his will, the greater is his fall; like one that standing upon a high clift, would cast himself down into a bottomless pit, he looketh still further, and he falleth in further and further, and yet can find no ground.

72. Thus he is an eternal enemy to the Heart of God, and all the holy angels; and he cannot frame any other will in himself. His angels and devils are of very many several sorts, all according to the eternal birth. For at the time of his creation he stood (in the kingdom of heaven) in the point, *locus,* or place (where the Holy Ghost in the birth of the Heart of God, in paradise, did open infinite and innumerable centres), in the eternal birth; in this seat or place, he was [3]bodied, and hath his beginning [4]in the opening of the centres in the eternal nature.

73. Therefore (as is mentioned before in the third chapter) when the birth of life sprang up, every essence had again a centre in itself, according to its own property or quality, and figureth a life according to its essences, *viz.* harshness, bitterness,

[1] fountain of poison.

[2] Viz. the cold fire.

[3] Or created.

[4] in the opening of the ground, as a building from the earth.

fire, and sound; and all further according to the
ability of the eternal birth, which is [1]confirmed in
the kingdom of heaven.

[1] Or estab-
lished.

74. Seeing then that they stood in heaven in
the time of their creation, therefore their quality
was also manifold; and all should have been and
continued angels, if the great fountain Lucifer
(from whence they proceeded) had not destroyed
them.   And so now also every one in his fall continueth in his own essences, only the second Principle is extinguished in them; and so it is also with
the soul of man, when the light of God goeth out
in it; but so long as that shineth therein, it is in
paradise, and eateth of the Word of the Lord, of
which shall be clearly spoken in its due place.

THE FIFTH CHAPTER

Of the third Principle, or creation of the material World, with the Stars and Elements; wherein the first and second Principles are more clearly understood.

1. BECAUSE I may happen not to be understood clearly enough by the desirous Reader, and shall be as one that is altogether dumb to the unenlightened (for the eternal and indissoluble band, wherein the essence of all essences standeth, is not easily nor in haste to be understood), therefore it is necessary that the desirous Reader do the more earnestly consider himself what he is, and from whence his reason and [1]senses do proceed, wherein he findeth the similitude of God, especially if he consider and meditate what his soul is, which is an eternal incorruptible spirit.

[1] inward senses, or thoughts.

2. But if the Reader be [2]born of God, there is no nearer way for him to come to the knowledge of the third Principle, than by considering the new birth, how the soul is new born by the love of God in the light, and how it is translated out of the prison or dungeon of darkness into the light by a

[2] Or be in true resignation.

second birth.   And now if you consider that darkness wherein it must be without the new birth ; and consider what the Scripture saith, and what every one findeth by experience, that falleth into the wrath of God, and whereof there are terrible examples ;   that the soul must endure irksome torment in itself, in the birth of the life of its own self, so long as it is in the wrath of God ; and then that if it be born again, exulting great joy ariseth in it ; and thus you find very clearly and plainly two Principles, as also God, paradise, and the kingdom of heaven.

3. For you find in the root of the original of the spirit of the soul, in itself, in the substance of the eternal birth and incorruptible eternal band of the soul, the most exceeding horrible inimicitious irksome [1] source, wherein the soul (without the light of God) is like all devils, wherein their eternal source consisteth, being an enmity in itself, a will striving against God [and goodness], it desireth nothing that is pleasant or good, it is a climbing up of pride in the strength of the fire, a bitter [fierce, odious malice, or] wrathfulness against paradise, against God, against the kingdom of heaven ; also against all creatures in the second and third Principles, lifting up themselves alone [against all this], as the bitterness [2] in the fire doth.

4. Now the Scripture witnesseth throughout, and the new-born man findeth it so, that when the soul is new-born in the light of God, then on

[1] Or torment, or working property.

[2] in wrath, or anger doth.

5

the contrary it findeth, how very humble, meek, courteous, and cheerly it is; it readily beareth all manner of crosses and persecution; it turneth the body from out of the way of the wicked; it regardeth no reproach, disgrace, or scorn, put upon it from the devil, or man; it placeth its confidence, refuge, and love, in the Heart of God; it is very cheerful; it is fed by the Word of God, in which there is a paradisical exulting and triumph; it cannot be [hurt, or so much as] touched by the devil. For it is in its own substance (wherein it stands in the first Principle of the indissoluble band) enlightened with the light of God; and the Holy Ghost, who goeth forth out of the eternal [1] birth of the Father in the Heart, and in the light of the Heart of God, he goeth forth in it, and establisheth it the child of God.

[1] generation, begetting, or working.

5. Therefore all that it doth (seeing it liveth in the light of God) is done in the love of God; the devil cannot see that soul, for the second Principle, wherein it liveth, and in which God and the kingdom of heaven stand, as also the angels, and paradise, is shut up from him, and he cannot get to it.

6. In this consideration you may find what I understand by a Principle. For a Principle is nothing else but a new birth, a new life: Besides, there is no more than 'one Principle wherein there is an eternal life, that is, the eternal Deity. And that would not have been manifested, if God had

created no creatures in himself (*viz.* angels and men), who understand the eternal and indissoluble band, and [1] how the birth of the eternal light is in God.

[1] Or the manner.

7. Thus now herein is understood how the divine essence in the divine Principle hath wrought in the root of the first Principle, which is the begettress, matrix, or genetrix in the eternal birth in the [2] *limbus*, or in the original water-spirit; by which operation at last, the earth and stones come forth. For in the second Principle (*viz.* in the holy birth) there is only spirit, light, and life; and the eternal wisdom hath wrought in the eternal inanimate genetrix, which is void of understanding (*viz.* in her own property) before the original of the light; out of which came the [3] dark chaos, which in the elevation of Lord *Lucifer* (when the light of God departed from him, and the fierceness of the source of the fire was kindled) became hard matter (*viz.* stones and earth), whereupon followed the gathering together of the earth, as also the spewing out of *Lucifer* from his throne, and the creating of the third Principle; and thereupon it followed, that he was shut up in the third Principle as a prisoner, expecting henceforth the [judgment or] sentence of God. Now whether it be not a shame, disgrace, and irksomeness to him to be so imprisoned between paradise and this world, and not to be able to comprehend either of them, I propose it to be considered.

[2] *Limbus* signifieth a seed, or concretion of matter.

[3] dust, dirt, or mud.

8. Thus now if we will speak of the third Principle, *viz.* of the beginning and birth of this world, then we must consider the root of the genetrix, or begettress, seeing every Principle is another birth, but out of no other essence; and so we may find, that in the first Principle in the indissoluble band (which in itself is inanimate, and hath no true life, but the [1]source of the true life is born by the moving spirit of God, which from eternity hath its original in the first Principle, and goeth forth from eternity in the second Principle, as in the birth of the Heart or Son of God) the matrix of the genetrix is set open, which is originally the [2]harshness; yet in the light it is the soft mother of the water-spirit. Thus it is seen and found clearly and plainly before our eyes, that the spirit of God hath wrought there in the matrix, so that out of the incomprehensible matrix (which is but a spirit) the comprehensible and visible water is proceeded.

9. Secondly, you [may] thus see the separation clearly by the stars and fiery heaven, that the eternal separation [or distinction] is in the eternal matrix; for you may see that the stars and the fiery heaven, and the watery, the airy, and earthly, are generated out of one mother, that they qualify with [or have influence upon] one another, and that the birth of their substance is in one another, also that one is the case or vessel to hold the other in, and yet they have not one and the same [property]

[1] Or working property.

[2] astringency, or tartness.

qualification [or condition].   Thus here in the
separation you [may] know, that the eternal matrix
hath a separation in itself, as is mentioned before
in the third chapter concerning the eternal birth
of the four anguishes, where the fire is generated
between harshness and bitterness, and the light in
the flash of fire, and so every source retaineth its
own due.

10. Understand it thus : as the spirit moved this
matrix, so the matrix wrought, and in the kindling
from the spirit of God in the fifth form of the
matrix, the fiery heaven of the constellations did
exist, which is a mere *quinta essentia*, or *quintessence*, born in the fifth form of the matrix, in
which place the light hath its original ; out of
which at last the sun is born [or brought forth],
wherewith the third Principle becometh opened and
manifested, which [sun] now is the life in the third
Principle, and the opener of the life of every life in
the matrix, in this place, or *locus* ; as the Heart of
God in paradise, in the immaterial heaven and
birth, openeth the eternal power of God, wherein
the eternal life continually springeth up, and
wherein the eternal wisdom continually shineth.
Thus also the light of the sun (which is sprung
up in the inanimate matrix) by the [flowing,
hovering, or] moving spirit in the matrix, openeth
the third Principle of this material world, which
is the third and beginning Principle ; which as to
this form taketh an end, and returneth into its

¹ Or devourer,
the most pure
elementary
air.
² Or finishing
of its time.

¹ether in the end of this ²enumeration, as the Scripture witnesseth.

11. And then all in this third Principle remaineth again in the first matrix; only that which hath been sown in this Principle, and that hath its original out of paradise, out of heaven, and out of the second Principle, (*viz.* man), that continueth eternally in the matrix. And if he have in this [life's] time attained the second Principle, so that he is born therein, it is well with him; but if he have not, then he shall remain still eternally in the matrix, yet not ³reach the light of God.

³ Or attain.

12. Now I know very well, that I shall not only in part be as it were dumb or obscure to the desirous Reader, but also tedious, and he will be somewhat troubled at me, in that I have written of the eternal mother (wherein the divine essence standeth); and that I now write, that this matrix is ⁴inanimate and void of understanding, out of which also a Principle void of understanding is generated; as is plain before our eyes, that in this world there is no true understanding, either in the stars, or in the elements; and also in all its creatures there is but an understanding to qualify [or to operate], to nourish itself, and to increase, as the matrix in itself is.

⁴ Or dumb.

13. Hereupon you are to know, that the matrix in the second Principle (which yet hath its original and eternal root in the first Principle) is but merely an eternal, beginningless, soft [or meek] spirit,

which hath no such fiery [1] intolerable light, but all
there is pleasant and cheerful, and the eternal
original matrix is not known there ; but the soft
light of the Heart of God maketh all courteous and
cheerful.

[1] Or light that cannot be endured, as is in the matrix of the first Principle.

14. Therefore also the spirit which goeth forth
in the soft matrix is the Holy Ghost; and God
dwelleth in himself, and he calleth himself an
angry, zealous [or jealous] God, only according to
the most original matrix, which is not manifested
in paradise ; and in the beginning also it was
forbidden to man to eat of the fruit [of] good and
evil, from the most original matrix. Neither
should man have known this most original matrix,
if he had not imagined [thought or longed] after it,
and eaten of the fruit thereof, whereby the matrix
presently took hold of him, captivated him, [acteth
or] qualifieth in him, nourisheth and also driveth
him, as is plain before our eyes.

15. And thus you are to know, that the second
Principle hath it [in its power], and there only
is wisdom and understanding ; also therein now is
the omnipotence [almightiness]. And this third
Principle is the second's proper own, not separate,
but one essence in it [and with it] all over, and yet
there is a birth between them, as may be seen
by the [2] rich man and *Lazarus*, the one being in
paradise, and the other in the most original matrix,
or hell.

[2] Luke xvi.

16. And therefore God [created or] generated

made known to angels and men.

the third Principle, that he might be [1]manifested by the material world: He having created the angels and spirits in the second Principle in the paradisical world, they could thereby understand the eternal [2]birth in the third Principle, also the wisdom and omnipotence of God, wherein they could behold themselves, and set their imagination merely [3]upon the Heart of God; in which [4]form they could remain in paradise, and continue to be angels; which the devils have not done, but they meant to rise up in the matrix, and domineer in great power over paradise, and all angelical [5]regions, upon which they fell out of paradise, and besides were driven out of their place (or *locus*) into [6]restraint, so that the matrix of this world also holdeth them captive.

[2] generating, working, or begetting.

[3] Or into.

[4] Or condition.

[5] principalities, thrones, and dominions.

[6] narrowness, or a corner.

[7] the universal place of this world, as far as the creating Word *Fiat* spreads itself.

17. For the [7]*locus* or space of this world was their angelical [dominion or] kingdom, where they were in the place of this world.

18. But though we speak of the paradisical essence, and also of the Principle of this world, of its power and wonderful birth, and what the divine and eternal wisdom is, yet it is impossible for us to utter and express it [all]; for the [8]lake of the deep can be comprehended in no spirit (whether it be angel or man); therefore the innumerable eternal [9]birth and wisdom maketh a wonderful eternal joy in paradise. This innumerable power and wisdom may now also be known by us men, in the third Principle, if we will take it into our consideration;

[8] fountain or well-spring.

[9] Or working.

if we look upon the starry heaven, the elements and living creatures, also upon trees, herbs, and grass, we may behold in the material world the similitude of the paradisical incomprehensible world; for this world is proceeded out of the first root, wherein stand both the material, and also the paradisical spiritual world, which is without beginning or transitoriness.

19. And now if we meditate and consider of the original of the four elements, we shall clearly find, see, and feel the original in ourselves, if we be men and not beasts, full of malice and gainsayings against God and the [1]matrix of this world. For the original is as well known in man, as in the deep of this world; although it seemeth wonderful to the unenlightened man, that any should [be able] to speak of the original of the air, fire, water, and earth, as also of the starry heaven; he supposeth this impossible to be known; thus he [2]swimmeth in his own mother, and desireth not to know it, neither was it good for man to know it; but since the fall of *Adam* hath cast us headlong into it, it is highly necessary for us to know it, that we may fly from the bestial man, and learn to know the true man.

[1] mother, the eternal nature, or root.

[2] glideth away in his thoughts imperceptibly.

20. And if you open the eyes of your mind, you will see that fire is in water, as may be seen in a storm of lightning, and yet it is no durable fire, though it be true fire, which setteth houses on fire, and burneth them. So also you may see that there

goeth forth from it a mighty forcible air, and that they are in one another; and besides, you see that water is generated in the storm.

21. But you will not find this root here, you must look into the [1]matrix, and there it is wholly manifest, and you may know it in all things, for the matrix of this world standeth in the eternal matrix, from which paradise and the kingdom of heaven have their original. Now as the eternal matrix is a birth that goeth forth, where, in the original, there is harshness, darkness, hardness, and anguish, so you may see, that when the spirit of God hath [2]kindled the inward matrix, then it becometh stirring, working, and active.

Or womb. The temporary matrix is the temporary nature, and the eternal matrix is the eternalnature.

[2] Or awakened.

22. For there is in the original, first, [3]harshness, which attracteth, shutteth up, maketh darkness, and sharp cold; but the tartness cannot endure the attracting; for the attracting in the cold maketh in the bitterness a sting [or prickle], which rageth and resisteth against the hard death, but not being able to come away out of the tartness (being its mother wherein it standeth), therefore it rageth very horribly, as if it would break the harshness [in pieces]; it flieth out upwards and sideways, and yet findeth no rest, till that the birth of the harshness fall into an aching horrible essence, like a brimstone-spirit, very rough, hard, stinging in itself [or kindling in itself], like a whirling wheel, and that the bitterness flieth up very swiftly, from whence proceedeth a twinkling flash; at which the

[3] astringent attraction.

dark harshness is terrified, and sinketh back as vanquished. And so when the bitterness findeth the mother overcome, and as it were half dead, or soft [or meek], it is terrified more than the mother. But the shriek or terror being past in the harsh mother, which is now half dead, or soft [pliable or meek], then the bitterness loseth its terrible right [or property], and becometh white, light, and clear; and thus is the kindling and birth of the fire, as is mentioned before.

23. Dear Reader, account not this ridiculous; that this birth (which also is just so in the [1] begin-ning of your life) may not trouble or confound you; and observe it further.

[1] in the mother's womb.

24. When God in the first matrix moved himself to create, and created the angels, he created them in paradise, in the light holy matrix (which is this and no other); but the matrix, with its fiery, dark, and harsh bitter property, remained altogether hidden; for the light of God from eternity preserved it, and kept it pleasant, clear, and bright. But when God moved himself to create, then it became manifested; for the angels were created out of the indissoluble band, out of the matrix, and were bodified from the moving spirit of God.

25. Now when God .had created great potent princely angels, and that in the place of the fourth form in the matrix, where the source of fire hath its original, they stood not, neither did they cast

¹ Or their minds into resignation.

their ¹imaginations forward into the fifth form, wherein the sprouting forth of paradise consisteth ; but they cast their imaginations back into themselves, and formed [or created] a will [or purpose] in the matrix, to domineer in the fire over the light of God and paradise. For the fiery matrix (*viz.* the abyss of hell) moved itself in the creation so hard, that *Lucifer* (that great prince) hath formed his will out of it, and is continued therein, supposing that so he should be a great and terrible lord in his whole place [of dominion].

26. Thus the devil moved the matrix, and the fiery form moved the devil ; for ²that also would be creaturely, as [well as] all the other forms in the matrix, which yet was opposite to the fifth form in the matrix, where in the meek and clear light the pleasant source of love springeth up, wherein the second Principle standeth eternally.

² the fiery form would have a creature of his own.

27. When this storm was in the creation (in the first Principle) the matrix became very big [or much impregnated] and kindled ; and every form in the matrix wrought [stirred or acted]. But because the anger and wrath had there elevated itself, and that this place could not thus subsist in paradise, therefore God moved this place yet more in the matrix, which was yet the more kindled, where then is to be the devil's bath [repository or dwelling-place], and the fourth form stood in the flash of the fire, which reflected back into the

mother, and [1]found the spirit of God in the [1] felt or perceived.
forming [or creation], where in a moment [that
fourth form] lost its wrathful [smart, fierce property,
authority or] right, and became in great joy, white,
clear, and [2]light: and in this place [or thing con- [2] Or bright.
sisteth or] standeth the *Fiat*, by which God created
heaven and earth: for before the *Fiat*, the third
Principle was not manifested, but there was merely
paradise in the place of this world.

28. But God seeing that the great prince *Lucifer*
would domineer in the matrix, in the strength of
the fire in his place, therefore he shut up the fifth
form in the matrix of paradise from him, for it is
shut up both in its inward corporeal form, and outwardly also.

29. For when the matrix became [3]thin again, [3] rarefied.
dead and vanquished, from the risen light, then
the material [matrix] turned to water, as we may
perceive; and in this kindling before the light of
the sun (when the matrix was still in the harsh
fierceness) the matrix attracted that which was
wrought together into a water-spirit, out of which
came the rocky cliffs, stones and the dark earth,
which before the time of the creation was but a
[4]chaos; and in that time sprang forth the third [4] dust, cloud, dirt, or puddle.
Principle, the fiery heaven, in the fifth form in
the matrix, by the *Fiat*, which the Father spake
through his Heart, or Son, by and in the going
forth of his spirit, who there, [5]upon the matrix in [5] the spirit moved upon the water.
the fifth form, framed the fiery heaven, as the

highly worthy *Moses* hath clearly written of it. For the matrix is the water-spirit in the original, in the first form; and now when it became material in the place of this world, then the spirit moved upon the water in the heavenly matrix, which is immaterial (from whence the material water is generated), and so formed the creatures.

30. Thus in this springing up [or going forth] the material matrix was extinguished, and the wrathfulness [tartness or fierceness] is come in the stead thereof. And the devil remained in the original of the matrix (which cannot be altered in eternity), between paradise and this world, in the dark matrix; and with the creation of the earth, he was thrust down from his high throne [or seat], where now the fiery starry heaven is.

THE SIXTH CHAPTER

Of the Separation in the Creation, in the third Principle.

1. IF we consider of the [1] separation and the springing forth in the third Principle of this world, how the starry heaven should spring up, and how every star hath a peculiar form and property in itself, in every of which a several centre is observed, so that every one of them is fixed [or steady] and master [or guider] of itself, and that every one of them ruleth in the matrix of this world, and [2] worketh and generateth in the matrix after their kind. And then afterwards, if we consider the sun, which is their king, heart, and life, without whose light and virtue [3] they could neither act nor effect any thing, but remain in the hard dark death ; and this world would be nothing (but a fierce rough hardness). And further, if we consider the elements of fire and water [and observe] how they continually generate one in another, and then how the constellations rule in them, as in their own propriety ; and also consider what the mother is, from whence all these things

[1] distinction, specific difference, form, or variation, whereby every thing hath its own peculiar essence.

[2] Or qualifieth.

[3] the stars.

79

must proceed; then we shall come to see the separation, and the eternal mother, the [1] genetrix of all things.

[1] Or bringer forth.

2. Nay, we have it clearly and plainly to be seen in ourselves, and in all things, if we would not be so mad, blind, and self-conceited, and would not be so drawn and led by a [2] school-boy, but did stick close to the schoolmaster himself, who is the master of all masters; for we see indeed that all things spring out of the eternal mother; and as she is in her own birth, so she hath generated this world, and so is every creature also generated. And as that [mother] is in her springing forth in multiplication, where every fountain [or source] hath another centre in it from the genetrix, and a separation [or distinction], but undivided and not asunder, so also this world is generated out of the eternal mother, which now is such another genetrix, and yet is not separated [or sundered] from the eternal [3] mother, but is come to be in a material manner, and it hath through the sun attained another light and life; which [light and life] is not the wise Master himself, but the wise Master (who is God) he keepeth that light and life, so that it standeth and continueth in the eternal matrix, and yet it is not the eternal wisdom itself.

[2] outward reason.

[3] Or nature.

3. Now because this birth [of the sun] hath a beginning through the will of God, and entereth again into its [4] ether, therefore it hath not the virtue or power of the wisdom; but it continually

[4] Or repository.

[1]worketh according to its kind, it vivifieth and
killeth; what it doth, it doth [not regarding
whether it be] evil, crooked, lame, or good, beautiful or potent, it causeth to live and to die, it
affordeth power and strength, and destroyeth the
same again; and all this without any premeditated
wisdom; whereby it may be perceived, that it is
not the divine providence and wisdom itself, as the
heathens supposed, and foolishly relied upon the
virtue thereof.

4. But if we would see the ground thereof,
we must only look upon the first mother in her
birth, and so we shall see and find it all. For
as the first mother (considering her in the original
without the light) is sour [or harsh], dark,
hard, and cold, and yet there is the [2]water-
spirit in the bringing forth, thus you may find
(when the material world sprang up) that God
then on the first day created the heaven and
the earth.

5. Now the heaven cometh out of the sour
matrix, which in the paradisical [heaven] is the
water-spirit; and out of that paradisical [water-
spirit or matrix] the material [heaven or matrix]
is created; as *Moses* writeth, that the heaven was
created out of the midst of the waters; and it is
very right. And also in that very hour the earth
and the stones, and all metals (the matrix of this
world being yet dark) were generated out of the
matrix.

[1] Or buildeth.

[2] Or spirit of the water.

6

6. For when the matrix was stirred, and that lord Lucifer would domineer in the fire, then the dark matrix attracted all that was wrought in the [1] birth together, from whence earth, stones, metals, brimstone and salt did proceed : Hereby the kingdom of prince Lucifer was shut up, and he remained in the inward centre captivated in the outward.

[1] out-birth.

7. But the virtue which was in the matrix, was that which could effect such things in the matrix ; for a stone is nothing else but a water, [2]mercury, salt, and brimstone, wherein an oil is hidden. Now the birth of the matrix hath such a form in its eternal essence, and [3] birth of its life. For first, there is the harshness [or sourness], fierceness [or eager strongness] and hardness, from whence the cold proceedeth. Now the sourness [or harshness] attracteth and sharpeneth the cold ; and in its attracting it maketh the bitter sting [or prickle] which pricketh and rageth, and cannot endure the hard attracting, but vexeth like a furious madness, it riseth up and rageth, and becometh like a brimstone-spirit.

[2] The original text, *Mercurius*.

[3] Or continual generation and subsistence.

8. And in this form in the wrath [or fierce strongness], in the watery sour mother, the sour bitter earth, brimstone and salt is generated, before the kindling of the sun in the matrix that is void of understanding. But the separation that is in it, is caused from the birth's standing in great anguish, and from its desiring the separation in the birth ; for the bitterness agreeth not with the

harshness [or sourness], and yet they are as mother and son, and as members one [1] of another; and it [1] must be so, or else nothing could be, for it is the eternal band, and the original of life.

9. Moreover, when the bitterness rageth, riseth up, and [2] vexeth in the [sour] harsh mother, then it falleth into a glimmering flash most terribly; in this form the mercurius, or venom, or poison is generated. For when the matrix perceiveth this flash of fire in its dark sour form, then it is terrified, and becometh dead in her hard sour property. And in this place death, poison, [3] withering and corruption are generated in the matrix, and also the noble life in the mercurius, and in the springing up of the third Principle.

10. And further, when the horror [or crack or shriek] of the fire is come into its harsh mother, and hath thus overcome its mother, then itself is much more terrified, for there it loseth its fierce or strong property, because the mother [hath] attained another [4] source; and out of the horror of the fire a [5] brightness is come to be, in which, in the inanimate matrix, the *materia* [or matter], in the midst of the horror [or crack], is come to be a soft and bright [6] mixed matter, *viz.* from the crack of the light [is proceeded] gold, silver, copper, tin, lead, etc. according as every place in the matrix stood in the wrestling centre.

11. For the birth in the whole space of this world (as far as Lucifer's kingdom reached) was

[1] in.

[2] acheth.

[3] falling away, or decaying and destruction.

[4] Or root.

[5] glance, or lustre.

[6] Or concrete.

Note.

thus; and therefore there are very different kinds of earth, metals, and other things in one place, than in another. And it is plain before our eyes, that all metals are mixed, which proceedeth from the [1] bringing forth *in infinitum*; which we well understand and see, but cannot utter, nor dare we speak it, for it troubleth us, and it reacheth into the Deity, which is without beginning, and eternal; therefore the creature must let it alone upon pain of the loss both of its reason and sense.

[1] Or out-birth.

12. But to declare this further: When the matrix stood thus in the birth, where the matter of the earth was generated, then the matrix with the kindling became water; you must understand it aright, not wholly in substance, but it hath generated the earth, stones, and metals, and yet the matrix continueth still; so also the water still continueth in the killing and overcoming; whereby the material world took its beginning, where the globe of the earth was drawn together in this moving, and standeth in the middle of the circle from above and from beneath as a point [or *punctum*].

Note.

13. And there in the centre, in the paradisical matrix, and in the paradisical heaven, the spirit of God stood in his own eternal seat, neither did it depart from thence, and moved upon the material water with the *Fiat*, and there formed the heaven, which was created out of the midst of the watery matrix; and he separated the root of the darkness

from the light in the matrix, in which darkness the devils remained, and they have not comprehended the matter in the matrix, nor the new light, which sprang up in the matrix. And so with this creation and separation the length of one day was finished, and out of the beginning and end, and morning and evening, was the first day, as *Moses* writeth.

14. But that we may so speak of the heaven, that the Reader might come to understand what that [heaven] is which God then created, [consider] what *Moses* writeth of it. God made a firmament between the waters, and separated the waters beneath the firmament from the waters above the firmament, and the firmament he called heaven, which is very right; but hitherto it hath been very ill understood.

15. Now observe, the heaven is the whole deep, so far as the *ethera*, or skies, have [1] given up themselves to the birth of this world, and that heaven is the matrix, out of which earth, stones, and the material water are generated. And there God separated the material water from the matrix. And here it is very plainly discerned, that the material water is as it were dead, or hath death in it; for it could not abide in the [2] moving mother, but was created [to be] upon the globe of the earth, and God called it sea [*Meer*]; in which [word] is understood, in the language of nature, as it were a springing [or growing] in death, or a life

[1] expanded, or spread.

[2] Viz. the air.

¹ the corrupti-
bility.
² That is, the
Reader will
not under-
stand it.
³ Or under-
stand.

in ¹corruption : ²Although herein I shall be as one that is dumb to the Reader, yet I ³know it very well, and I am very well satisfied therewith. But because the bestial man is not worthy to know it, therefore I will not here cast the Pearl before the swine ; but for the children of God, which will be benefited by it, the spirit of God will certainly teach and instruct them in it.

16. Now when the heaven became clear [or pure], and cleansed from the earth and the dark mist [or dust] in the concretion [or driving together], then in the matrix of the heaven there were the three elements, fire, air and water, which are three in one another, in one mother; and that mother is here called the heaven ; therefore henceforward in my writing, I shall use the word *heaven* instead of the word *matrix*.

17. For the heaven is the matrix, and is called heaven because of the separation, because the fifth essence of heaven is severed, and set in the higher heaven, where the matrix is more fiery, as it is properly understood in the language of nature, and is plain before our eyes. But here the quality, birth and property of the heaven ought to be described, because the four elements sprang out of it, as out of their mother; and because the virtue of every life consisteth therein, therefore the original of the four elements must be described, wherein it will first truly be understood what the heaven is.

THE SEVENTH CHAPTER

Of the Heaven and its eternal Birth and Essence, and how the four Elements are generated; wherein the eternal Band may be the more and the better understood, by meditating and considering the material World.

The great Depth.

1. EVERY spirit seeth no further than into its mother, out of which it hath its original, and wherein it standeth; for it is impossible for any spirit in its own natural power to look into another Principle, and behold it, except it be regenerated therein. But the natural man, who in his fall was captivated by the matrix of this world, whose natural spirit [1] moveth between two Principles, *viz.* [1] wavereth. between the divine and the hellish, and he standeth in both the gates, into which Principle he falleth, there he cometh to be regenerated, whether it be as to the kingdom of heaven, or the kingdom of hell; and yet he is not able in this [life] time to see either of them both.

2. He is in his own essence and substance a two-fold man. For his soul (in its own substance) is

out of the first Principle, which from eternity hath no ground nor beginning; and in the time of the creation of man in paradise, or the kingdom of heaven, the soul was truly [1]bodified by the *Fiat* in a spiritual manner; but with the first virtue [or power] which is from eternity, in its own first virtue or power it hath remained inseparably in its first root, and was illustrated [or made shining bright] by the second Principle, *viz.* by the Heart of God; and therewith standing in paradise, was there, by the moving spirit of God, breathed into the matrix of the third Principle, into the starry and elementary man. And now therefore he may understand the ground of heaven, as also of the elements and of hell, as far as the light of God shineth in him; for if that light be in him, he is born in all the three Principles; but yet he is only a spark risen from thence, and not the great source, or fountain, which is God himself.

3. And therefore it is that Christ saith: *If you had faith as a grain of mustard-seed, you might say to the mountain, Cast thyself into the sea, and it shall be done.* And [2]in this power men have raised the dead, and healed the sick, by the word, and the virtue and power of the spirit, or else they could not have been able to have done such things, if they had not stood in the power of all the three Principles.

4. For the created spirit of man, which is out of the matrix of this world, that ruleth (by the virtue

of the second Principle in the virtue of the light)
over and in the virtue of the spirit of the stars and
elements very mightily, as in that which is its proper
own.   But in the fall of *Adam* we lost this great
power, when we left paradise, and went into the
third Principle, into the matrix of this world, which
presently held us captive in restraint.   But yet we
have the knowledge [of that power] by a glance [or
glimmering], and we see as through a dim or dark
glass the eternal [1] birth.

> [1] Or operative propagation.

5. And although we move thus weakly or im-
potently in all the three births, and that the gate
of paradise is so often darkened to us, and that the
devil doth so often draw us into the hellish gate,
and that also the elements cover the [2] sidereal gate,
and wholly cloud them, so that we oftentimes move
in the whole matrix, as if we were deaf, dumb, or
half dead, yet if the paradisical light shineth to us,
we may very well see into the mother of all the
three Principles; for nothing can hinder us, the
threefold spirit of man seeth every form and quality
in its mother.

> [2] Or the dominion or influences of the stars.

6. Therefore though we speak of the creation of
the world, as if we had been by at present, and had
seen it, none ought to marvel at it, nor hold it for
impossible.   For the spirit that is in us, which one
man inherits from another, that was breathed out
of the eternity into *Adam*, that same spirit hath
seen it all, and in the light of God it seeth it still;
and there is nothing that is far off, or unsearchable:

For the eternal birth, which standeth hidden in the centre of man, that doth nothing [that is] new, it knoweth, worketh and doth even the same that ever it did from eternity; it laboureth for the light and for the darkness, and worketh in great anguish; but when the light shineth therein, then there is mere joy and knowledge in its working.

7. So that when the heaven, and the birth of the elements are spoken of, it is not a thing afar off, or that is distant from us, that is spoken of; but we speak of things that are done in our body and soul; and there is nothing nearer us than this birth, for we live and move therein, as in the house of our mother; and when we speak of heaven, we speak of our native country, which the enlightened soul can well see, though indeed such things are hidden from the body.

8. For as the soul of man moveth and swimmeth between the virtue of the stars and elements, so the created heaven also moveth between paradise and the kingdom of hell, and it swimmeth in the eternal matrix; its limit reacheth as far as the *ethera* [skies or receptacle] hath yielded itself up to the creation, so far as the kingdom of Lucifer did reach, where yet no end is to be found: For the virtue or power of God is without end, but our sense reacheth only to the fiery heaven of the stars, which are a [1]propagation in the fifth form of the eternal mother (or a *quinta essentia*), wherein the separation in the time of the third Principle (or in the beginning

[1] Or outbirth, issue, or offspring.

of this world), the virtue or power of the matrix
was [1] separated, where now the separation is thus
moved : And then every essence in the propagation, in the manifold centres of the stars, hath a
[2] longing desire, one after another, and a continual
will to infect [impregnate, or mix influences];
and the one essence, or virtue, is the [3] meat and
drink, as also the chest [case, or receptacle] of
the other.

[1] Or divided into parts, or varied.

[2] attracting.

[3] food.

9. For as in the paradisical Principle the Holy
Ghost in the Trinity of the Deity continually goeth
forth, and floweth very softly, immovably and
imperceptibly as to the creature, and yet formeth
and fashioneth all in the paradisical matrix, so also
doth the third Principle. After that the matrix
became visible and material, every virtue in the
matrix hath had a great attractive longing towards
another, a continual springing, blossoming, and
fading again like a bud, or some boiling seething
matter, wherein the sourness, coldness, and [eager
fierce] strongness, attract without ceasing; and
this attracting, prickle [or sting], stirreth always
without ceasing, and striveth [or resisteth], so that
the sour matrix (because of the inward, hellish,
or most original matrix) standeth continually in
anguish, with a great desire of the light, which it
espieth in the root of the fire, and is continually
affrighted at it, and becometh mild, soft, and
material; whereby the elementary water is continually generated.

10. In this manner you must understand the four elements, which yet are not four divided things, or essences, but one only essence: And yet there are four differences, or distinctions in this birth; and each element lieth in the other, as in a chest, and it is its receptacle, also it is a member therein. Understand and consider the ground aright, which followeth: The [1]sourness is the matrix, and a cause of all things, which in its own substance is very dark, cold, and as nothing; but the eternal Deity being there, and speculating or beholding itself in the sourness, therefore the dark sourness is desirous after the divine virtue, and attracteth; although there is no life or understanding in the sourness, yet it is the ground of the first essence, and the original whence something cometh to be: Here we can search no further into the ground of the Deity, for it troubleth [disturbeth, or confoundeth] us.

[1] Or astringency is the root of the mother.

11. Now the sourness (in its lust or great longing [or panting] after the light) attracteth continually, and in its own substance it is nothing else but a vehement hunger, very dry, and as [a *vacuum* or] nothing at all, a desiring will, as the darkness after the light; and its hunger, or attracting, maketh the bitterness, the woe [or lamentation] that it cannot be satiated, or mollified, from whence the anguish ariseth, so that the will, or prickle [or sting] is rubbed, [or [2]struck] in itself, from the lust of the desiring, and it will not

[2] As steel and a flint strike fire.

yield itself to the dark nothing, or dead will, but
setteth its desire and anguish, and also its [eager
or] strong will so very hard towards the hidden
light of God, that thereby the will becometh a
twinkling flash, like a sparkling or [1] crackling fire, [1] As when you
whereby the sourness, that is so very aching, is throw water
continually filled, and as it were deadened, whereby into the fire.
the sour spirit cometh to be soft, sweet, and
material, even water.

12. But the bitterness being so very much
affrighted at the flash of fire in the sourness, it
catcheth its mother (the sourness) which is become
material from the crack, and flieth out, and is
clouded or [2] swelled from the material sourness, as [2] impregnated.
if it also were material, and moveth, and strength-
eneth itself continually in the mother; and that is
the element called air in this world, which hath its
original in the watery mother, and the water hath ·
its original from the air, and the fire hath its
original from the longing anguish; and the earth
and stones took their beginning in the strong
attraction at the fall of Lucifer, when the sourness
was so fierce, strong, rising, and attractive, which
attraction is stopped again by the light in the third
Principle.

13. Thus it may very plainly be understood,
that the light of God is a cause of all things, and
you may hereby understand all the three Principles:
For if the power, virtue, and light of God were not,
then there would be also no attractive longing in

the dark eternity, and also the sour desire (which is the mother of the eternity) would be nothing at all; and it may be understood, that the divine virtue shineth in everything, and yet it is not the thing itself, but the spirit of God in the second Principle; and yet the thing is his ray [glance or lustre], which thus proceedeth from the longing, or attracting will. But now the Heart of God is in the Father, [in] the first will, and the Father is the first desiring or longing after the Son, and the Son is the virtue and [1] light of the Father, from whence the eternal nature becometh always longing; and so from the Heart of God, in the eternal dark matrix, [it] generateth the third Principle. For [2] so God is manifest, but otherwise the Deity would remain hidden eternally.

[1] lustre, or brightness.

[2] Or thereby.

14. Now therefore we say (as the Scripture informeth us) that God dwelleth in heaven, and it is the truth. Now mark, *Moses* writeth, that God created the heaven out of the midst of the waters, and the Scripture saith, God dwelleth in heaven; therefore we may now observe, that the water hath its original from the longing of the eternal nature after the eternal light of God; but the eternal nature is made manifest by the longing after the light of God, as is mentioned before; and the light of God is present every where, and yet remaineth hidden to nature; for nature receiveth only the virtue of the light, and the virtue is the heaven wherein the light of God dwelleth and is hidden,

and so shineth in the darkness. The water is the *materia*, or matter that is generated from the heaven, and therein standeth the third, which again generateth a life and comprehensible essence, or substance, out of itself, *viz.* the elements and other creatures.

15. Therefore, O noble man, let not Antichrist and the devil befool you, who tell you that the Deity is afar off from you, and direct you to a heaven that is situated far above you; whereas there is nothing nearer to you than the heaven is. You only stand before the door of heaven, and you are gone forth with *Adam* out of the paradisical heaven into the third Principle; yet you stand in the gate, do but as the eternal mother doth, which by great desiring and [1] longing after the kingdom [1] Or seeking. of God, attaineth the kingdom of heaven, wherein God dwelleth, wherein paradise springeth up; do you but so, set all your desire [2] upon the Heart of [2] into. God, and so you will pass in by force, as the eternal mother doth; and then it shall be with thee as Christ said, *The kingdom of heaven suffereth violence, and the violent take it by force*: So you shall make to yourself friends in heaven with your unrighteous *Mammon*, and so you come to be the true similitude and image of God, and his proper own; for all the three Principles, with the eternity, are in you, and the holy paradise is again generated in you, wherein God dwelleth. Then where will you seek for God? Seek him in your soul only

that is proceeded out of the eternal nature, wherein the [1] divine birth standeth.

16. O that I had but the pen of man, and were able therewith to write down the spirit of knowledge. I can but stammer of the great mysteries like a child that is beginning to speak; so very little can the earthly tongue express what the spirit comprehendeth and understandeth; yet I will venture to try whether I may procure some to go about to seek the Pearl, whereby also I might [2] labour in the works of God, in my paradisical garden of roses; for the longing of the eternal [3] matrix driveth me on to write and exercise myself in this my knowledge.

17. Now if we will lift up our minds, and seek after the heaven wherein God dwelleth, we cannot say that God dwelleth only above the stars, and hath inclosed himself with the firmament which is made out of the waters, in which none can enter except it be opened (like a window) for him; with which thoughts men are altogether befooled [and bewildered]. Neither can we say (as some suppose) that God the Father and the Son are only with angels in the uppermost inclosed heaven, and rule only here in this world by the Holy Ghost, who proceedeth from the Father and the Son. All these thoughts are void of the very knowledge of God. For then God would be divided and circumscriptive, like the sun that moveth aloft above us, and sendeth its light and virtue to us,

[1] Or divine working.

[2] Or work.

[3] mother of nature.

whereby the whole deep becometh light and active all over.

18. Reason is much befooled with these thoughts; and the kingdom of Antichrist is begotten in [1] these thoughts, and Antichrist hath by these opinions set himself in the place of God, and meaneth to be God upon earth, and ascribeth [2] divine power to himself, and stoppeth the mouth of the spirit of God, and will not hear him speak; and so strong delusions come upon them, that they believe the spirit of lies, which in hypocrisy speaketh strong delusions, and seduceth the children of hope, as St *Paul* witnesseth.

[1] Which possess the minds of straying Christians.

[2] divine authority, *Jus divinum*.

19. The true heaven, wherein God dwelleth, is all over, in all places [or corners], even in the midst [or centre] of the earth. He comprehendeth the hell where the devils dwell, and there is nothing without God. For wheresoever he was before the creation of the world, there he is still, *viz.* in himself; and is himself the essence of all essences: All is generated from him, and is originally from him. And he is therefore called God, because he alone is the good, the heart, or [that which is] best; understand, he is the light and virtue [or power], from whence nature hath its original.

20. If you will [3] meditate on God, take before you the eternal darkness, which is without God; for God dwelleth in himself, and the darkness cannot in its own power comprehend him; which darkness hath a great [desire of] longing after the

[3] think, or apprehend anything of God.

7

[1] speculating as in a glass.

[2] Or active property.

light, caused by the light's [1] beholding itself in the darkness, and shining in it. And in this longing or desiring, you find the [2] source, and the source taketh hold of the power or virtue of the light, and the longing maketh the virtue material, and the material virtue is the inclosure to God, or the heaven; for in the virtue standeth the paradise, wherein the spirit which proceedeth from the Father and the Son worketh. All this is incom-

[3] creature, or natural man.

prehensible to the [3] creation, but not impossible to be found in the mind; for paradise standeth open in the mind of a holy soul.

21. Thus you [may] see how God created all things out of nothing, but only out of himself;

[4] that which is procreated, viz. the four elements.

[5] Or springing properties.

and yet the [4] out-birth is not from his essence [or substance], but it hath its original from the darkness. The [5] source of the darkness is the first Principle, and the virtue [or power] of the light is the second Principle, and the out-birth, [generated] out of the darkness by the virtue of the light, is the third Principle; and that is not called God: God is only the light, and the virtue of the light, and that which goeth forth out of the light is the Holy Ghost.

22. You have a similitude [of this] in yourself. Your soul which is in you giveth reason to you, whereby you think [consider, and perceive]; that representeth God the Father: The light which shineth in your soul, whereby you know the virtue [or power in you], and lead [and direct and order]

yourself with; that representeth God the Son, or the Heart, the eternal power and virtue: And the mind, in which the virtue of the light is, and that which proceedeth from the light wherewith you govern your body; that representeth the Holy Ghost.

23. The [1] darkness that is in you, which longeth after the light, that is the first Principle; the virtue or power of the light which is in you, whereby you can see in your mind without [bodily] eyes, that is the second Principle; and the longing [power or] virtue, that proceedeth from the mind, and attracteth and filleth [or impregnateth] itself, from whence the material body groweth, that is the third Principle. And you [may] understand very exactly, how there is an inclosure [stop, or knot] between each Principle; and how God is the beginning and the first virtue [or power] in all things; and you understand, that in this gross [sluggish, or dull] body, you are not in [2] paradise. For that [outward body] is but a misty [excrementitious, dusky, opaque procreation, or] out-birth in the third Principle, wherein the soul lieth captive, as in a dark dungeon: Of which you shall find a very large description, when we come to write about the fall of *Adam.*

24. Now mark, when God would manifest himself by the material world, and the matrix stood in the anguishing birth, wherein the Creator moved the first Principle to the creating of angels, then

[1] Or blindness of understanding.

[2] Or in the divine joy, wherein God and the angels dwell.

the matrix stood undivided in the inward ¹essence; for there was then no comprehensibility, but spirit only and the virtue of the spirit. The spirit was God, and the virtue was heaven, and the spirit wrought in the virtue, so that thereby the virtue became attracting and longing, for the spirit beheld itself in the virtue; and therein the spirit created the virtue from whence the angels came to be. And thus the virtue became the dwelling of the angels, and the paradise wherein the spirit wrought; and the spirit longed after the light, and the light shone in the virtue; so there is a paradisical joy, and pleasant sport therein; and thus God is manifested.

25. Now thus the eternal light, and the virtue of the light, or the heavenly paradise, moveth in the eternal darkness; and the darkness cannot comprehend the light; for they are two several Principles; and the darkness longeth after the light, because that the spirit beholdeth itself therein, and because the divine virtue is manifested in it. But though it hath not comprehended the divine virtue and light, yet it hath continually with great lust lifted up itself towards it, till it hath kindled the root of the fire in itself, from the beams of the light of God; and there arose the third Principle: And it hath its original out of the first Principle, out of the dark matrix, by the ²speculating of the virtue [or power] of God. But when the kindled virtue in this springing up [of the third Principle]

² beholding, imagining, or reflection.

in the darkness became fiery, then God put the *Fiat* therein, and by the moving spirit, which goeth forth in the virtue of the light, created the fiery source in a bodily manner, and severed it from the matrix, and the spirit called the fiery created properties stars, for their quality.

26. Thus it is plain to our sight how the starry heaven (or as I may better render it to the enlightened Reader), the quintessence (or the fifth form in the birth), is severed from the watery matrix; or else there would have been no ceasing from the generating of stones and earth, if the fiery [1]nature had not been severed: But because [1] property or kind. the eternal essence (*viz.* God) would manifest himself in the dark matrix, and [hath desired] to make the nothing something, therefore he hath severed the kindled virtue, and made the matrix clear or pure.

27. And thus now the matrix standeth incomprehensibly, and longeth after the fiery nature [or condition], and the fiery nature longeth after the matrix. For the spirit of God (which is a spirit of meekness) [2]beholdeth itself in the watery matrix; [2] speculateth, or imagineth. and the matrix receiveth virtue from thence. Thus there is a constant will to generate and work, and the whole nature standeth in a great longing and anguish, willing continually to generate the divine virtue, God and paradise being hidden therein, but it generateth after its kind, according to its ability.

28. Now when God had severed the matrix with [or from] its fiery form, and would manifest himself with this world, then he put the *Fiat* into the matrix, and spake out of himself, [saying], *Let there be herbs, grass, trees, and beasts, every one according to its kind*: This Speaking was the Heart, or the virtue [or power] of the eternal Father: But the spirit which had the *Fiat*, went from the eternal Father (in the virtue of the Heart of God) forth with the will (and the will was the *Fiat*) and [1] made the out-birth in the third Principle material, visible, and comprehensible, each according to its essence; as the virtue was, so was also its body. For there the fiery matrix, or the constellation, gave its virtue to the *Fiat*; and the watery matrix, with the elements, received the virtue, and so were impregnated, and each element generated its own creatures out of itself; as also each form in the fiery and watery nature out of themselves; and yet it became no separable essence, but only every creature was separated according to its kind, according to the eternal virtue, which arose in the longing by the lust, and became the third Principle, which was not before time [began].

29. Thus the starry heaven ruleth in all creatures, as in its proper own; it is the [husband or] man; and the matrix, or the watery form, is its [wife or] woman, which it continually impregnateth; and the matrix is the genetrix, which bringeth forth the child which the heaven

[1] created.

[1] begetteth; and that is the created heaven in the [1] maketh, or formeth.
third Principle, from whence the elements are pro-
ceeded; *viz.* the watery matrix, out of which the
visible water generated itself, and still always doth
generate itself in the anguish.

30. Therefore *Moses* writeth, that *God created
the heaven out of the midst of the waters*: [This
you must] understand [to be] out of the eternal
watery matrix, which is but a spirit, wherein the
paradise is, and the holy heaven, *viz.* the divine
virtue, which the dark matrix lusted after in its
hunger, out of which the visible matrix of the four
elements is proceeded; out of which the essence of
all essences, that now are, were created by the
Fiat through the eternal spirit of God.

31. For every form in the matrix hath its visible
creatures, and such as are invisible to human eyes;
which creatures in part as to us are as it were but
mere [2] figured spirits, as the fire hath spirits and [2] shapes, and forms of appearance.
creatures that are invisible to our material eyes,
and we cannot see them: There are also in the
air invisible spirits, which we see not; for the air
being immaterial, so are also the spirits thereof:
The water hath material creatures, which are not
visible to us; and because they are not out of the
fire nor air, they are of another [3] quality, and are [3] property.
hidden [as] to the fiery and airy [spirits], except
they will manifest themselves.

32. As fire, air, water, and earth, lie in one case
[or chest], and they four are but one thing, and

yet of four distinct differences, and none of them can comprehend, nor retain the other, and somewhat of one of the four being [1] fixed in every creature, that creature cannot bind itself as to that, but is manifested therein, and according to that spirit is comprehensible and perceptible, and yet is incomprehensible to the spirits of the other elements.

[1] Or predominant.

33. For all things are come to be something out of nothing : And every creature hath the centre, or the circle of the birth of life in itself; and as the elements lie hidden in one another in one only mother, and none of them comprehendeth the other, though they are members one of another, so the created creatures are hidden and invisible to one another. For every creature looketh but into its mother that is fixed [or predominant] in it. The material creature seeth a material substance, but an immaterial substance (as the spirits in the fire and in the air) it seeth not; as the body seeth not the soul, which yet dwelleth in it; or as the third Principle doth not comprehend, nor apprehend the second Principle wherein God is; though indeed itself is in God, yet there is a [2] birth between : As it is with the spirit of the soul of man, and the elementary spirit in man, the one being the case [chest] or receptacle of the other; as you shall find about the creation of man.

[2] Or Principle.

THE EIGHTH CHAPTER

Of the Creation of the Creatures, and of the Springing up of every [1]growing Thing; as also of the Stars and Elements, and of the Original of the [2]Substance of this World.

[1] vegetable, or fruit.

[2] Or essence.

1. IN the beginning of the last preceding chapter, it is mentioned that it is not strange for a man to write, speak, and teach of the creation of the world, though he was not present when it was doing, if he have but the knowledge in the spirit. For there he seeth in the mother, as in a glass, the genetrix of every thing; for one thing always lieth in another, and the more is sought, the more is found, and there is no need to cast the mind beyond this world; for all is to be found in this world, yea in every thing that liveth and moveth. Whatsoever any looketh upon, and searcheth into, he shall find the spirit with the *Fiat* therein; and the divine virtue [or power discovereth, or] [3]beholdeth itself in all things, as it is written, *The word is near thee, even in thy heart and lips.* For when the light of God dawneth, or breaketh forth in the centre of the spirit of the soul, then the spirit of

[3] appeareth.

¹ Or creating. the soul seeth very well the ¹creation of this world, as in a clear glass, and nothing is afar off.

2. Therefore now I direct the Reader to the creatures, that he may search into them, and so he shall find all things, and that more wonderfully than any man can write or speak, if we be born of God. We must not ²think with our understanding and skill, of God's making or creating, as of a man that maketh somewhat, as a potter maketh a vessel of a lump of clay, or a stone-cutter or carver maketh an image after his pleasure; and if it doth not please him, then he breaketh it again: No, the works of God, in the creation of the world, were altogether fixed and steadfast, good and perfect, as *Moses* writeth: *And God saw all that he had made, and behold it was very good.*

² Or funda-
mentally con-
ceive.

3. For he took not one lump after another, or many lumps together, and made beasts of them, that is not likely; and it is much more a bestial than a human thought. But, as is mentioned before, after that the devil was fallen with his legions, (who had his throne ³in the place of this world, standing bodily after the manner of a spirit, in the first Principle, and ⁴thoroughly enlightened all over with the second Principle, truly dwelling in paradise, and in the divine virtue [or power], and yet with pride fell from the light of God, and caught at his own mother, the root of the fire, thinking to domineer over the meekness of the Heart of God), then his dwelling continued to be

³ *in loco.*

⁴ with lustre
or brightness.

the first Principle in the fiery dark matrix; and God created the out-birth out of the matrix, for a Principle; and in the eternal matrix, in the longing will, he opened the centre or birth of life; and there (after the manner of the Deity, as the eternal Deity from eternity hath always generated) arose [and sprang up] the third Principle, in which the Deity standeth as it were hidden, yet forming, imagining, or imprinting itself powerfully in all things; which is incomprehensible and unprofitable for the devil.

4. Yet the third Principle is a similitude of the paradisical world, which is spiritual, and standeth hidden therein. And thus God manifesteth himself; and seeing the spiritual world of the angels in the place of this world continued not, therefore he gave another Principle to this place, wherein a light springeth up still, and where there is a pleasant refreshment; for the purpose of God must stand, and the first creatures must continue in darkness, rather [than that the purpose of God should fail].

5. So the matter of this world, as also the stars and elements, must not be looked upon, as if God were not therein. His eternal wisdom and virtue [or power] hath formed itself with the *Fiat* in all things, and he himself is the master-workman; and all things went forth in the *Fiat*, every thing in its own essence, virtue and property. For as every star in the firmament hath a property different

from the other; thus is it with the mother also, out of which the fifth ¹essence of the stars went forth. For when the fiery form of the stars was separated from her, she was not presently severed from the first eternal birth-right, but she kept her first eternal virtue. Only the rising power of the fire is severed from her, so that she is become a pleasant refreshment, and a kind mother to her children.

6. Now when God on the first day had gathered together the lump of the earth in the great deep of this world, then the deep became purified, yet [the deep between the firmament and the earth, though it was cleansed from dregs, was] dark, and had no light in the matrix; but the fifth essence, that is, the fifth form in the matrix, shone as a fire, wherein the spirit of God with the *Fiat* moved upon the watery matrix; and the earth was naked, bare, and void; neither had it so much as one spire of grass.

7. Now saith *Moses, And God said, Let there be light, and there was light.* This light now was the fifth form in the matrix. For the fifth essence was not yet created in the matrix, nor separated till the fourth day, when God created the sun and stars out of it, and separated the light from the darkness; where then the light got the virtue of the glance, or splendour, into itself for its own, and the root of the fire in the centre remained hidden in the darkness.

8. On the second day, God created the firmament of the heaven, *viz.* the strong inclosure [fence, or stop] to the darkness of the original matrix, that it might no more kindle itself, and generate earth and stones. And therefore he made the inclosure or firmament out of the midst of the waters, which stayeth the might [force, or power] of the fire, and became the visible heaven, whence the creatures are proceeded, from whence now the elements, fire, air, and water proceed.

9. The third day God, by the *Fiat*, divided the waters upon the earth, and created them for several places, that there might be a dwelling upon the earth, and so the earth became dry. Now when this was done, then God did seek the creature, and the eternal Father spake (that is, he wrought through the Son, who is his Heart and glance) [or lustre] in the *Fiat*, in the earth ; and there budded the life through death ; and grass, herbs, and all manner of trees and plants sprang up, every one according to the eternal ¹source, as it had been ¹ fountain. before. Thus every essence became visible, and God manifested his manifold virtue with the manifold herbs, plants, and trees, so that every one that doth but look upon them, may see the eternal power, virtue, and wisdom of God therein ; if he be born of God he may know in every spire of grass his Creator, in whom he liveth. Thus in this time sprang up all that grew [or was] in the Earth.

[1] *This was found written in the manuscript copy apart by itself, so that it is not known whether it be the author's, or no.*

[1] *If men would not be blind, they might here see the Mystery of the Man Christ's remaining in Death till the third Day, and his bringing of Life out of the Earth.*

10. And the matrix of the earth stood still till the third day, as it were in death, in respect of the great storm : But in the *Fiat* the life sprang up through the death, and the eternal virtue [or power] and wisdom of God (which hath formed itself together in the *Fiat*) discovered itself on the blossoming earth, where the similitude of the paradisical world may be clearly seen.

11. For although many thousand several herbs stand one by another in one and the same meadow, and one of them is fairer and hath more virtue than another, yet one of them doth not grudge at the form of another, but there is a pleasant refreshment in one [2]mother : So also there is a distinct variety in paradise, where every creature hath its greatest joy in the virtue and beauty of another ; and the eternal virtue and wisdom of God is without number and end ; as you found before in the third chapter concerning the opening of the centres of the eternal life. You shall find no book wherein the divine wisdom may be more searched into, and found, than when you walk in a flowery fresh springing meadow, there you shall see, smell, and taste the wonderful power and virtue of God ; though this be but a similitude, and the divine

[2] The earth.

virtue in the third Principle is become material; and God hath manifested himself in a similitude. But [this similitude] is a loving schoolmaster to him that seeketh, he shall there find many of them.

12. On the fourth day, God took the place of this world rightly at the heart: For therein he created the [1] wise master out of his eternal wisdom in the third Principle, *viz.* the sun and stars; herein men may first rightly see the Deity, and the eternal wisdom of God, as in a clear glass, though indeed the essence or substance that is visible to the eye is not God himself, but it is the goddess in the third Principle, which in the end goeth into her ether again, and taketh her end.

[1] Or the wise men's masters, or teachers.

13. Though men must not cast the Pearl in the way that the beasts may tread it under foot, much less must men throw it among the grains [or husks] to be devoured by the swine; (for that would not be beneficial to the wanton world, because that seeketh nothing thereby but to misuse itself therewith; for the devil whom the world serveth, doth teach it, that when it learneth the ground of the heaven, and of the stars, to will presently to be a god, as *Lucifer* did): Yet I will write somewhat of the beginning and virtue or power of the stars, (because man and all creatures live in the virtue, working, and essences of them, and that every creature receiveth its property from them), for the sake of him that seeketh, who would willingly fly from the bestial man, and would fain

live in the true man, who is the image and similitude of God ; for to such it is very highly necessary
to be known ; also for the lily's sake which groweth
[1 midnight.] in the tree of the sour wrath towards the [1] north in
the matrix.

14. *Moses* writeth, *God said, Let there be lights
in the firmament of heaven, which may separate
and distinguish day and night, and be for signs,
for times and seasons, for days and years; and to
be for lights in the firmament of heaven, to shine
upon the earth; and it was so. And God made
two great lights, the greater light to rule the day,
and the lesser light to rule the night: Also, he
made the stars. And God set them in the firmament of heaven, that they might shine upon the
earth, and rule the day and the night, and separate
the light from the darkness.*

15. And though *Moses* hath written very rightly,
that they should govern the day and the night,
and should separate the light from the darkness,
and make times and seasons, years and days, yet it
is not plain enough to be understood by the desirous
Reader. For there is found a very high thing in
the virtue and power of the stars; [which is] that
every life, growth, colour, and virtue, thickness and
thinness, smallness and greatness, good and evil, is
moved and stirred by their power. For this cause
the wise heathens did rely upon them, and honoured
them as god. Therefore I will write somewhat of
their original, as far as is permitted to me at this

time, for their sakes that seek and desire the Pearl. But I have written nothing for the swine, and other bestial men, who trample the Pearl into the dirt, and scorn and contemn the spirit of knowledge; such as they, may, with the first world, expect a deluge, or flood of fire; and seeing they will bear no angelical image, therefore they must bear the images of lions, dragons, and other evil beasts, and worms [or creeping things]. And if they will not admit of good counsel that God may help them, then they must look to find by experience whether the Scriptures of prophecy lie to them or no.

16. The Evangelist St *John* writeth of the originality of the essence and creatures of this world, so very highly and exactly, as may be read in no other place of Scripture in the Bible: *In the beginning was the Word, and the Word was with God, and that Word was God: This was in the beginning with God, all things were made by it, and without it was nothing made that was made. In it was the life, and the life was the light of men, and the light shone in the darkness, and the darkness hath not comprehended the light.*

17. Mark what *John* saith: *In the beginning of the creation, and before the times of the world, was the Word, and the Word was God, and in the Word was the light, and it shone in the dark-ness, and the darkness could not comprehend the light.* Wherein may be clearly understood, that the eternal light is God; and that it hath its

8

eternal original in the eternal virtue or power; and that it is the eternal Word which shone in the darkness. Seeing then that Word created all things in all places, therefore it also was in all places, for without it was nothing made.

18. Now that Word had no matter out of which it made any thing, but it created all things out of the darkness, and brought them to light, that it might shine forth, appear, and present itself. For in it was the life, and it gave the light to the creature, and the creature is out of its virtue, and the virtue became material, and the light shineth therein, and the material virtue cannot comprehend it, for that is in darkness. But seeing the material virtue cannot comprehend the light, which from eternity shineth in the darkness, therefore God hath given that [material virtue] another light, which proceedeth out of the virtue (*viz.* the sun), which shineth in the creature, that so the creature is manifested in the light.

19. For as the Deity is the virtue [or power] and light of paradise in the second Principle, so the sun is the virtue [or power] and light of this material world in the third Principle. And as the Deity shineth in the darkness in the first Principle, so the sun shineth in the darkness in the third Principle. And as the Deity is the eternal virtue and the spirit of the eternal life, so the sun is the spirit and the virtue in the [1] corruptible life.

¹ Or transitory life.

20. So now a spirit is nothing else but a spring-

ing will, and in the will there is the anguish to the birth, and in the anguish the fire generateth itself, and in the fire the light, and from the light the will becometh friendly, pleasant, mild and sweet, and in the sweet will the kingdom and the glory generate themselves. Thus the light keepeth the might [or power]; and if that be put out, then the virtue [or power] and glory cease, and the kingdom also.

21. God, who is the eternal light, he is the eternal will; he shineth in the darkness, and the darkness hath comprehended the will: And in that will (which hath comprehended the darkness) the anguish riseth up, and in the sour [harsh] anguish the fire, and in the fire the light, and out of the light [cometh] the virtue [or power], and out of the virtue the kingdom. So now out of the fire [came] the constellations, and moreover the sun, and out of the virtue came the heaven; and the kingdom is God's. All this was in the first will in the creation, one with another; wherein God severed the fiery will from the mild will of the light, and called the fiery [will] stars, and the mild [will] heaven, in respect of the virtue of each of them.

22. The sun is the [1] goddess in the third Prin- [1] petty god. ciple; in the created world (understand, in the material virtue) it went forth out of the darkness in the anguish of the will, in the way and manner of the eternal birth. For when God set the *Fiat* in the darkness, then the darkness received the will of God, and was impregnated [2] for the birth. The [2] to.

will causeth the [sour] harshness, the harshness causeth the attracting, and the stirring of the attracting to mobility causeth the bitterness, which is the woe, and the woe causeth the anguish, and the anguish causeth the moving, breaking, and rising up. Now the sour harshness cannot endure the jerking, and therefore attracteth the harder to itself; and the bitterness or the attracting will not endure to be stayed, but breaketh and stingeth so very hard in the attracting, that it stirreth up the heat, wherein the flash springeth up, and the dark [sourness or] harshness is affrighted by the flash, and in the shriek the fire kindleth, and in the fire the light. Now there would be no light if the shriek in the harshness had not been, but there would have remained nothing but fire; yet the shriek in the harshness of the fire killeth the hard harshness, so that it sinketh down as it were to the ground, and becometh as it were dead and soft; and when the flash perceiveth itself in the harshness, then it is affrighted much more, because it findeth the mother so very mild, and half dead in weakness; and so in this shriek its fiery property becometh white, soft, and mild, and it is the kindling of the light, wherein the fire is changed into a white clarity [glance, lustre, or brightness].

23. In such a manner as this the sun rose up in the *Fiat*, and out of the sun (in its first kindling) [arose] the other planets, *viz.* upwards, out of the raging bitterness, *Mars* [arose], which the splendour

of the sun stayed [or upheld] when it discovered
[1] it : And out of the virtue of the sun, which raised [1] *Mars.*
itself higher [arose] *Jupiter*, imprisoned in the
centre of the *Fiat* : And out of the chamber of
anguish [arose] *Saturnus* : And downwards, *Venus*
[arose] from the soft mildness, when the harshness
was overcome, and was soft, sweet, and sinking
down like water. And when the light kindled,
then out of the sour harsh wrath came love and
humility to be, running downwards : And out of
the overcome virtue in the sour harshness [arose
Mercurius], wherein standeth the knowledge of
what was in the original before the light : But
when the light made the virtue in the place of the
sun material, as it were in an earthly manner
[arose] the moon.

24. This the world comprehendeth not, but
scorneth it, therefore I will here no further cast the
Pearl before the swine, for there belongeth another
light to this knowledge ; therefore I will pass that
by, and go on.

25. Out of the anguish of darkness (when God
spake the [Word] *Fiat* therein) came forth all
things : The anguish hath its original in the *Fiat*,
and the *Fiat* [hath its original] in the will, and the
will is eternal without original ; for it is (in God)
the matrix of the genetrix.

26. God is invisible, and the will also is invisible,
and the matrix also is invisible, and yet they are
in substance, and are from eternity, and continue

in eternity. And the Word is the virtue of the will; and the virtue [or power] maketh the *Fiat*, and the *Fiat* maketh the kingdom, and it is all alike eternal in one only substance: The will hath generated the Word from eternity; and the Word the virtue, and the virtue the spirit, and in the spirit is the light, and in the light is the power, understanding, and knowledge; otherwise it were altogether nothing.

27. That light hath wrought in the knowledge, and in the understanding, and generated a similitude of its substance; and the substance which wrought was the *Fiat*, and the *Fiat* formed the similitude which was generated out of the will, and made it visible; and the similitude was generated out of the darkness, out of the eternal nothing; and yet somewhat was there, *viz.* the originalness of the anguish, out of which the eternal will [1] generateth itself from eternity.

[1] Or taketh its eternal original.

28. Now the similitude also hath received such a will out of the *Fiat*, as the eternal will is; and it hath generated the virtue [or power], and the virtue is the heaven; and the light which is become shining in the virtue, is the sun, and that worketh in the virtue, so that there is understanding and knowledge: or else all in this world would be an immovable substance, and all would lie still, and so neither herb nor grass would grow.

29. Therefore in the *Fiat* is arisen out of the anguish the similitude of the knowledge and under-

standing, and that is the constellation; and it is the fifth form of the birth in the *Fiat*, and the *Fiat* hath severed the forms in the birth, so that every essence is several; as hard, soft, thick, thin, hot, cold, bitter, tart, sour, sweet, and so forth, as we see : And the spirit continued in the matrix of the heaven, which goeth out from thence (*viz.* the air), and the spirit receiveth the understanding from the constellation; for it is a member of the other in one only mother.

30. Now the matrix (*viz.* the created heaven) in the *Fiat*, together with the stars, is the similitude of all that was from eternity, though not visible; and the *Fiat* is in the similitude; and the paradise, wherein the angels dwell, is hidden in the matrix; and God is shining in the paradise, and yet incomprehensible; as the glance [or lustre] of the sun cannot be comprehended.

31. And God is immense [immeasurable], and the similitude is also immeasurable; he is in the similitude, and the similitude comprehendeth him not; the similitude is his work, and he is the Master-Workman thereof; the constellation is his instrument, and the [1] matrix, with the elements, are the *materia* [matter or materials] out of which the [2] Master cutteth and fashioneth his work.

[1] the created heaven.

[2] the *Fiat.*

32. Now the master always worketh on and on without consideration, what he lighteth upon that he maketh; for the consideration is in the work. And therefore it is that the whole nature standeth in

anguish and longing, to be freed from the vanity; as also the Scripture witnesseth. Because it tasteth the paradise in itself, and in the paradise the perfection, therefore it groaneth and lifteth itself up towards the light of God and paradise, and so bringeth forth in its anguish always something that is fairer, higher, and new; as may sufficiently be found and understood in the mind of man; and it is very visible to a small understanding, that in works always some special thing is brought to light, and if you be not blind, you may see this in men, beasts, yea even in herbs and grass.

33. Thus on the fourth day, by the *Fiat*, out of the virtue, he prepared the similitude of his substance [and fitted it] to be a matrix, which should generate all whatsoever was a similitude of his substance, out of the wisdom which was in him from eternity; that so all forms might be brought forth and become visible, which were from eternity in the matrix. And the similitude of the unsearchable manifold varieties and virtues are the stars, which altogether give [or send] their virtue into the matrix of the heaven, and the heaven giveth that same spirit to the creatures. This is the course of all creatures after the same essence [or substance], and they are formed after the same spirit, which is their virtue, spirit, and life.

34. When God had finished this on the fourth day, he saw it, and considered it, *and it was good,* as *Moses* writeth. Then God desired in his external

will, that this kingdom or Principle [of this world] should also be creaturely, like the perfect paradisical kingdom, that there should be living creatures therein.   And the will set the virtue (that is, the Word) in the *Fiat*; and then the matrix generated all manner of [living] creatures on the fifth day, every one after its kind.   You must understand by the word *kind*, as many various [forms] as the matrix is [of]; as you may observe it in the constellation.

35. Now I shall fall into the school of the master in his [1] *Pontificalibus*, who will ask out of what the beasts, fowls, fishes, and worms were made ; for he will have it, that all of them were made out of the earth, and will prove it out of *Moses*, and he understandeth as much of *Moses* as of paradise, which he will have to be altogether corporeal.   Therefore there is a gross deadness in the understanding ; and though I write plain enough, yet I shall be still dumb to that deadened soul which is void of understanding, and yet I cannot help it ; for it is said, *You must be born anew, if you will see the* [2] *kingdom of God.*   Would you fain know [out of what the beasts are made], then lay aside your [3] bonnet of pride that is in your mind, and walk along into the paradisical garden of roses, and there you shall find an herb ; if you eat of it, your eyes will be opened, so that you shall see and know what *Moses* hath written.

36. The [4] glosses that are put upon *Moses* from reason, will not shew you paradise, much less the

[1] cornered cap, or the crown of his degree.

[2] the divine region or government.

[3] cap or hood of self-conceited wisdom.

[4] and marginal notes.

Creator. The Prophets and Apostles learned more in the paradisical school in one hour, than the doctors in their [1] schools in thirty years. One's own wisdom availeth nothing. God giveth it to him whom he loveth, for nothing. It cannot be bought for money nor favour, as king *Solomon* will tell you.

37. If we will be still so very earthly minded, as to think that God made all the beasts of a lump of earth, of what then is their spirit made? seeing that earth is not very flesh, and the blood is not mere water. Besides, the earth and the water is not life; and though the [2] air cometh in it, yet it still remaineth such an essence as springeth only in the *Fiat*, and the tincture which riseth up in the fire, and from whence the noble life is stirred, is hidden.

38. *Moses* writeth, *Let there come forth all manner of* [3] *beasts, every one according to its kind.* Now then the question is, Out of what should they come forth? Answer, Out of the matrix. What is the matrix out of which they should come forth? It is the four elements, which are together in the earth. The *Fiat* brought forth the beasts [or living creatures] very [4] indigestedly, as they are in the essence, not from heaven, but out of the matrix of the earth; and the matrix of the earth is one [and the same] thing with the matrix in the deep above the earth, and [hath] one [and the same] [5] dominion. The constellation ruleth in all [things], and it is the *limbus*, or the [6] masculine, wherein the tincture consists, and in the matrix of the earth is the

[1] the universities.

[2] Or breath.

[3] animals, or living creatures.

[4] Without order.

[5] rule or governing.

[6] *Mars.*

aquastrish [or watery] spirit; they come forth only out of the matrix of the earth, that they might be of the essence of the earth, that so they might eat of the fruits that grow out of the earth. For every spirit lusteth after its mother from whence it came.

39. Now then if the beasts [or animals' nature] were merely out of a lump of earth, then they would eat earth, but seeing [1] it is proceeded out of the matrix of the earth by the *Fiat*, therefore it desireth also such food as the matrix affordeth out of its own essence; and that is not earth, but flesh. Yet this flesh now is a [2] mass whence the [3] body cometh, and the spirit of the constellation maketh the [4] tincture therein; which [spirit] ruleth over all as in one mother, and in every life it maketh the understanding. For the spirit of the constellation ruleth in all things, in the earth, stones, metals, elements and creatures.

[1] the bestial nature.

[2] Or concretion.
[3] corpus.
[4] Or penetrating the life and the blood.

40. For in the beginning of the creation, at the time when the earth became material, all was generated out of one only substance, and there was no more done but a separation made of one [5] from another: therefore in every separation there must needs be always a vehement hunger of one [6] after another. An example whereof you have in propagation; for the sake whereof the separation was so made: For you see that there is a male and a female; and that the one continually desireth copulation with the other, that they may [7] generate. This is a great hidden secret. Observe, when the

[5] part.

[6] part.

[7] engender.

Creator by the *Fiat* separated the matrix from the aquaster [or watery mother]; for the first form is heavenly and incorruptible, as long as the kingdom of this world standeth, and the root of the first form [1] holdeth paradise.

[1] touchth or reacheth.

I will set it down more intelligibly [or plainly]
for the simplest Reader's sake.

41. Observe, as hath been often mentioned, that as in the *Fiat*, in the aching matrix (*viz.* the dark harshness [or sourness]) the fire rose up in the breaking-wheel in the kindling; and that in the fiery, the light of the sun, and of all the stars [sprang up] (which is [done] in the harsh matrix, which from the light is become thin, lowly, and material water), and the pleasant source of love [sprang up], so that one form vehemently loveth the other, in respect of the kind, meek light, which was come into all forms; so now the soft meekness was become a new child, which was not the dark originality in the anguishing nature. But this child was the paradise, yet being it stood not in the materia [or matter], therefore the matrix of the harshness could not comprehend it; but [2] it yielded itself forth very desirously, and longing with great earnestness (according to the fire and bitterness) to comprehend the pleasant source of love, and yet could not comprehend it, for [3] it was paradisical; and thus it still stood in great longing, and generated water.

[2] the matrix.

[3] the source of love.

42. But now God separated the fire (*viz.* the fifth essence or form) from the water, and out of that made the stars; and the paradise is hid in the matrix. Therefore now the mother of the water desireth with great earnestness the mother of the fire, and seeketh the child of love; and the mother of the fire seeketh it in the mother of the water, where it was generated, and there is between them a continual vehement hunger one after another to copulate.

43. Now God said, *Let all manner of beasts come forth, every one after its kind*; and so there came forth out of the essence of every one's kind, a male and a female. And thus the spirit of the stars, or the spirit in the form of fire, had now by its longing copulated with the watery [spirit], and two sexes sprang out of one essence; the one according to the *limbus* in the form of fire, and the other according to the aquaster [or spirit of the water] in the watery form; yet so [blended or] mixed, that they were alike as to the body. And so the male was qualified according to the *limbus*, or form of fire, and the female according to the aquaster in the watery form.

44. And so now there is a vehement desire in the creatures. The spirit of the male seeketh the loving child in the female, and the female in the male; for the irrationality of the body in the unreasonable creatures knoweth not what it doth; the body would not, if it had reason, move so

eagerly towards propagation; neither doth it know anything of the impregnation [or conception], only its spirit doth so burn and desire after the child of love, that it seeketh love, (which yet is paradisical), and it cannot comprehend it; but it maketh a [1] semination only, wherein there is again a centre to the birth. And thus is the original of both sexes, and their propagation; yet it doth not attain the paradisical child of love, but it is a vehement hunger, and so the propagation is acted with great earnestness.

[1] Or sowing of seed.

45. But that I now write, that the stars rule in all beasts, and other creatures; and that every creature received the spirit of the stars in the creation, and that all things still stand in the same regimen; this the simple will hardly believe, though the doctor knoweth it well, and therefore we direct them to experience. Behold, a male and female beget young ones, and that often; now they come forth out of one only body, and yet are not of one kind, [nor of the same] colour and virtue, nor [shape or] form of body. All this is caused by the alteration of the stars; for when the seed is sown, the [2] carver maketh an image according to his [3] pleasure; [4] yet according to the first essence, he cannot alter that; but he giveth the spirit in the essence to it according to his power [or ability or dominion], as also manners, and senses, colour and gesture like himself, to be as he is; and as the constellation is in its essence

[2] the fashioner, or the *Fiat*.

[3] Or desire.

[4] As of a lion a lion, of a sheep a sheep.

at that time (when the [creature] draweth breath) [first in its mother's body], whether [the essence] be in evil or in good, [inclined] to biting, worrying and striking, or to meekness [or loving kindness and gentleness]; all as the [1] heaven is at that time, [1] Or the matrix. so will also the spirit and the beast be.

THE NINTH CHAPTER

Of the Paradise, and then of the Transitoriness of all Creatures; how all take their Beginning and End; and to what End they here appeared.

The Noble and most precious Gate [or Exposition] concerning the reasonable Soul.

1. NO money, nor goods, nor art, nor power, can bring you to the eternal rest of the eternal soft meekness of paradise, but only the noble knowledge; into that you may wrap up your soul. That is the Pearl which no moth can eat, nor thief can steal away; therefore seek after it, and then you will find the noble treasure.

2. Our wit [skill and understanding] is so very hard ¹knit up, that we have no more any knowledge of paradise at all. And except we be again born anew by water and the Holy Ghost, the veil of Moses lieth continually before our eyes when we read his writings, and we suppose that was paradise whereof Moses said: GOD placed ²him in the Garden of Eden which he had planted, that he might till it.

¹ cold, frozen, or shut up.

² *Adam.*

128

3. O beloved man, that is not paradise, neither doth *Moses* say so ; but that was the Garden in Eden, where they were tempted; the exposition whereof you may find about the fall of *Adam.* The paradise is the divine joy ; and that was in their mind, when they were [standing] in the love of God.   But when disobedience entered, they were driven out, and saw that they were naked ; for at that instant the spirit of the world caught them, in which there was mere anguish, necessity, turmoil, and misery, and in the end corruptibility and death.   Therefore it was of [1] necessity that the [1] needful. eternal Word did become flesh, and bring them into the paradisical rest again ; whereof you shall find [the exposition] in its due place, about the fall of *Adam.*

4. Paradise hath another Principle ; for it is the divine and angelical joy, yet not without the [2] place [2] *extra locum.* of this world.   Indeed it is without the virtue and source [or active property] of it ; neither can the spirit of this world comprehend it, much less a creature ; for it standeth not in the anguishing [3] birth.   And although it thus taketh its original, [3] operation. yet it consisteth in exact perfection, mere love, joy, and mirth ; wherein there is no fear, neither misery nor death: No devil can touch it, and no beast can [4] reach it.   [4] Or attain it.

5. But when we will speak of the source [or fountain] and joy of paradise, and of its highest substance, what it is, we have no similitude of it

9

in this world, we stand in need of angelical tongues and knowledge to express it; and though we had them, yet we could not express it with this tongue. It is well understood in the mind, when the soul rideth in the chariot of the bride, but we cannot express it with the tongue; yet we will not cast away the [1] A, B, C, but prattle [or stammer] with the children, till another mouth be given us to speak withal.

[1] that little which we can express of it.

6. When God had created the beasts, he brought them to *Adam*, that he should give them their names, every one according to its essence and kind, as they [the beasts] were qualified [or according to the quality and condition they were of]. Now *Adam* was in the Garden of Eden in *Hebron*, and also in paradise at once, yet no beast can come into paradise; for it is the divine [2] joy, wherein there is no unclean thing, also no death or corruptible [or transitory] life; [3] much less is there the knowledge of good and evil. Yet *Moses* writeth of it, that in the Garden of Eden there was the Tree of Temptation, which bore the knowledge of good and evil; which indeed was no other tree than like the trees we now eat of, in the [4] corruptibility; neither was it any other garden, than such as we now have, wherein earthly fruits (good and evil) grow; as is before our eyes.

[2] Or habitation, or refreshment.

[3] therefore the Garden of Eden is not paradise.

[4] Or in the transitory body.

7. But the paradise is somewhat else; and yet no other place, but another Principle, where God and the angels dwell, and where there is perfection,

where there is mere love, joy, and knowledge; where no misery is : which [paradise] neither death nor the devils touch, neither do they know it : And yet it hath no wall of earth or stones about it, but there is a great gulf [or cliff] between paradise and this world, so that they who would pass from hence thither, cannot; and they who would come from thence to us, cannot either; and the hell and the kingdom of darkness is between them.   And none can come therein but by a new birth; which Christ spake of to *Nicodemus*.   The souls of the saints [holy] and regenerate must enter into it (by the death of darkness), whom the Arch-Shepherd with the angels bringeth thereinto upon his [1] bride-chariot: Of which you shall find [an exposition] in its proper place in order.

[1] Note, the bride-chariot is the true resignation into the bosom of the Father.

8. But seeing somewhat is lent me from the grace of the power [or divine virtue] of God, that I might know the way to paradise; and seeing it behoveth every one to work the works of God, in which he standeth; of which God will require an account from every one, what he hath done in the labour of his day's work in this world; and will require the work (which he gave every one to do) with increase, and will not have them empty; or else he will have that unprofitable servant to be bound hand and foot, and cast into darkness; where he must be fain to work, yet in the anguish, and in the forgetting of the day-labour which was given him to do here [or of the talent which he

had received here] wherein he was found an unprofitable servant.

9. Therefore I will not neglect my day-labour, but will labour as much as I can on the way; and although I shall scarce be able to [1] tell the letters, in this so high a way, yet [2] it shall be so high, that many will have enough to learn in it all their life long: He that supposeth that he knoweth it very well, he hath not yet learnt the first letter of paradise, for no doctors are to be found on this way in this school, but only [3] scholars [or learners].

10. Therefore let not my Master of Arts (in his [4] hood and tippet) think himself so cunning in this matter, nor pour out his mockings so presumptuously [against the children of God], for so long as he is a scorner [or mocker] he knoweth nothing of this. He ought not to think his cap becometh him so finely; nor ought he to boast of his human calling, as if he did sit in his calling [5] by the ordinance of God, whereas he is not set or confirmed therein from God, but by the favour of man. He ought not so much to prohibit [and forbid] the way to paradise, which himself doth not know: He must one day give a heavy account of his [6] ordination by the favour of man; because he boasteth of a divine calling, and yet the spirit of God is far from him, therefore he is a liar, and belieth the Deity.

11. Therefore let every one take care what he doth: I say again, that whosoever he be that intrudeth himself to be a pastor [or [7] shepherd]

[1] Much less to spell or read.
[2] my labour.

[3] children going to school.

[4] Or crowned hat.

[5] by holy orders, divine institution, or divine right.

[6] Or institution.

[7] Or minister.

without the divine calling, without the knowledge
of God, he is a thief and a murderer; he entereth
not through the door into paradise, but he creepeth
in with the dogs and the wolves, into the den of
thieves, and he doth it but for his belly's sake, and
his own honour [and esteem]; he is no pastor [or
shepherd], but he dependeth on the great whore,
upon Antichrist; and yet he supposeth that he is
a pastor [or shepherd]; but he is not known in
paradise.

12. Christ teacheth us and warneth us faithfully
of the times that were to come, wherein they shall
say, *Lo here is Christ,* or, *Lo there he is; he is in
the wilderness; he is in the chamber; go not
forth, believe it not; for as the lightning breaketh
forth in the east, and shineth to the west, so will
the coming of the Son of Man be.*

13. Therefore, O child of man, see whether it be
not so; where the false pastors [or shepherds],
without the divine calling, always wrangle [strive,
contend, and dispute]; and every one of them
saith, [1] Follow me, here is Christ, there is Christ,
and they judge [and condemn] one another, and
give one another over to the devil; they abandon
unity, and forsake the love wherein the spirit of
God is [2] generated; and cause bitterness, and lead
astray the simple plain people, to think that Christ
is such a wrangling shepherd [pastor, priest, or
minister], and doth so grapple with [3] his opponents,
in raising war and murder, as they do; and that

[1] Or come and resort to me.

[2] acteth or worketh.

[3] tho adverse party.

the spirit of God must needs be in such doings [which are accounted zeal for God]; and that this must be the way to paradise.

14. Christ said, *Love one another, thereby shall men know that ye are my disciples; if any smite thee on one cheek, turn to him the other cheek also; if you be persecuted for my name's sake, then rejoice, for your reward is great in the kingdom of heaven*: But now there is nothing taught but mere ignominy [reproach, and revilings]: they that are dead many hundred years ago, and are in the judgment of God, and some also may be in paradise, these must be judged, and condemned, and cursed by the wrangling shepherds [or contentious priests]. Doth the Holy Ghost speak by them, as they cry out and say he doth? Whereas they are still full of gall and bitterness, and nothing but covetousness and vengeance is kindled in them, and they are far from the way of paradise.

15. Therefore, thou child of man, take heed, let not your ears be tickled: When you hear the false shepherds [or pastors] judge and condemn the children of Christ, that is not the voice of Christ, but of Antichrist; the way to paradise hath quite another entrance; your heart must with all your power and strength be directed to God [or goodness]; and as God desireth that all men should be saved, so his will is that we should help to bear one another's burthen [and bear with one another], and friendly, soberly, and modestly meet one

another with entreaties in the Holy Ghost, and
seek with earnestness the [salvation and] welfare
of our neighbour in humility, and wish heartily
that he might be freed from vanity, and enter
with us into the [1] garden of roses.

[1] Into the
sweet smell-
ing pleasant
peacefulness.

16. The knowledge that is in the infinite God
is various and manifold, but every one should
rejoice in the gifts and knowledge of another, and
consider, that God will give such superabundant
knowledge in the paradisical world, of which we
have here (in the variety and difference of gifts)
but a type: Therefore we must not wrangle nor
contend about gifts and knowledge; for the spirit
giveth to every one according to his essence in the
wonderful God, to express that [gift he hath] after
his own form [or manner]; for that [form], in the
perfection of love in paradise, will be a very inward
hearty sport of love, where every one shall speak
from his knowledge of the great wonders of the
[2] holy birth.

[2] the holy
paradisical
bringing
forth.

17. O, what [3] sharp thorns the devil hath
brought into the sport of love, that we practise
such proud contention in the noble knowledge,
insomuch that men bind up the Holy Ghost with
laws! What are laws in the kingdom of Christ,
who hath made us free, that we should walk in
him in the Holy Ghost? To what purpose are
they invented, but for the pleasure of Antichrist,
who thereby doth strut in might and pomp, and
is God on earth? O fly from him, thou child of

[3] bitter envy.

man, the time is come for us to awake from the sleep of Antichrist. Christ cometh with the fair lily out of paradise in the valley of *Jehosaphat*: It is time for them to trim their lamps that will go to the marriage [of the Lamb].

The Gate [or the Exposition].

18. Paradise consisteth in the power [and virtue] of God: It is not corporeal, nor [1] comprehensible; but its corporeity or comprehensibility is like the angels, which yet is a bright, clear, visible substance, as if it were material; but it is figured merely from the virtue [or power], where all is transparent and shining, where also the centre of the birth is in all things, and therefore the birth is without measure or end.

19. I give you a similitude in the mind of man, from which the thoughts are generated, which have neither number nor end, (for every thought hath a centre to generate again other thoughts), and thus is the paradise from eternity to eternity. But being the light of God is eternal, and shineth without wavering or hindrance, therefore also in the birth there is an unchangeable substance, wherein all things spring up in mere perfection, in great love.

20. For the spirit of knowledge intimateth this, that there are fruits and things that grow in paradise, as well as in this world, in such a form or figure, but not in such a source [or property]

[1] palpable.

and palpability.   For the matter or body of it is power, and it groweth in the heavenly [1] *limbus*; [1] soil or earth. its root standeth in the matrix, wherein there is neither earth nor stone; for it is in another Principle.   The fire in that [Principle] is God the Father; and the light is God the Son; and the air is God the Holy Ghost; and the virtue [or power] out of which all springeth is heaven and paradise.

21. As we see that here out of the earth there spring plants, herbs, and fruits, which receive their virtue from the sun, and from the constellation: so the heaven or the heavenly *limbus* is instead of the earth; and the light of God instead of the sun; and the eternal Father instead of the virtue of the stars.   The depth of this substance is without beginning and end, its breadth cannot be [2] reached, [2] fathomed. there are neither years nor time, no cold nor heat; no moving of the air; no sun nor stars; no water nor fire; no sight of evil spirits; no knowledge nor apprehension of the affliction of this world; no stony rock nor earth; and yet a figured substance of all the creatures of this world.   For all the creatures of this world have appeared to this end, that they might be an eternal figured similitude; not that they continue in this spirit in their substance, no not so: All the creatures return into their [3] ether, and the spirit corrupteth [or fadeth], [3] receptacle. but the figure and the shadow continue eternally.

22. As also all words (both the evil and the

good) which were here spoken by a human tongue, they continue standing in the shadow and figured similitude, and the good reach paradise in the Holy Ghost; and the false [evil] and wicked ones reach the abyss of hell. And therefore it is that Christ said, *Man must give an account of every idle* [or unprofitable] *word*; and when the harvest cometh, then all shall be separated. For the Scripture saith also, That every one's works shall follow him, and all shall be tried by the fire of nature; and all false [or evil] works, words, and deeds, shall remain in the fire of nature (which shall be the hell); at which, when the devils hear it, they tremble and quake.

23. All shall remain in the shadow, and every thing in its own source [or property]; therefore it will be an eternal shame to the wicked, that they shall see in the eternity all their works and words, as a menstruous cloth, which shall stick full of the wrath of God, and shall burn, according to their essence, and according to their here-kindled source [or property].

24. For this world is like a field, wherein good seed is sown, into which the enemy casteth weeds [or tares], and goeth his way, which grow together until the time of the harvest, when all [the fruit] shall be gathered, and brought into the barn; of which Christ also saith, *That the tares* [or weeds] *shall be tied up in bundles, and cast into the fire, and the wheat shall be brought into the barn.*

The Holy Gate.

25. Reason (which is gone forth with *Adam* out of paradise) asketh, Where is paradise to be had [or found]? Is it far off, or near? Or, when the souls go into paradise, whither do they go? Is it in this world, or without the place of this world above the stars? Where is it that God dwelleth with the angels? And where is that desirable native country where there is no death? Being there is no sun nor stars in it, therefore it cannot be in this world, or else it would have been found long ago.

26. Beloved reason, one cannot lend the key to another to [unlock] this [withal]; and if any one have a key, he cannot open it to another, as Antichrist boasteth that he hath the keys of heaven and hell. It is true, he may have the keys of both in this [life] time; but he cannot open with them for anybody else; every one must unlock it with his own key, or else he cannot enter therein. For the Holy Ghost is the key; when he hath that key, then he may go both in and out.

27. There is nothing that is nearer you than heaven, paradise, and hell, unto which of them you are inclined, and to which of them you tend [or walk], to that in this [life] time you are most near: You are between both. And there is a birth between each of them; you stand in this world between both the gates, and you have both the

births in you: God beckoneth to you in the one gate, and calleth you; and the devil beckoneth to you in the other gate, and calleth you; with whom you go, with him you enter in. The devil hath in his hand power, honour, pleasure, and [worldly] joy, and the root of these is death and hell-fire. On the contrary, God hath in his hand, crosses, persecution, misery, poverty, ignominy, and sorrow; and the root of these is a fire also, and in the fire [there is] a light, and in the light the virtue, and in the virtue [or power] the paradise, and in the paradise [are] the angels, and among the angels, joy. The [1]gross eyes cannot behold it, because they are from the third Principle, and see only by the splendour of the sun; but when the Holy Ghost cometh into the soul, then he regenerateth it anew in God, and then it becometh a paradisical child, and getteth the key of paradise, and that soul seeth into the midst thereof.

[1] Or dim fleshly eyes.

28. But the gross body cannot see into it, because it belongeth not to [paradise], it belongeth to the earth, and must putrify, or rot, and rise in a new virtue [or power] (which is like paradise) in Christ, at the end of days; and then it also may dwell in paradise, and not before: It must lay off the third Principle, [viz.] this skin [fleece or covering], which father *Adam* and mother *Eve* are gotten into, in which they supposed they should be wise when they should wear all the three Principles manifested in them; if they had rather worn two hidden

in them, and had stayed in the [1] one, it had been good for us ; of which further about the fall.

[1] In the Principle of light.

29. Thus now in the essence of all essences, there are three several distinct properties, which yet are not parted asunder, with one source [or property] far from the other ; but they are in one another as one only essence, and yet the one doth not comprehend the other. As these three elements, fire, air, water, are all three in one another, and neither of them comprehendeth the other ; and as one element generateth another, and yet is not of the essence nor source [or property] thereof; so the three Principles are in one another, and one generateth the other, and yet no one of them all comprehendeth the other, and none of them is the essence [or substance] of the other.

The Depth in the Centre [or Ground].

30. As hath been often mentioned, God is the essence of all essences, wherein there are two essences in one, without end, and without original ; viz. the eternal light, that is, God, or the good ; and then the eternal darkness, that is, the [2] source ; and yet there would be no source in it if the light were not. The light causeth that the darkness longeth after [or is in anguish for] the light, and this anguish is the source of the wrath of God (or the hellish fire) wherein the devils dwell : From whence God also calleth himself an angry, zealous [or jealous] God. These are the two Principles, the

[2] the nature or the working property.

original of which we know nothing of, only we know the [1] birth (therein), the indissoluble band, which is as followeth :

31. In the originalness of darkness, there is [2] harshness and austereness, this harshness causeth that it be light; for harshness is a desirousness, an attracting; and that is the first ground of the willing [or longing] after the light, and yet it is not possible to comprehend it; and the attracting in the will is the [sting or] prickle, which the desirousness attracteth, and the first stirring [or moving]. Now the prickle cannot endure the attracting in the will, but resisteth, flieth up, and yet cannot get away from thence; for it is generated in the attracting. But because it cannot remove from thence, nor endure the attracting, therefore there is a great anguish, a desirousness [or longing] after the light, like a furiousness, and like a breaking whirling wheel; and the anguish in the bitterness riseth up in the [3] wrath after the light, but cannot get it, being desirous in the anxiety to lift up itself above the light, yet doth not overcome, but is infected [impregnated or mingled] with the light, and attaineth a twinkling flash; and as soon as the harshness, or the hardness (viz. the darkness) getteth the same into it, it is terrified, and instantly goeth away into its [4] ether: And yet the darkness continueth in the centre. And in this horror [terror or shriek] the hardness or harshness becometh mild, soft [supple], and thin; and the

[1] Or working activity.

[2] sourness, tartness, sharpness, astringency, or attraction.

[3] fierceness.

[4] Or receptacle.

flash is made in the bitterness, which flieth up thus
in the prickle: Thus the prickle discovereth itself
in the mother, which so terrifieth the mother with
the flash, that she yieldeth herself to be overcome;
and when the prickle strengtheneth itself in the
mother, and findeth her so mild, then that is
much more terrified, and loseth its [fierce, strong]
wrathful propriety, and in the twinkling of an
eye becometh white, clear, and bright, and flieth
up very joyfully, trembling with great delight
[lust] and desire; and the mother of harshness
from the light cometh to be sweet, mild, thin,
and material, even water. For she loseth not the
essence of the harsh condition, and therefore the
essence attracteth continually to it out of the
mildness, so that out of the nothing, somewhat
cometh to be, *viz.* water.

32. Now as is mentioned before, when the joy
riseth up from the mother, as the light cometh into
her (which yet she cannot [1] comprehend) then the
joy (in the ascending will) hath a centre in it again
and generateth out of itself again a very soft and
pleasant source [or fountain], an humble, amiable
source, which is immaterial; for then there can be
generated nothing that is more pleasant and full of
joy [and refreshment], therefore here is the end of
nature; and this is the warmth of the *Barm*, or as
I may say the *Barmhertzigkeit* [the mercifulness].
For here nature neither seeketh nor desireth further
any [2] birth more: it is the perfection.

[1] Or take hold of.

[2] Or working.

33. Now in this pleasant source, the moving spirit (which in the original, in the kindling, was the bitter aching spirit) springeth forth very joyfully without removing, and it is the Holy Ghost; and the sweet [1]source [or fountain] which is generated in the centre from the light, is the Word or Heart of God; and in this joy is the paradise; and the birth is the eternal Trinity: In this you must dwell, if you will be in paradise; and the same must be born [or generated] in you, if you will be the child of God, and your soul must be in it, or else you cannot enjoy nor see the kingdom of God.

[1] well-spring.

34. Therefore the [2]stedfast *faith* and confidence thus bringeth us into God again: For it getteth the divine centre [3]of regeneration in the Holy Ghost, or else there is nothing that availeth: Other matters which men do here, are but [4]essences, which follow him in the shadow, wherein he shall stand; for as there is the birth in the holy Deity, which in the original standeth in the willing [desiring] and aching property, before the light [breaketh forth], so also must thou, O man (that art gone forth out of paradise), in anguish, longing, and in a desirous will, go into the birth again, and so thou shalt attain paradise again, and the light of God.

[2] sure, or strong, firm.

[3] to the.

[4] works.

35. Behold, thou reasonable soul, to thee I speak, and not to the body, thou only apprehendest it: When the birth is thus continually

generated, then every form hath a centre to the regeneration; for the whole divine essence [or substance] standeth in continual and in eternal [1] generating (but unchangeably) like the mind of [1] working. man, the thoughts being continually generated out of the mind, and the will and desirousness out of the thoughts. Out of the will and desirousness [is] the work [generated] which is made a substance, in the will, and then the mouth and hands go on to perform what was substantial in the will.

36. Thus also is the eternal birth, wherein the virtue [or power] is continually generated from eternity; and out of the virtue the light; and the light causeth and maketh the virtue. And the light shineth in the eternal darkness, and maketh in the eternal mind the [desiring] attracting will; so that the will in the darkness generateth the thoughts, the lust and the desirousness, and the desirousness is the attracting of the virtue, and in the attracting of the virtue is the mouth that expresseth the *Fiat*, and the *Fiat* maketh the *materia* [or matter], and the spirit separateth it, and formeth it according to the thoughts.

37. Thus is the birth (and also the first original) of all the creatures; and [2] it standeth yet in such [2] the creation of the a [3] birth in the essence; and after such a manner creatures. it is, out of the eternal thoughts (*viz.* the wisdom [3] Or working. of God) by the *Fiat*, brought out of the matrix; but being come forth out of the darkness, out of

the ¹ out-birth, out of the centre, (which yet was generated in the time, in the will), therefore it is not eternal, but corruptible [or transitory], like a thought; and though it be indeed material, yet every ² source taketh its own into itself again, and maketh it to be nothing again, as it was before the beginning.

38. But now, nothing corrupteth [or is transitory], but only the spirit in the will, and ³ its body in the *Fiat*; and the figure remaineth. eternally in the shadow. And this figure could not thus have been brought to light and to visibility, that it might subsist eternally, if it had not been in the ⁴ essence; but now it is also incorruptible, for in the figure there is no ⁴ essence: The centre in the ⁵ source is broken asunder, and gone into its ether [receptacle, or air]; and the figure doth neither good nor evil, but it continueth eternally to the [manifestation of the] deeds of wonder and the glory of God, and for the joy of the angels.

39. For the third Principle of the material world shall pass away, and go into its ether, and then the shadow of all creatures will remain, also of all growing things [vegetables or fruits], and of all that ever came to light; as also the shadow and figure of all words and works, and that incomprehensibly; also without understanding or knowledge, like a nothing, or shadow, in respect of the light.

40. This was the unsearchable purpose of God

in his will; and therefore he thus [1] created all
things; and after this time there will be nothing
but only light and darkness; where the source [or
property] remaineth in each of them (as it hath
been from eternity), where the one shall not
comprehend the other, as it hath also not been
done from eternity.

[1] Brought them to light in a four elementary essence or substance.

41. Yet whether God will create anything more
after this [world's] time, that my spirit doth not
know; for it apprehendeth no further than [what
is] in its centre wherein it liveth, in which the
paradise and the kingdom of heaven standeth; as
you may read [afterwards] about the creation of
man.

42. And so now the angels and blessed men
[will] remain in the birth of the light; and [2] the
spirits of alteration out of light into the source
[or torment], together with the spirits of the
wicked men, [will remain] in the eternal darkness,
where no recalling is to be found; for the spirits
cannot go into the corruptibility [or transitoriness]
again. They are created out of the [3] *limbus* of
God, out of the harsh matrix, out of which the
light of God existeth from eternity; and not like
the beasts out of the [4] out-birth, which went forth
out of the *limbus* of the conceived purpose of God,
which is finite [or taketh an end], and hath been
[or appeared] here, only that it might be an eternal
shadow and figure.

[2] the spirits that were turned out of the light into darkness.

[3] divine power and virtue.

[4] Or progeneration.

43. The eternal will is incorruptible [or intran-

sitory] and unchangeable [or unalterable]; for the Heart of God is generated out of it, which is the end of the nature and of the willing. If the [1]spirits of the source [or torment] had put their imagination and their desiring will [2]forward into the light of meekness, into the end of nature, they would have continued angels; but seeing they out of pride would fain be above the meekness, and above the end of nature, and awakened the centre, they found nothing more; for from eternity there had been nothing more [than the end of nature]; and therefore they awakened the [3]centre of the source [or torment] in themselves. The same they now have, and they were thrust out of the light into the darkness.

[1] Or the spirits of the working nature.

[2] into resignation.

[3] Or ground of the working properties.

44. If you be born of God, then you [may] thus understand God, paradise, the kingdom of heaven and hell, and the entrance in, and end of, the creatures, [and] the creation of this world; but if not, then the veil is as well before your eyes as it was upon *Moses*. Therefore saith Christ, *Seek, and you shall find; knock, and it shall be opened unto you: No son asketh his father for an egg, that he should give him a scorpion:* Also, *My Father will give the Holy Spirit to them that ask it.*

45. Therefore, if you do not understand this writing, then do not, as Lucifer did in taking the spirit of pride, presently fall [4]a-mocking and deriding, and ascribe it to the devil; but seek the humble lowly Heart of God, and that will

[4] mocking that which you understand not.

bring a small grain of mustard-seed (from the
[1] tree of paradise) into your soul; and if you [1] Or fruit or growth.
abide in patience, then a great tree will grow out
of that [seed], as you may well think that the like
hath come to pass with this author.   For he is to
be esteemed as a very simple person, in comparison of the great learned men: But Christ saith,
My Power is strong in the weak: Yea Father, it
hath so pleased thee to hide these things from the
wise and prudent, and thou hast revealed them to
babes and sucklings; and that the wisdom of this
world is foolishness in thy sight.   And although
now the children of the world are wiser in their
generation than the children of light; yet their
wisdom is but a corruptible substance [essence or
thing], and this wisdom continueth eternally.

46. Therefore seek for the noble Pearl; it is
much more precious than this [whole] world; it
will never more depart from you: And where the
Pearl is, there will your heart be also: You need
not here ask any further after paradise, joy, and
the heavenly delightfulness; seek but the Pearl,
and when you find that, then you find paradise,
and the kingdom of heaven, and you will be so
taught, as being without it you cannot believe.

47. It may be, you will turmoil yourself [with
hard labour], and seek for it in art, supposing to
find [2] it there: O no, you need not; it lieth not [2] this deep and high wisdom.
therein.   The doctor that is without this way
knoweth it not.   But if he also hath found this

¹ Or a more
public person,
or *Publicus.*

Pearl, then he is a ¹person greater for the public benefit than I; as St *Paul* was above the other Apostles, yet in one [and the same] way of gentle meekness, as becometh the children of God. Whatsoever is wanting here that you long after, seek further, and you will find the ground, according to the desire [or longing] of your soul.

THE TENTH CHAPTER

Of the Creation of Man, and of his Soul,
also of God's ¹breathing in.

The pleasant Gate.

1. I HAVE perused many master-pieces of writing, hoping to find the ²Pearl of the Ground of Man; but I could find nothing of that which my soul lusted after. I have also found very many contrary opinions. And partly I have found some who forbid me to search [or seek], but I cannot know with what ground or understanding, except it be that the blind grudge at the eyes of them that see. With all this my soul is become very disquiet within, and hath been as full of [pain and] anguish as a woman at her travail, and yet nothing was found in it, till I followed the words of Christ, when he said, *You must be born anew, if you will see the kingdom of God* : which at first stopped up my heart, and I supposed that such a thing could not be done in this world, but [that it should first be done] at my departure out of this world. And then my soul first was in anguish to the birth, and would very willingly have tasted

² The high and deep wisdom of God.

151

the Pearl; and gave itself up in this way more vehemently to the birth, till at last it obtained a jewel. According to which [received jewel] I will write, for a Memorial to myself, and for a light to them that seek. For Christ said, *None lighteth a candle and putteth it under a bushel, but setteth it upon a table, that all that are in the house may see by the light of it.* And to this end he giveth the Pearl to them that seek, that they should impart it to the poor for their health, as he hath very earnestly commanded.

2. Indeed *Moses* writeth, *That God made man of the dust of the earth.* And that is the opinion of very many: And I should also not have known how that was to be understood, and I should not have learned it out of *Moses*, nor out of the [1]glosses which are made upon it; and the veil would have continued still before my eyes, yet in great trouble. But when I found the Pearl, then I looked *Moses* in the face, and found that *Moses* had written very rightly, and that I had not rightly understood it.

[1] expositions, or interpretations of it.

3. For after the fall God said also to *Adam* and *Eve, Earth thou art, and to earth thou shalt return again*: And if I had not considered the [2]*limbus* (out of which the earth was), I should have been so blind still: That [*limbus*] shewed me the ground of what *Adam* was before and after the fall.

[2] the power, or the eternal substantiality.

4. For no such earth or flesh as we carry about

us can subsist in the light of God : Therefore also Christ said, *None goeth to heaven, but the Son of Man who is come from heaven, and who is in heaven.* Thus our flesh before the fall was heavenly, out of the heavenly *limbus*. But when disobedience came, in the lust of this world, to generate itself in another centre, then it [the flesh] became earthly ; for by the biting of the earthly apple in the Garden of *Eden*, the earthly dominion [or kingdom] took its beginning : And the mother of the great world instantly took the [1] little world into its power [or virtue], and made it to be of a bestial [2] kind, both in [3] form and in substance.

[1] man.

[2] Or property.

[3] shape.

5. And if the soul had not been [4] within it, then *Adam* would have continued to be an unreasonable beast ; but being the soul out of the *limbus* had been breathed into *Adam* by the Holy Ghost, therefore now the [5] mercifulness (*viz.* the Heart of God) must do its best again, and bring again the centre out of the heavenly *limbus*, and himself become flesh, and by the *Fiat* generate the new man in the soul, which is hidden in the old. For the old belongeth only to the corruptibility, and goeth into its ether, and the new remaineth for ever. But how this came to pass, you have the following fundamental information of it, wherein, if you be regenerated from God, you may see the old and new man into the very heart, because you have the Pearl ; but if not, then you shall scarce see

[4] Or in the midst, or centre of it.

[5] *Barmhert-zigkeit.*

here the old *Adam*, and you shall not so much as look upon the new.

6. The veil of *Moses* must be done away, and you must look *Moses* in the face, if you will behold the new man; and without the Pearl, you shall not be able to take away the veil, nor know [what] *Adam* [was] before his fall. For *Adam* himself after the fall did no more know the first man; and therefore he was ashamed of his monstrous form [or shape], and hid himself behind the trees in the garden; for he looked on himself, and saw that he had a bestial form, and thereupon he gat instantly bestial members for propagation, which the *Fiat* in the third Principle created on him, through the spirit of the great world.

7. Men must not think, that man before his fall had bestial members to propagate with, but heavenly [members], nor any [1] entrails; for such a stink, and [filthy] source [or property], as man hath in his body, doth not belong to the Holy Trinity in paradise, but to the earth; it must go again into its ether. But man was created immortal, and also holy, like the angels; and being he was created out of the *limbus*, therefore he was pure. Now in what manner he is, and out of what he was made, it followeth further:

8. Behold, when God had created the third Principle, after the fall of the devils, when they fell from their glory (for they had been angels, standing in the place of this world) yet nevertheless

[1] Or guts.

he would that his will and purpose should stand; and therefore he would give to the place of this world an angelical [1]host again, which should [1] Or company. continue to stand for ever. And now he having created the creatures, whose shadows after the changing of the world should continue for ever, yet there was no creature found that could have any joy therein [in the shadows], neither was there any creature found that might manage the beasts in this world; therefore God said, *Let us make man an image like unto us, which may rule over all the beasts, and creatures upon the earth; and God created man to be his image, after the image of God created he him.*

9. Now the question is: What is God's image? Behold, and consider the Deity, and then you will light upon it. For God is not a bestial man; but man should be the image and similitude of God, wherein God should dwell. Now God is a spirit, and all the three Principles are in him: And he would make such an image, as should have all the three Principles in him, and that is rightly a similitude of God; *And he created him,* etc. Whereby *Moses* may be rightly understood, that God created him, and not made him of a lump of earth.

10. But the *limbus* out of which he created him is the matrix of the earth; and the earth was generated out of it; yet the *materia* [or matter] out of which he created him was a *massa,* a *quinta*

essentia, out of the stars and elements; which instantly became earthly, when man awakened the earthly centre, and did instantly belong to the earth and corruptibility.

11. But yet this *massa* was out of the heavenly matrix, which is the root of the [1] out-birth, or [the root] of the earth. The heavenly centre ought to remain [2] fixed; and the earthly ought not to be awakened. And in this virtue [and power] he was lord and ruler over the stars and elements; and all creatures should have stood in awe of him, and he should have been incorruptible; he had the virtue and properties of all manner of creatures in him, for his virtue was out of the virtue [or power] of the understanding. Now then he ought to have all the three Principles, if he were to be the similitude of God, [*viz.*] the [3] source of the darkness, and also of the light, and also the [3] source of this world: And yet he should not live and [4] act in all three, but in one of them only, and that in the paradisical [property], in which his life [quickened] arose, [or did exist].

12. Now that this is demonstratively and certainly thus, [appeareth] in that it is written, *And God breathed into him the [5] living breath, whereby man became a living soul.* All other creatures which were produced out of the corruptible [6] *limbus* by the *Fiat*, in all those the will in the *Fiat* had awakened the spirit in their centre, and every creature's spirit went forth out of the essence and

[1] Or pro-generation.

[2] stedfast, chief, master, or predominant.

[3] working property.

[4] Or qualify.

[5] Or breath of life.

[6] substantiality, or nature.

property of its own self, and mixed afterwards with the spirit of the great world of the stars and elements, and that ought not to have been in man; his spirit ought not to have mixed itself [or been united] with the spirit of the stars and elements. The two Principles (*viz.* the darkness and the spirit of the air) ought to have stood still in such a substance [as should be the image of God]; and therefore he breathed into him the [1] living breath; understand God's breath, that is, the paradisical breath or spirit, [*viz.*] the Holy Ghost; that should be the breath of the soul, in the centre of the soul. And the spirit which went forth out of the *limbus*, or out of the *quinta essentia* (which is of the [2] condition of the stars) that was to have power over the fifth essence of this world. For man was in one only essence [or substance], and there was also but one only man that God thus created, and he could have lived for ever. And although God had brought the stars again into their ether, and also had withdrawn the matrix of the elements, and the elements also, back into nothing, yet man would have continued still. Besides, he had the paradisical centre in him, and he could have generated again out of himself, out of his will, and have awakened the centre; and so should have been able, in paradise, to generate an angelical [3] host, without misery or anguish, also without tearing [rending or dividing of himself]; and such a man he ought to have been, if he must

[1] Or breath of life.

[2] kind, or property, or nature.

[3] Or company.

continue in paradise, and be eternal without decay ; for paradise is holy, and in that respect man also ought to have been holy, for the virtue [and power] of God and paradise consisteth in holiness.

The deep Gate of the Soul.

13. The soul of man, which God hath breathed into him, is out of the eternal Father ; yet understand it aright ; there is a difference [to be observed, you must] understand, [that it is] out of his unchangeable will, out of which he generateth his Son and Heart from eternity, out of the divine centre, from whence the *Fiat* goeth forth, which maketh separation, and hath in [1] it all the essences of the eternal birth [or all manner of things which are in the eternal birth]. Only the birth of the Son of God, that very centre which the Son of God himself is, he hath not ; for that centre is the end of nature, and not creaturely. This is the highest centre of the fire-burning love and mercy of God, the perfection [or fulness]. Out of this centre no creature cometh, but it appeareth [or shineth] in the creature, *viz.* in angels, and in the souls of holy men ; for the Holy Ghost, and the omnipotence [or almightiness] which frameth the eternal will in the eternal Father, goeth forth out of this [centre].

14. Now therefore the soul standeth in two gates, and toucheth two Principles, *viz.* the eternal darkness, and the eternal light of the Son of God,

[1] the soul.

as God the Father himself doth. Now as God the Father [1] holdeth his unchangeable eternal will to generate his Heart and Son, so the angels and souls keep their unchangeable will in the Heart of God. Thus it [the soul] is in heaven and in paradise, and enjoyeth the unutterable joy of God the Father which he hath in the Son, and it heareth the inexpressible words of the Heart of God, and rejoiceth at the eternal, and also at the created images, which are not in essence [or substance], but in figure.

[1] keepeth or retaineth.

15. There the soul eateth of all the words of God; for the same are the food of its life; and it singeth the paradisical [2] songs of praise concerning the pleasant fruit in paradise, which groweth in the divine virtue [or power] of the divine *limbus*, which is the food of the [3] body; for the body eateth of the *limbus*, out of which it is, and the soul eateth of God and of his Word, out of which it is.

[2] Hallelujahs.

[3] the heavenly and eternal paradisical body.

16. Can this be no joy and rejoicing? And should not that be a pleasant thing, with the many thousand sorts of angels to eat heavenly bread, and to rejoice in their communion and fellowship? What can possibly be named which can be more pleasant? Where there is no fear, no anger, no death: where every voice and speech is salvation, power, strength, and might, be to our God; and this voice going forth into the eternity. Thus with this sound the divine virtue of paradise goeth forth; and it is a mere growing in the divine centre

of the fruits in paradise. And there is the place where St *Paul* heard words unutterable, that no man can express. Such a man was *Adam* before his fall. And that you may not doubt, that this is very sure and most truly thus, look upon the circumstances.

17. When God had created *Adam* thus, he was then in paradise in the joyfulness; and this clarified [or [1] brightened] man was wholly beautiful, and full of all manner of knowledge; and there God brought all the beasts to him (as to the great lord in this world), that he should look upon them, and give to every one its name, according to its essence and virtue, as the spirit of every one was figured in it. And *Adam* knew all what every creature was, and he gave every one its name, according to the quality [or working property] of its spirit. As God can see into the heart of all things, so could *Adam* also do, in which his perfection may very well be observed.

[1] illustrious or shining.

18. And *Adam* and all men should have gone wholly naked, as he then went; his clothing was the clarity [or brightness] in the virtue [or power]; no heat nor cold touched him; he saw day and night [clearly] with open eyes; in him there was no sleep, and in his mind there was no night, for the divine virtue [and power] was in his eyes; and he was altogether perfect. He had the [2] *limbus*, and also the [3] matrix in himself; he was no [male] or man, nor [female or] woman; as we

[2] seed.
[3] womb.

in the resurrection shall be [neither]. Though indeed the knowledge of the marks [of distinction will] remain in the figure, but the *limbus* and the matrix not separated, as now [they are].

19. Now man was to dwell upon the earth as long as it was to stand, and manage [rule and order] the beasts, and have his delight and recreation therein: But he ought not to have eaten any earthly fruit, wherein the corruptibility [or transitoriness] did stick. It is true he should have eaten, but only with the mouth, and not into the body; for he had no [entrails, stomach, or] guts, nor any such hard dark flesh, it was all perfect; for there grew paradisical fruit for him, which afterwards [1] went away, [2] when he went out of paradise: And then God cursed the earth, and the heavenly *limbus* was drawn from him, together with that fruit, and he lost paradise, God, and the kingdom of heaven. For before sin, when paradise was upon the earth, the earth was not bad [or evil, as now it is].

20. If *Adam* had continued in innocency, then he should in all fruits have eaten paradisical fruit, and his food should have been heavenly, and his drink [should have been] out of the mother of the heavenly water of the source [or fountain] of the eternal life. The [3] out-birth touched him not, the element of air he had no need of in this manner [as now]; it is true, he drew breath from the air, but he took his breath from the incorruptibility, for he

[1] Or disappeared.
[2] because that he.
[3] Or the material water.

11

¹ Or was not united.

did not ¹mingle with the spirit of this world, but his spirit ruled powerfully over the spirit of this world, over the stars, and over the sun and moon, and over the elements.

21. This must be *Adam's* condition; and thus he was a true and right image and similitude of God. He had no such hard bones in his flesh [as we now have], but they were strength, and such [a kind of] virtue; also his blood was not out of the

² Or watery mother.

tincture of the ²aquastrish matrix, but it was out of the heavenly matrix. In brief, it was altogether heavenly, as we shall appear [and be] at the Day of the Resurrection. For the purpose of God standeth, the first image must return and come again and continue in paradise; and seeing it could be done in no other form, [way, or manner], nor [that which was lost] be restored again, therefore God would rather spend his own Heart; his eternal will is unchangeable, that must stand.

22. And when God had created man, then he planted a garden in *Eden* towards the east, and placed him therein, and caused to spring up and grow all manner of fruit, delightful to behold, and all sorts of trees good to eat of; and the Tree of Life in the midst of the garden, and the Tree of Knowledge of Good and Evil. And when God had placed man in the garden, he commanded him, and said, *You shall eat of every tree in the garden, but of the Tree of Knowledge of Good and Evil thou shalt not eat; for in the day that thou eatest*

thereof, thou shalt die the death. Here the veil
lieth upon *Moses*, and they must be sharp [or
piercing] eyes that can behold the face of *Moses.*
God hath not without cause let *Moses* write this so
very mystically [hiddenly and obscurely].

23. For what needed God to care so much for
the biting of an apple, as to destroy so fair a
creature for it? Doth he not forgive many greater
sins? And he so exceedingly loved man, that he
spared not his only Son, but let him become man,
and gave him unto death. And could he not
forgive a small sin? Seeing he was omniscient [or
knew all things], therefore why did he let the Tree
of Knowledge of Good and Evil grow?

24. Reason judgeth thus, that if God would not
have had it so, *Adam* should not have eaten of
it, or else he should not have forbidden that tree
only; sure he made it for a stumbling-stock to him.
Thus the reason of one [sort or] party judgeth.
The reason of the other party will mend the
matter, which is indeed somewhat the wiser, but
not much: They say, God tempted *Adam*, [to try]
whether he would continue in his obedience or
not; and when he became disobedient, then God
threw mighty anger and wrath upon him, and
cursed him to death; and that his wrath could
not be quenched, except he be reconciled in such a
manner. This reason of this party maketh God to
be a mere unmercifulness, like an evil man of this
world, who yet will be reconciled, when he hath

once revenged himself sufficiently; and this reason hath no knowledge at all of God, nor of paradise.

25. O beloved soul! it is a very [1] heavy business, at which the very heavens might well stand amazed. In this temptation there is a very great matter hidden in *Moses,* which the unenlightened soul understandeth not : God did not regard a bit of an apple or pear, to punish so fair a creature for it : The punishment cometh not from his hand, but from the [2] *spiritus majoris mundi,* from the spirit of the great world, from the third Principle. God intended most mercifully towards man, and therefore he spared not his own Heart, but let it become man, that he might deliver man again. You ought not to have such thoughts. God is love, and the good in him is no angry thought; and man's punishment was not but from himself, as you shall [find or] read in its due place.

[1] For which the curse came.

[2] Or macrocosm.

The Secret Gate of the Temptation of Man.

26. Since many questions fall to be in this place (for the mind of man seeketh after its native country again, out of which it is wandered, and would return again home to the eternal rest) and since it is permitted to me in my knowledge, I will therefore set down the deep ground of the fall, wherein men may look upon the eyes of *Moses* : If you be born of God, then it may well be apprehended by you, but the unenlightened mind cannot hit the mark; for if the mind desireth to see what

is in a house, it must then be within that house;
for from hearsay, without seeing it oneself, there is
always doubting whether a thing be as is related.
But what the eye seeth, and the mind knoweth,
that is believed perfectly, for [the eye and the
mind] apprehendeth it.

27. The mind searcheth wherefore man must be
tempted, whereas God had created him perfect;
and seeing God is omniscient [and knoweth all
things], the mind therefore always layeth the blame
upon God; and so do the devils also; for the mind
saith, If the Tree of Knowledge of Good and Evil
had not sprung up, then *Adam* had not fallen.

28. O beloved reason! if you understand no
more than so, then shut up the eyes [of your mind]
quite, and search not; continue under patience in
hope, and let God alone [he will do well enough],
or else you will fall into the greatest unquietness,
and the devil will drive you into despair, who continually [pretendeth or] giveth it [1] forth, that God
did will evil, [and that] he willeth not that all men
should be saved, and therefore he created the tree
of anger.

[1] The devil saith it in the mind.

29. Beloved mind, put such thoughts away from
thee, or else thou wilt make of the kind and loving
God, an unmerciful and hostile will, but leave off
such thoughts of God, and consider thyself what
thou art; in thyself thou shalt find the Tree of the
Temptation, and also the will to have it, which
made it spring up; yea the source [lust or quality]

whence it sprang up standeth in thee, and not in God; [this must be understood] that when we will speak of the pure Deity (which manifesteth itself in the second Principle through the Heart of God) it is thus, and not otherwise.

30. But when we consider [or mean] the original of the first Principle, then we find the [nature, property, or] species of the tree, and also the will to the tree. We find there the abyss of hell and of anger [and wrath]; and moreover we find the will of all the devils, we find the envious will of all the creatures of this world, wherefore they all are the enemies of one another, and do hate, bite, worry, kill and devour one another. My beloved reason, here I will shew you the Tree of the Temptation, and you shall look *Moses* in the face: Keep your mind [1] stedfast, that you may apprehend it.

[1] fixed, or upon it.

31. I have often given you to understand in this book already, what the essence of all essences is; but because it is most of all highly necessary in this place to know the ground [thereof], therefore I will [2] set it you down all at large, and very fundamentally, so that you shall know it in yourself; yea you shall understand it in all creatures, and in all things that are, or that you look upon, or at any time may possibly think on; all these shall be witnesses. I can bring heaven and earth, also the sun, stars, and elements for a witness, and that not in bare words and promises only, but it shall be set before you [very convincingly and]

[2] Or explain.

very powerfully in their virtue and essence; and you have no virtue [or power, or faculty] in your body, that shall not [convince you and] witness against you; do but not suffer the lying spirit, the old serpent, to darken your mind, who is the inventor of a thousand [1] tricks.

[1] Or sleights, shifts, fetches, arts.

32. When he seeth that he cannot catch [or overcome] man, by making him [2] doubtful of the mercy of God, then he maketh him careless, so that he accounteth all as nothing. He maketh his mind very drowsy, so that he esteemeth very lightly of himself, as if all were not worth the looking after: Let things be as they will, he will not break his heart [or trouble his head] with it. Let the [3] Pope look after it, they must answer for it. Thus the mind carelessly passes it over, like a whirlwind or stream of water; concerning which Christ said, The devil stealeth the word out of their hearts, that they do not apprehend it, nor believe it, that they might be saved; so that it taketh no root.

[2] Or despair.

[3] priest, minister, or learned, who take upon them *cura animarum*.

33. Or else if the Pearl should grow, and the lily bud forth, [4] he should be revealed, and then every one would fly from him, and he should stand in great shame. This trade he hath driven ever since the beginning of the world: And though he resisteth never so vehemently, yet a lily shall grow in his supposed kingdom, whose smell reacheth into the paradise of God, in spite of all his raging and tyranny; this the spirit of God doth witness.

[4] the devil.

34. Behold, thou child of man, if thou wilt easily

draw near to this knowledge, take but thy mind before thee, and consider it, and therein thou wilt find all.   You know, that out of it proceedeth joy and sorrow, laughter and weeping, hope and doubting, wrath and love, lust to a thing and hate of the thing : you find therein wrath and malice, also love, meekness, and well-doing.

35. Now the question is, May not the mind stand in one only will (*viz.* in mere love) like God himself?   Here sticketh the mark, the ground, and the knowledge : Behold, if the will were in one only essence, then the mind would also have but one quality that could give the will to be so, and it should be an immovable thing, which should always lie still, and should do no more but that one thing always : in it there would be no joy, no knowledge, also no art or skill of anything at all, and there would be no wisdom in it : also if the quality were not *in infinitum*, it would be altogether a nothing, and there would be no mind nor will to anything at all.

36. Therefore it cannot be said, that the total God in all the three Principles is in one only will and essence ; there is a distinction [or difference to be observed] : Though indeed the first and the third Principles be not called God, neither are they God, and yet are his essence [or substance], out of which from eternity the light and Heart of God is always generated, and it is one essence [or being], as body and soul in man are.

37. Therefore now if the eternal mind were not, out of which the eternal will goeth forth, then there would be no God. But now therefore there is an eternal mind, which generateth the eternal will, and the eternal will generateth the eternal Heart of God, and the Heart generateth the light, and the light the virtue, and the virtue the spirit, and this is the Almighty .God, which is one unchangeable will. For if the mind did no more generate the will, then the will would also not generate the Heart, and all would be a nothing. But seeing now that the mind thus generateth the will, and the will the Heart, and the Heart the light, and the light the virtue, and the virtue the spirit, therefore now the spirit again generateth the mind; for it hath the virtue, and the virtue is the Heart; and it is an indissoluble band.

The Depth.

38. Behold now, the mind is in the darkness, and it conceiveth its will to the light, to generate it; or else there would be no will, nor yet any [1] birth : This mind standeth in anguish, and in a [1] working. longing [or is in labour]; and this longing is the will, and the will conceiveth the virtue; and the virtue fulfilleth [satisfieth or impregnateth] the mind. Thus the kingdom of God consisteth in the virtue [or in power], which is God the Father, and the light maketh the virtue longing to [be] the

will, that is God the Son, for in the virtue the light is continually generated from eternity, and in the light out of the virtue goeth the Holy Ghost forth, which generateth again in the dark mind the will of the eternal essence.

39. Now behold, dear soul, that is the Deity, and that comprehendeth in it the second or the middlemost Principle. Therefore God is only good, the love, the light, the virtue [or power]. Now consider, if the mind did not stand in the darkness, there would no such eternal wisdom and skill be; for the anguish in the will to generate, standeth therein; and the anguish is the quality, and the quality is the [1] multiplicity [or variety], and maketh the mind, and the mind again maketh the multiplicity [or plurality].

[1] plurality.

40. Now, dear soul, see all over round about you, in yourself, and in all things: What find you therein? You find nothing else but the anguish, and in the anguish the quality, and in the quality the mind, and in the mind the will to grow and generate, and in the will the virtue [or [2]power], and in the virtue the light, and in the light its forth-driving spirit; which maketh again a will to generate a twig [bud or branch] out of the tree like itself; and this I call in my book the *centrum*, [the centre], where the generated will becometh an essence [or substance], and generateth now again such [another] essence; for thus is the mother of the genetrix.

[2] faculty or ability.

41. Now the anguish hath the first Principle [1] in possession; seeing it standeth in the darkness, it is another essence than the essence in the light is, where there is nothing else but mere love and meekness, where no source [or torment] is discovered; and the quality which is generated in the centre of the light, is now no quality, but the eternal skill and wisdom of whatsoever was in the anguish before the light [brake forth]: This wisdom and skill now always cometh to help the conceived will in the anguish, and maketh in itself again the centre to the birth, that so the sprout may generate itself in the quality, *viz.* the virtue, and out of the virtue the fire, and out of the fire the spirit, and the spirit maketh in the fire the virtue again, that thus there [may] be an indissoluble band. And out of this mind which standeth in the darkness, God generated the angels, which are flames of fire, yet [2] shining through and through with the divine light. For in this mind a spirit can and may be generated, and not else; for before it in the Heart and light of God, there can no spirit be generated, for the Heart of God is the end of nature, and it hath no quality; therefore also nothing cometh out of it more, but it continueth unchangeably in the eternity, and it shineth in the mind of the quality of the darkness, and the darkness cannot comprehend it.

42. Now therefore in the anguishing mind of the darkness, is the inexpressible [or unutterable] source [or rising property], from whence the name quality

[1] under its power.

[2] Or thoroughly enlightened.

existeth, as from many sources [or wells] into one source, and out of these many sources [running] into one source springeth forth the plurality of skill, so that there is a multiplicity [or variety of it]. And the spirit of God out of the light cometh to help every skill [or science, or knowledge], and in every skill of the sources in the quality (by its kind ¹infecting of the love) it maketh again a centre, and in the centre a source [or spring] is generated again, as a twig out of a tree, where again there springeth forth a mind in the anguish. And the spirit of love, with its infecting [or infusing] of kindness, maketh all, every thought in the will, and [that] essentially.

¹ infusion.

43. For the will in the centre climbeth aloft till it generateth the fire, and in the fire is the substance and essentiality generated. For it is the spirit thereof, and the end of the will in the dark mind, and there can be nothing higher generated in the anguish than the fire, for it is the end of nature, and it generateth again the anguish and the source, as may be perceived. Now therefore the dark anguishing [aching, or anxious] mind hath not only one substance, *viz.* one being [or essence] in itself, but many, or else no quality could be generated ; and yet it is truly but one [being, essence, or] substance, and not many.

44. Thou dear soul, thus saith the high spirit to thee ; yield up thy mind here, and I will shew it thee. Behold, what doth comprehend thy will, or

wherein consisteth thy life? If thou sayest, In water and flesh: No, it consisteth in the fire, in the warmth. If the warmth were not, then thy body would be stiff [with cold], and the water would dry away; therefore the mind and the life consisteth in the fire.

45. But what is the fire? First, there is the darkness, the hardness, the eternal cold, and the dryness, where there is nothing else but an eternal hunger. Then how cometh the fire to be? Dear soul, here [in the fire's coming to be] the spirit of God (*viz.* the eternal light) cometh to help the hunger; for the hunger existeth also from the light: Because the divine virtue beholdeth itself in the darkness, therefore the darkness is desirous [and longing] after the light; and the desirousness is the will.

46. Now the will or the desirousness in the dryness cannot [1] reach the light; and therein consisteth the anguish in the will [longing] after the light; and the anguish is attractive, and in the attracting is the woe, and the woe maketh the anguish greater, so that the anguish in the [2] harshness attracteth much more, and this attracting in the woe is the bitter [sting or] prickle, or the bitterness of the woe; and the anguish reacheth after the [sting or] prickle with attracting, and yet cannot [3] comprehend it, because it resisteth, and the more the anguish attracteth, the more the [sting or] prickle raveth and rageth.

[1] Or attain.

[2] sourness, or astringency.

[3] Or catch it.

47. Now therefore the anguish, bitterness, and woe in the [sting or] prickle, are like a brimstone-spirit, and all spirits in nature are brimstone: They [torment, or] cause the anguish in one another, till that the light of God cometh to help them; and then there cometh to be a flash, and there is its end, for it can climb no higher in nature; and this is the fire, which becometh shining in the flash, in the soul, and also in the mind. For the soul reacheth the virtue of the light, which doth put it into meekness; and in this world it is the burning fire: In hell it is immaterial, and there it is the eternal fire, which burneth in the [1] quality.

[1] Or property.

48. Now, thou dear soul, here you see in a glass how very near God is to us, and that he himself is the heart of all things, and giveth to all virtue [power] and life. Here Lucifer was very [2] heedless, and became so very proud, that when this brimstone-spirit in the will of the mind of God was created, then he would fain have flien out above the end of nature, and would drive the fire out above the meekness; he would fain have had all burn in the fire; he would have ruled [or domineered]: The sparks of fire in the brimstone-spirit did elevate themselves too high; and these spirits pleased not the Creator, or the spirit in the *Fiat*, and [therefore] were not [established] angels, although in the first mind (when the centre was opened to the [creation of the] spirits) he came to help them,

[2] careless, inconsiderate.

and [[1] beheld] them as well as the other angels : [1] Or reflected on them.
But they indeed generated a fiery will, when they
should have opened their centre to the regeneration
of their minds, and so should have generated an
angelical will.

49. The first will, out of which they were created,
that was God's, and that made them good ; and the
second will, which they as obedient [children]
should have generated out of their centre in meek-
ness, that was evil : And therefore the [2] father, for [2] the gene-
generating such a child, was thrust out from the will which he
virtue of God, and so he spoiled the angelical generated.
kingdom, and remained in the source of the fire :
And because the [3] evil child of their mind did turn [3] the will that was born out
away from the meekness, therefore they [4] attained of their mind.
what they desired. For the mind is the god and [4] Or came to be.
the creator of the will ; that is free from the eternal
nature, and therefore what it generateth to itself,
that it hath.

50. Now if you ask, Wherefore came not the
love of God to help them again ? No, friend, their
mind had elevated itself, even to the end of nature,
and it would fain have gone out above the light of
God ; their mind was become a kindled source of
fire in the fierce wrath, the meekness of God cannot
enter into it, the brimstone spirit burneth eternally :
In this manner he is an enemy to God, he cannot
be helped ; for the centre is burning in the flash :
his will is still, that he would fain go out above the
meekness of God ; neither can he get [frame, or

create] any other [will], for his source hath revealed the end of nature in the fire, and he remaineth an unquenchable source of fire; the heart of God in the meekness, and the Principle of God, is close shut up from him, and that even to eternity.

51. To conclude, God will have no fiery spirit in paradise, they must remain in the first Principle, in the eternal darkness; if they had continued as God had created them (when the meekness shone [or appeared] to them), and had put the centre of their minds into the meekness, then the light of God should for ever have [1]shone through them, and they should have eaten of the *Verbum Domini* [the Word of the Lord]; and they should, with the root of their original, have stood in the first Principle, like God the Father himself; and with the will in the mind [they should have stood] in the second Principle: Thus they should have had a paradisical source [quality or property], and an angelical will; and they should have been friendly in the [2]*limbus* of Heaven, and in the love of God.

[1] Or thoroughly enlightened them.

[2] Or heavenly earth.

THE ELEVENTH CHAPTER

Of all Circumstances of the Temptation.

1. NOW the highest question is, What that is which caused the mind of the devil so to elevate itself, and that so great a number of them are fallen in their high-mindedness [or pride]? Behold, when God set the *Fiat* in the will, and would create angels, then the spirit first separated all qualities, after that manner as now you see there are many kinds of stars, and so the *Fiat* created them [several]. Then there were created the princely [angels], and the throne angels, according to every quality (as hard, sour, bitter, cold, fierce, soft, and so forth, [1] in the essences, till to the end of nature) out of the source of the fire ; a similitude whereof you have in the stars, how different they are.

[1] in the springing essential powers.

2. Now the thrones and princely angels, are every one of them a great fountain ; as you may perceive the sun is, in respect of the stars, as also in the blossoming earth. The great fountain-vein [or well-spring] in the source, was in the time of the *Fiat* in the dark mind, the prince or throne-

angel: There out of each fountain came forth again a centre in many thousand thousands; for the spirit in the *Fiat* manifested itself in the nature of the darkness, after the manner of the eternal wisdom. Thus the manifold various properties that were in the whole nature, went forth out of one only fountain, according to the ability of the eternal wisdom of God; or as I may best render it to be understood by a similitude; as if one princely angel had generated out of himself, at one time, many angels; whereas yet the prince doth not generate them, but the essences; and the qualities go forth with the centre in every essence, from the princely angels, and the spirit created them [1] with the *Fiat*, and they continue standing essentially. Therefore every [2] host (which proceeded out of one [and the same] fountain) gat a will in the same fountain, which was their prince (as you see how the stars give all their will into the virtue [or power] of the sun); of this, much must not be said to my [3] Master in Arts, he holdeth it impossible to know such things, and yet in God all things are possible, and to him a thousand years are as one day.

[1] by

[2] Or company.

[3] The learned in reason.

3. Now of these princely angels one is fallen (for he stood in the fourth form of the matrix of the genetrix in the dark mind, in that place in the mind where the flash of fire taketh its original) with his whole host that was proceeded from him: Thus the fiery kind [condition or property] moved

him to go above the end of nature, (*viz.* above the Heart of God), that kind stood so [1]hard kindled in him. [1] Or fiercely.

4. For as God said to the matrix of the earth, *Let there come forth all kinds of beasts*, and the *Fiat* created beasts out of all the essences; and first divided the matrix, and after that the essences and qualities; and then he created them out of the divided matrix, male and female. But because the creatures were material, therefore every kind [species or generation] must thus propagate itself from every essence; but with the angels not so, but [their propagation was] sudden and swift; as God's thoughts are, so were they.

5. But this is the ground: every quality [or source] would be creaturely, and the fiery [property] elevated itself too mightily, into which Lucifer had [2]brought his will; and so it went with *Adam* as to the tempting tree, as it is written; and God suffered all sorts of trees to spring up in the Garden of *Eden*; and in the midst of the garden the Tree of Life, and the Tree of the Knowledge of Good and Evil. [2] Or set his delight or pleasure in it

6. *Moses* saith: God suffered to spring up out of the earth all sorts of trees pleasant to look upon, and good for food. But here is the veil in *Moses*, and yet in the Word it is bright, clear, and manifest, that the fruits were pleasant to behold, and good to eat, wherein there was no death, wrath, or [3]corruptibility, but [it was] paradisical fruit, of [3] corruption.

which *Adam* could live in clarity [or brightness] in the will of God, and in his love in perfection in eternity; only the death stuck in the Tree of Knowledge of Good and Evil, that only was able to bring man into another image.

7. Now we must needs clearly [conceive, or] think, that the paradisical fruit which was good, was not so very earthly, for (as *Moses* himself saith) they were of two sorts; the one good to eat and pleasant to behold, and the other had the death and corruptibility in it: In the paradisical fruit there was no death nor corruptibility; for if there had been any death or corruptibility therein, then *Adam* had eaten death in all the fruits; but seeing there was no death therein, therefore the fruit could not be so altogether earthly; though indeed it sprang out of the earth, yet the divine virtue of the second Principle was imprinted therein, and yet they were truly in the third Principle, grown [or sprung] out of the earth, which God cursed as to the earthly food, that no paradisical fruit did grow any more out of the earth.

8. Besides, if *Adam* had eaten earthly fruit, he must then have eaten it into his body, and have had guts [or entrails]: And how could such a stink [and dung] (as we now carry in the body) have been in paradise in the holiness of God? Moreover, he would, by eating earthly food, have eaten of the fruit of the stars and elements, which would presently have infected [or qualified] in

him, as was done in the fall; also so his fear over all the beasts would have ceased. For the essences of the beasts would presently have been like the human essences in virtue [and power], and [1] one would have domineered more strongly over the other.

[1] Or the stronger would have domineered over the weaker.

9. Therefore it was quite otherwise with *Adam*; he was a heavenly paradisical man, he should have eaten of the heavenly paradisical fruit, and in the virtue [or power] of that [fruit] he should have ruled over all beasts [or living creatures], also over the stars and elements: No cold nor heat should have touched him, or else God would not have created him so naked, but like all beasts, with a rough [or hairy] skin [or hide].

10. But the question is, Wherefore grew the earthly Tree of the Knowledge of Good and Evil? For if that had not been, *Adam* had not eaten of it: Or wherefore must *Adam* be tempted? Hearken, Ask your mind about it, wherefore it so suddenly generateth and conceiveth in itself a thought of anger, and then of love? Dost thou say [it cometh] from the hearing and seeing of a thing? Yes, that is true, this God also knew very well; and therefore he must be tempted. For the centre of the mind is free, and it generateth the will from hearing and seeing, out of which the imagination and lust doth arise.

11. Seeing *Adam* was created an image and

whole similitude of God, and had all three Principles in him like God himself, therefore also his mind and imagination should merely have looked into the Heart of God, and should have set his lust and [desire, or] will thereon; and as he was a lord over all, and that his mind was a threefold spirit, in three Principles in one only essence, so his spirit also, and the will in the spirit, should have stood open [or free] in one only essence, *viz.* in the paradisical heavenly [essence]. And his mind and soul should have eaten of the Heart of God, and his body [should have eaten] of the heavenly *limbus*.

¹ Or virtue or power.

12. But seeing the heavenly ¹ *limbus* was manifested through the earthly, and was in the fruit in one only essence, and *Adam* so too, therefore it behoved *Adam* (having received a living soul out of the first Principle, and breathed in from the Holy Ghost, and enlightened from the light of God standing in the second Principle) not to reach after the earthly matrix.

13. Therefore God here also gave him the command, not to lust after the earthly matrix, nor after her fruit, which stood in the corruptibility, and transitoriness, but the spirit of man ² not. He should eat of the fruit, but no otherwise than of the paradisical kind and property, [and] not of the earthly essences. For the paradisical essences had imprinted themselves in all fruits, therein they were very good to eat of, after an angelical manner,

² not in the corruptibility.

and also pleasant to behold, or corporeal, as *Moses* also saith. Now it may be asked, What then was properly the tempting in *Adam*?

The Gate of Good and Evil.

14. We have a very powerful testimony hereof, and it is known in nature, and in all her children, in the stars and elements, in the earth, stones, and metals; especially in the living creatures, as you see, how they are evil and good, *viz.* lovely creatures, and also venomous evil beasts; as toads, adders, and serpents [or worms]; so also there is poison and malice in every sort of [1]life of the third Principle : And the [fierceness or] strongness must be in nature, or else all were a death, and a nothing.

[1] Or living thing.

The Depth in the Centre.

15. As is mentioned before, the eternal mind standeth thus [2] in the darkness, and vexeth itself, and longeth after the light, to generate that; and the anguish is the source, and the source hath in it many forms, till that it reacheth the fire in its substance, *viz.* [it hath] bitter, sour, hard, cold, strong, darting forth, or flashing; in the root of itself sticketh the joy and pain alike; *viz.* when it cometh to the root of the fire, and can reach the light, then out of the wrath [or sternness] cometh the great joy. For the light putteth the stern form into great meekness; on the contrary, that

[2] Or unknown.

form which cometh only to the root of the fire,
that continueth in the ¹ wrath.

¹ Or grimness, fierceness.

16. As we are to know, that when God would manifest the eternal mind in the darkness, in the third Principle ² with this world, then first all forms in the first Principle till fire were manifested, and that form now which comprehended the light, that became angelical and paradisical; but that which comprehended not the light, that remained to be wrathful, murderous, sour and evil, every one in its own form and essence. For every form desired also to be manifested, for it was the will of the eternal essence to manifest itself. But now one form was not able to manifest itself alone in the eternal birth, for the one is the member of the other, and the one without the other would not be.

² Or by.

17. Therefore the eternal Word, or Heart of God, wrought thus in the dark and spiritual matrix, which in itself, in the originalness without the light, would be [as it were] dumb [or senseless], and hath generated a corporeal and palpable [or comprehensible] similitude of its essence, in which all the forms were brought forth out of the eternal formation, and brought into essence. For out of the spiritual form, the corporeal [form] is generated, and the eternal Word hath created it by the *Fiat*, to stand thus.

18. Now then, out of these forms, out of the matrix of the earth, by the *Fiat*, in the Word,

went forth all the creatures of this world; also
trees, herbs, and grass, every one according to its
kind; as also worms, evil and good, as every form
in the matrix of the genetrix had its original.
And thus it was also with the fruits in the paradise
of this world in the Garden of *Eden*; when the
word was spoken, *Let there come forth all sorts
of trees and herbs*, then out of all forms [or the
genetrix or womb] trees and herbs came forth and
grew, which were altogether good and pleasant;
for the word in the *Fiat* had [1] imprinted itself in
all the forms.

[1] imaged or imagined.

19. But then the darkness and source [or pain]
were in the midst in the centre, wherein death,
the wrathfulness, decay, and the corruptibility did
stick; and if that had not been, this world would
have stood for ever, and *Adam* would not have
been tempted: [2] They also, like a [3] death (or a
corrupting worm of the source) did work together,
and generate the Tree of Good and Evil in the
midst of its seat [or place], because death stuck in
the midst of the centre, by which this world will
be kindled in the fire at the end of the days.   And
this source is even the anger of God, which by the
Heart or light of God in the eternal Father is continually put into the meekness; and therefore the
Word or Heart of God is called the eternal
mercifulness of the Father.

[2] the darkness, and source, or pain.

[3] *mors.*

20. Seeing then all the forms of the eternal
nature were to come forth [it is so come to pass],

as you may see in toads, adders, worms, and evil beasts; for that is the form which sticketh in the midst in the birth of all creatures, *viz.* the poison [venom], or brimstone-spirit; as we see that all creatures have poison and gall; and the life of the creatures sticketh in the power [or might] of it [the poison]; as you may find before in this book, in all the chapters, how the eternal nature taketh its original, how it worketh, and how [or after what manner] its essence [being or substance] is.

21. Now thus the tree of the strong [tartness, or wrath] (which is in the midst of nature) grew also in the midst of the Garden of *Eden*; and was (according to the ability of its own form which it hath from the eternal quality in the originalness) the greatest and the mightiest [tree]. And here it may be seen very clearly, that God would have preserved and had man to be in paradise, for he forbad him this tree, and caused other fruit enough [besides] to grow in the forms and essences.

The Gate of the Tempting.

22. St *Paul* saith, *God foresaw* [or elected] *man, before the ground* [or foundation] *of the world was laid*: Here we find the ground so very [plain or] fair, that we have a delight to write on, and to seek the [1] Pearl. For behold, in the eternal wisdom of God, before the creation of the world, the fall of the devils, and also of man, appeared in the eternal matrix, and was seen. For the eternal

[1] Wisdom.

Word in the eternal light knew very well, that if it came to manifest the fountain of the eternal birth, that then every form would break forth; yet it was not the will of the love in the Word of the light, that the forms of the tart [sour, strong wrath] should elevate themselves above the meekness; but it had such a mighty [or potent] form, that it is so come to pass.

23. Therefore the devil also, in regard of the might of the tart [strong fierce wrath], was called a prince of this world in the [angry strong] fierceness, of which you shall find [more] about the fall. And therefore God created but one man; for God would that man should continue in paradise, and live eternally; and on the contrary, the sternness [or strong fierce wrath] would tempt him, [to try] whether he would put his imagination and will wholly into the Heart of God, and into paradise, wherein he was.

24. And because *Adam* was drawn forth out of the strong [stern, sour] essences, therefore he must be tempted, [to try] whether his essences (out of which his imagination and lust proceeded) could stand in the heavenly quality, and whether he would eat of the *Verbum Domini* [the Word of the Lord]; and [to try] which essence, whether the paradisical, or the strong [fierce, wrathful], would overcome in *Adam*.

25. And this was the purpose of God, therefore to create but one man, that the same might be

tempted [and tried] how he would stand, and that upon his fall he might the better be helped: And the Heart of God did before the foundation of the world in his love foreintend [or prepurpose] to come to help [him]; and when no other remedy could do it, the Heart of God himself would become man, and regenerate man again.

26. For man is not fallen out of strong [fierce, angry] pride, like the devil; but his earthly essences have overcome his paradisical essences, and brought them into the earthly lust, and in that regard he hath grace again bestowed upon him.

The highest, strongest, and the mightiest Gate of the Temptation in Adam.

[1] not only in this chapter, but in all these writings.

[2] Or womb, or lap.

27. Here I will faithfully admonish the Reader, deeply to consider *Moses*, for [1] here, under the veil of *Moses*, he may look upon the face of *Moses*: Also he may see the second *Adam* in the [2] love of the virgin: Also he may see him in his temptation, and upon the cross; as also in death; and lastly, in the virtue of the resurrection at the right hand of God: Also you may see *Moses* on mount *Sinai*; and lastly, the clarification [or transfiguration] of Christ, *Moses* and *Elias* on mount *Tabor*: Also you may see herein the whole Scripture of the Old and New Testaments: Also you find herein all the Prophets from the beginning of the world hitherto, and all the might and power of all tyrants, wherefore things have gone so, and must still go [as they

do] : Lastly, you find the golden gate of the
omnipotence [or almightiness], and of the great
power in the love and humility; and wherefore
the children of God must still be tempted ; and
wherefore the noble grain of mustard-seed must
grow in storms, crosses, and misery, and wherefore
it cannot be otherwise : Also herein you find the
essence of all essences.

28. And it is the gate of the lily, concerning
which the spirit witnesseth, that it will [1] hereafter [1] shortly.
grow in the wrathful tree, and when it groweth,
it will bring us true knowledge, by its pleasant and
fragrant smell, in the Holy Trinity; by which
smell Antichrist [2] will be stifled, and the tree of [2] *Note, we must yet con-*
the stern anger be broken down, and the beast *ceal the exposi-*
enraged, which hath its might and strength from *tion of this verse.*
the tree for a time, till it be dry and fiery, because
it can get no more sap from the wrathful tree that
is broken down ; and then it will smell [or lift up
itself] in the [fierce, tart] [3] wrath against the tree [3] Or rage.
and the lily, till the tree (of which the beast did
eat and was strong) destroyeth the beast, and his
power remaineth in the fire of the originalness.
And then all doors [will] stand open in the great
tree of nature, and the priest *Aaron* [will] give
his garment and fair ornament to the Lamb, that
was slain and is [alive] again.

29. Reader, who lovest God; hereby it will be
shewn thee, that the great Mysteries [4] meet us, [4] Or are im-*parted to us.*
concerning the hidden things that were in *Adam*

before his fall, and that yet there are much greater after his fall, when he was as it were dead, and yet living; and here is shewn the [1] birth of the eternal essence, and wherefore it still must thus have been, that *Adam* must have been tempted, and wherefore it could not have been otherwise; though reason continually [2] gainsayeth it, and allegeth God's omnipotency, that it was in him to hinder, or suffer the doing of it.

30. Beloved reason, leave off your thoughts, for with these thoughts and conceits you know not God, nor the eternity. Then how will you with such thoughts know the similitude which God generated out of the eternal mind? It hath here been sundry times mentioned to you, that the mind (which yet is the greatest essence in man) doth not stand [3] in a source.

31. If we think of [or consider] the incliner, what that was which inclined and drew *Adam* to that which was forbidden, that he should lust contrary to the command of God, whereas he was yet in great perfection, then we shall find the eternal mind, out of which *Adam* was also created; and that because he was an extract out of the eternal mind, out of all essences of all the three Principles, therefore he must be tempted [to try] whether he could stand in paradise: For the Heart of God desired that he should continue in paradise, but now he could not continue in paradise, except he did eat paradisical fruit;

[1] Or continual working.

[2] speaketh against it.

[3] in a working property, but is free.

therefore now his Heart should have been wholly [1]inclined towards God; and so he should have lived in the divine centre, and God had wrought in him.

[1] given up to God.

32. Now what opposed him, or what drew him from paradise to disobedience, so that he passed into another image [form or condition]? Behold, thou child of man, there was a threefold strife in *Adam*, without *Adam*, and in all whatsoever *Adam* beheld. Thou wilt say, What was it? It was the three Principles; first, the kingdom of hell, the power of the wrath; and secondly, the kingdom of this world, with the stars and elements; and thirdly, the kingdom of paradise, that desired to have him.

33. Now these three kingdoms were in *Adam*, and also [2]without him; and in the [3]essences there was a mighty strife, all drew as well in *Adam* as without *Adam*, and would fain have him; for he was a great lord [come] out of all the [powers or] virtues of nature. The Heart of God desired to have him in paradise, and [would] dwell in him; for it said, it is my image and similitude. And the kingdom of wrath [and of the fierce tartness] would also have him; for it said, he is mine, and he is [proceeded] out of my fountain, out of the eternal mind of the darkness; I will be in him, and he shall live in my might, for he is generated out of [that which is] mine; I will, through him, shew great and strong power. The kingdom of

[2] *extra.*

[3] essential virtues or powers that went forth from the three Principles.

this world said, he is mine; for he beareth my image, and he liveth in [that which is] mine, and I in him; he must be obedient to me, I will tame him and compel him, I have all my members in him, and he in me; I am greater than he, he must be my [1] householder, I will shew my fair wonders and virtues in him, he must manifest my wonders and virtues, he shall keep and manage my herds, I will clothe him with my fair glory; as now it is to be seen.

[1] Or steward.

34. But when the kingdom of the fierceness, of the wrath, of death, and of hell, saw that it had lost, and could not keep man, then it said, I am [2] death, and a worm, and my virtue [or power] is in him, and I will grind him and break him to pieces, and his spirit must live in me; and although thou world supposeth that he is thine, because he beareth thy image, yet his spirit is mine, generated out of my kingdom; therefore take what is thine from him, I will keep that which is mine.

[2] mors.

35. Now what did the virtue in *Adam*, in this strife? It flattered with all the three [kingdoms]. It said to the Heart of God, I will stay in paradise, and thou shalt dwell in me: I will be thine, for thou art my Creator, and thou hast thus concreted [or extracted] me out of all the three Principles, and created me: Thy refreshment is pleasant, and thou art my bridegroom, I have received of thy fulness, and therefore I am impregnated [or with child], and I will bring forth a virgin, that my

kingdom may be great, and that thou mayest have mere joy in me: I will eat of thy fruit, and my spirit shall eat of thy virtue [or power]; and thy name in me shall be called *IMMANUEL*, God with us.

36. And when the spirit of this world perceived that, then it said, Wherefore wilt thou only eat of that which thou comprehendest not, and drink of that which thou feelest not? Thou art not yet merely a spirit, thou hast from me all the kinds of comprehensibility in thee; behold, the comprehensible fruit is sweet and good, and the comprehensible drink is [1] mighty and strong, eat and drink from me, and so thou shalt come to have all my virtue and beauty; thou mayest in me be mighty [and powerful] over all the creatures, for the kingdom of this world shall be thy own, and thou shalt be lord upon earth.

[1] powerful, and full of virtue or strength.

37. And the virtue in *Adam* said, I am upon earth, and dwell in this world, and the world is mine, I will use it according to my lust [will, and pleasure]. Then came the command of God (which was [2] received in the centre of God, out of the circle [or circumference] of the eternal life), and said, *In the day that thou eatest of the earthly fruit, thou shalt die the death*: This command was comprehended or enclosed (and hath its original in the eternal Father) in the centre, where the eternal Father continually from eternity generateth his Heart or Son.

[2] enclosed, conceived, or comprehended.

13

¹ Or have nothing to do.

38. Now when the worm of darkness saw the command of God, it thought with itself, here thou wilt ¹not prevail, thou art spirit without body, and contrariwise, *Adam* is corporeal, thou hast but a third part in him, and besides, the command is in the way; thou wilt even slip [or creep] into the essences, and flatter with the spirit of this world, and take a creaturely form upon thee, and send a legate [or ambassador] out of my kingdom, clothed in the form of a serpent, and wilt persuade him to eat of the earthly fruit, and then the command destroyeth his body, and the spirit remaineth [to be] mine. Here now the legate [or ambassador], the devil, was very willing [and ready] at this, especially because *Adam* in paradise was in his place, where he should have been; and [he] thought [with himself], Now thou hast an opportunity to be revenged; thou wilt mingle lies and truth so together, that *Adam* may not [observe or] understand it, [the treachery], and so thou wilt tempt him.

Of the Tree of Knowledge [of] Good and Evil.

² might.

39. I have told you before, out of what ²power the tree is grown; *viz.* that it grew out of the earth, and hath wholly had the nature of the earth in it, as at this day all earthly trees are [so] (and no otherwise, neither better nor worse), wherein corruptibility standeth, as the earth is corruptible, and shall pass away in the end, when all shall

go into its ¹ether, and nothing else shall remain ¹ Or recep-
of it besides the figure. Now this was the ^tacle.
tree which stood in the midst of the garden in
Eden, whereby *Adam* must be tempted in all
essences; for his spirit should rule powerfully
over all essences, as the holy angels, and God
himself doth.

40. Besides, he was created by the Word, or
Heart of God, that he should be his image and
similitude, very powerfully in all the three Principles, [and be] as great as a prince or throne-angel.
But this tree standing thus in the garden, and of all
the trees that only did bear earthly fruit, therefore
Adam looked so often upon it, because he knew
that it was the Tree of Knowledge of Good and
Evil, and the virtue of the tree pressed him to it
so very hard (which virtue was also in him) that
the one lust infected [poisoned or mingled with]
the other: And the spirit of the great world
pressed *Adam* so very hard, that he became infected,
and his virtue [or power] was overcome. Here
the paradisical man was undone, and then said the
Heart of God, It is not good that man [should]
be alone, we will make him a help [or consort]
to be with him.

41. Here God saw his fall, and that he could
not stand, because *Adam's* imagination and lust
was so eager after the kingdom of this world, and
after the earthly fruit, and that *Adam* would not
generate a perfect paradisical man out of himself,

but an infected [poisoned man], according to the lust, and would fall into corruptibility. And the text in *Moses* soundeth further very right, thus, *And God let a deep sleep fall upon man, and he slept [or fell asleep].*

THE TWELFTH CHAPTER

Of the Opening of the Holy Scripture, that the Circumstances may be highly considered.

The Golden Gate, which God affordeth to the last World, wherein the Lily shall flourish [and blossom].

1. LOVING Reader, I had need have an angelical tongue for this description, and thou an angelical mind, and then we should well understand one another: But seeing we have them not, therefore we will express the great deeds of God with the earthly tongue, according to our [received] gift and knowledge, and open the Scripture to the Reader, and give him occasion to consider further, whereby the Pearl might be sought and found at last; therefore we will work in our day-labour, [1] according to our duty, till the [2] Pearl of the lily be found.

2. Reason asketh: How long was *Adam* in paradise before his fall, and how long did the temptation last? I cannot tell thee that, out of *Moses'* description of the creation, for it is for great cause concealed: Yet I will shew thee the wonders of God, and [3] expound them, according to

[1] and lead them that come after us into it.
[2] Or gate.
[3] Or search into them.

197

the knowledge that is given me, whereby thou mayest the better learn to [1] consider the temptation and the fall of *Adam*.

[1] Or understand.

3. Beloved reason, look into the glass of the actions and deeds of God. When God appeared to *Moses* in the [2] burning bush, he said, *Pull off thy shoes; for here is a holy place*: What was that? Answer: God shewed [*Moses*] thereby his earthly birth. For he would give him a law, wherein man should live (if it were possible), and attain salvation: But who was it that gave the law, and commanded man to live therein? Answer: It was God the Father, out of his centre, and therefore it was done with fire and thunder; for there is no fire and thunder in the Heart of God, but kind love.

[2] Or fire flaming.

4. Hereupon reason will say, Is not God the Father one [and the same] essence with the Son? Answer: Yes, [they are] one essence and will. By what means then did he give the law? Answer: By the spirit of the great world; because *Adam* after the fall, and all men, lived [3] therein, therefore it must be tried, whether man could live [4] therein, in confidence towards God. Therefore he established it with great wonders [or miracles], and gave [5] it clarity [shining brightness or glory]; as may be seen in *Moses*, who had a [glorious bright] shining face. And when he had chosen to himself this people, he destroyed the children of unbelief, and brought [6] them out with wonders into the wilder-

[3] in the spirit of the great world.
[4] in the law.
[5] the law.
[6] his chosen.

ness ; and there it was tried whether men could live in perfect obedience under this clarity [glory or brightness].

5. What was done there ?   Answer : *Moses* was called by God (out from [among] the children of *Israel*) up into mount *Sinai,* and stayed there forty days : And then he would try the people whether it were possible for them to put their trust [or confidence] in God, that they might be fed with [1] heavenly bread, that so they might attain perfection.   And there now stood the mind *majoris mundi,* of the [2] great world ; and on the contrary, the eternal mind of God, in strife one against another ; God required obedience, and the mind of this world required [or desired] the pleasure of this transitory life, as eating, drinking, playing, dancing ; therefore they chose them moreover their belly-god, a Golden Calf, that they might be free and live without law.

[1] manna.

[2] Or macrocosm.

6. Here you see again, how the three Principles strove one against another about man : The law that was given to *Adam* in the Garden of *Eden* brake forth again, and desired to have obedience ; in like manner, also, the spirit of strong [fierceness or] wrath brake forth again in the false fruit and voluptuousness, and sought the corruptible life. And this strife now lasted forty days, before they set up the calf, and fell [wholly like *Adam*] from God ; so long the strife of the three Principles continued.

7. But now, when they were fallen away from God, [as *Adam* was], then came *Moses* with *Joshua*, and saw the apostasy [or falling away], and brake the tables in pieces, and led them into the wilderness; where they must all die, except *Joshua* and *Caleb*: For the clarity [or brightness] of the Father in the fire, in the first Principle, could not bring them into the Promised Land; and although they did eat manna, yet it did not help [in] the trial, only *Joshua*, and at length *JESUS*, must do it.

8. And when the time came, that the true Champion [or Saviour] returned again out of paradise, and became the child of the virgin, then [1] was renewed. the strife of the three Principles [1] came again. For there he was again set before the tempting tree, and he must endure the hard brunt before the tempting tree, and stand out the temptation of the three Principles, which was not possible for the first *Adam* to do. And there the strife continued forty days and forty nights, just so long as the strife with *Adam* in paradise continued, and not an hour longer; and then the Champion [or Saviour] overcame. Therefore open your eyes aright, and look upon the Scripture aright; although it be brief and obscure [to reason], yet it is very true.

9. You find not in *Moses*, that *Adam* was driven out of paradise the first day; the temptation of *Israel*, and of Christ, informeth us quite otherwise. For the temptation of Christ is to a tittle (in all

circumstances) the same with the temptation of *Adam*.

10. For *Adam* was tempted forty days in paradise, in the Garden of *Eden*, before the tempting tree, [and tried] whether he could stand, whether he could set his inclination on the Heart of God, and only eat of the *Verbum Domini* [the Word of the Lord]; and then [if he had stood], God would have given him his body (the heavenly *limbus*) to eat, that he should eat it in his mouth, not into his body ; he should have brought forth the child of the virgin out of himself ; for he was neither man nor woman [male nor female]; he had the matrix, and also the man [or masculine nature] in him, and should have brought forth the virgin full of modesty and chastity out of the matrix, without rending of his body.

11. And here is the strife in the Revelation of *John*, where a woman brought forth a son, which the dragon and the [1] worm would devour; and there stood the virgin upon the earthly moon, and despiseth the earthiness, and treadeth it under feet. And so should *Adam* also have trodden the earthiness under foot, but it overcame him ; therefore afterwards the child of the virgin (when it had overcome the tempting tree) must also enter into the first death of the strong [fierce] wrath in the death, and overcome the first Principle.

[1] Or serpent.

12. For he stood forty days in the temptation in the wilderness, where there was no bread nor drink,

then came the tempter, and would have brought him from obedience, and said, *He should out of the stones make bread*; which was nothing else, but that he should leave the heavenly bread (which man receiveth in faith and in a strong confidence in God), and put his imagination into the spirit of this world, and live therein.

13. But when the child of the virgin laid the heavenly bread before him, and said, Man liveth not only ¹from this world, ¹from the earthly eating and drinking, then came the second way [or kind] of temptation forth, *viz.* the might [power, dominion, and authority] of this world; the prince of the wrath [or strong fierceness] would give him all the power of the stars and elements, if he would put his imagination into him, and pray to [or worship] him. That was the right scourge [or whip] wherewith *Adam* was ²scourged, [*viz.*] with the might, riches, and beauty of this world, after which at last *Adam* lusted, and was taken; but the child of the virgin laid before him that the kingdom was not his, [*viz.*] belonging to the prince of the [fierce, strong] wrath, but [it belonged] to the Word and Heart of God; he must worship God, and serve him only.

14. The third temptation was the same into which the devil also was fallen, ³with high-mindedness [or pride], when he [Christ] was tempted to have flien from above, from the pinnacle of the temple, and should have elevated himself above humility and

¹ Or by, or of.

² Or driven on with.

³ Or out of.

meekness; for the meekness maketh the angry Father, in the originalness, soft and joyful, so that the Deity [thus] becometh a soft and pleasant essence.

15. But lord Lucifer would (in the creation) have fain been above the meekness of the Heart of God, above the end of nature; therefore he would fain also have persuaded the son of the virgin to fly without wings, above the end of nature, in pride; of which shall be handled in its due place at large. I have brought this in thus, but in brief, that my writing may be the better understood, and how it stands with [or upon] the ground [or foundation] of the Scripture, and is not any new thing, neither shall there be any thing new [in them], but only the true knowledge, in the Holy Ghost, of the essence of all essences.

Of Adam's *Sleep*

16. *Adam* had not eaten of the fruit before his sleep, till his wife was created out of him; only his essences and inclination had eaten of it in the spirit by the imagination, and not in the mouth; and thereupon the spirit of the great world captivated him, and mightily [1]qualified in him [or infected him]. [1] Or wrought upon him. And then instantly the sun and stars wrestled with him, and all the four elements wrestled so mightily and powerfully, that they overcame him; and [so] he sank down into a sleep.

17. Now to an understanding man it is very easy

to be found and known, that there neither was, nor should be any sleep in *Adam*, when he was in the image of God. For *Adam* was such an image as we shall be at the resurrection of the dead, where we shall have no need of the elements, nor of the sun, nor stars, also [of] no sleep, but our eyes shall be always open eternally, beholding the glory of God, [1] from whence will be our meat and drink; and the centre in the [2] multiplicity, or springing up of the birth, affordeth mere delight and joy; for God will bring forth out of the earth into the kingdom of heaven no other [kind of] man, than [such a one] as the first [was] before the fall; for he was created out of the eternal will of God; that [will] is unchangeable, and must stand; therefore consider these things deeply.

_{[1] Or which will be.}
_{[2] Or propagation.}

18. O thou dear soul, that swimmest in a dark [3] lake, incline thy mind to the gate of heaven, and behold what the fall of *Adam* hath been, which God did so greatly loathe, that [because of it] *Adam* could not continue in paradise : behold and consider the sleep, and so you shall find it all. Sleep is nothing else but [4] an overcoming; for the sun and the stars are still in a mighty strife, and the element of water, [*viz.*] the matrix, is too weak for the fire and the stars, for that [element] is the [being] overcome in the centre of nature, as you find before in many places.

[3] Or bath.

[4] Or a being overcome.

19. And the light of the sun is as it were a god in the nature of this world, and by its virtue ⌈and

influence] it continually kindleth the stars [or constellations], whereby the stars [or constellations] (which are of a very terrible and anguishing essence) continually exult in triumph very joyfully. For it [the sun] is an essence like the light of God, which kindleth and enlighteneth the dark mind of the Father, from whence, by the light, there ariseth the divine joy in the Father.

20. And so it [the sun] maketh a triumphing, or rising [to be] in the [1] matrix of the water, always like a [2] seething; for the stars altogether cast their virtue [or influence] into the matrix of the water, as [3] being therein; in like manner also now the matrix of the water is continually seething and rising, from whence cometh the [4] growing in trees, plants, grass, and beasts. For the uppermost regimen [or dominion] of the sun and stars, and also of the elements, ruleth in all creatures, and it is a blossom or bud from them, and without their power, there would be in this world, in the third Principle, no life, nor mobility, in any manner of thing, nothing excepted.

[1] root or mother.
[2] Or boiling.
[3] the stars being in the matrix.
[4] vegetation.

21. But the living creatures, as men, beasts, and fowls, have the tincture in them, for in the beginning they were an extraction [taken] from the quality of the stars and elements by the *Fiat*. And in the tincture [there] standeth the continual kindling fire, which continually draweth the virtue or *oleum* [the oil] out of the water; from whence cometh the blood, in which the noble life [5] standeth.

[5] Or is.

22. Now the sun and the stars [or constellations] continually kindle the tincture, for it is fiery; and the tincture kindleth the body, with the matrix of the water, so that they are always boiling [rising] and seething. The stars [or constellations] and the sun are the fire of the tincture, and the tincture is the fire of the body, and so all are seething. And therefore when the sun is underneath, so that its beams [or shining] is no more [upon a thing], then the tincture is weaker, for it hath no kindling from the virtue of the sun. And although the virtue of the stars and the quality are kindled from the sun, yet all is too little, and so it becometh feeble [or as it were dead]. And when the tincture is feeble, then the virtue in the blood (which is the tincture) is wholly weak, and sinketh into a sweet rest, as it were dead or overcome.

23. But now in the tincture only is the understanding, which governeth the mind, and maketh the [thoughts or] senses; therefore all is as it were dead, and the constellation now only ruleth in the root of the first Principle, where the Deity, like a glance [lustre] or virtue, worketh in all things: There the starry spirit in the glance of the glass of the divine virtue in the element of fire looketh into the matrix of the water, and setteth his jaws open after the tincture, but that is void of power; and therefore he taketh the virtue of the tincture (*viz.* the mind) and mingleth [or qualifieth] with it, and then the mind sealeth the elements, and

worketh therein dreams and [1]visions, all according [1] representations.
to the virtue of the stars; for [2]it standeth in the [2] the mind consisteth.
working and quality of the stars; and these are the
dreams and visions of the night in the sleep.

The Gate of the highest Depth of the Life of the Tincture.

24. Though the doctor, it may be, knoweth what the tincture is, yet the simple and unlearned do not, who many times (if they had the art) have better gifts and understanding than the doctor, therefore I write for those that seek; though indeed I hold, that neither the doctor, nor the alchemist, hath the ground of the tincture, unless he be born again in the spirit; such a one seeth through all, whether he be learned or unlearned; with God the peasant is as acceptable as the doctor.

25. The tincture is a thing that separateth, and bringeth the pure and clear from the impure; and that bringeth the life of all sorts of spirits, or all sorts of essences, into its highest [pitch] degree [or exaltation]. Yea it is the cause of the shining, or of the lustre: It is a cause that all creatures see and live. But its form is not one and the same [in every thing]; it is not in a beast, as in man; so also it is different in stones and herbs; although it is truly in all things, yet in some things strong, and in some weak.

26. But if we search what it is in essence and property, and how it is generated, then we find a

very worthy [precious] noble ¹substance in its
birth, for it is come forth from the virtue, and the
fountain of the Deity, which hath imprinted ²itself
in all things. And therefore it is so secret and
hidden, and is imparted to the knowledge of none
of the ungodly, to find it, or to know it. And
although it be there, yet a vain, false [or evil] mind
is not worthy of it, and therefore it remaineth
hidden to him : And God ruleth all in all incomprehensibly and imperceptibly to the creature ; the
creature passeth away it knoweth not how ; and
the shadow and the figure of the tincture continueth eternally ; for it is generated out of the
eternal will : But the spirit is given to it by the
Fiat, according to the kind of every creature ; also
in the beginning of the creation it was implanted
and incorporated in jewels, stones, and metals,
according to the kind of every one.

27. It was from eternity in God, and therefore
it is eternally in God. But when God would create
a similitude of his essence, and that it should be
generated out of the darkness, then it stood in the
flash of fire that went forth, in the place where
the fifth form of the birth of love generateth itself
in the similitude. For it was generated out of
the fountain of the will, out of the Heart of God,
and therefore its shadow continueth in the will of
God eternally ; and for the sake thereof also the
shadow of all creatures, and of every [essence]
substance [or thing], which was ever generated

in the similitude, remaineth eternally; for it is
the similitude of God, which is generated out of the
eternal will; yet its spirit continueth not eternally
in the third Principle of this world; that ceaseth,
or passeth away with the ceasing of the springing,
or the ceasing of the life.

28. For all whatsoever liveth in the third
Principle, corrupteth [or passeth away], and goeth
into its ether and end, till [it cometh] to the figure
of the tincture; and that continueth standing
eternally as a shadow or will, without spirit or
mobility: But in the second Principle the tincture
continueth eternally standing in the spirit, and in
the substance [or essence], all very powerfully, *viz.*
in angels and men, as also in the beginning [or
first springing] of every substance; for their centre
to the birth is eternally fixed [or stedfast].

Of its [the Tincture's] Essences and Property.
The deep Gate of Life.

29. Its essence is the flash in the circle [or
circumference] of the springing of the life, which
in the water maketh the glance and shining; and
its root is the fire; and the stock is the [sour]
harshness. Now the flash separateth the bitterness
and harshness from the water; so that the water
becometh soft [fluid], and clear, wherein then the
[1] sight of all creatures doth consist, so that the [1] Or faculty
of seeing.
spirit in the flash in the matrix of the water doth
see; and the flash standeth therein like a glance

14

¹ fulfilleth or satisfieth.

[or lustre], and ¹filleth the spirit of the essences; from which the essence draweth vehemently to itself; for it is the [sour] harshness, and the flash continually separateth the darkness from the light, and the impure from the pure; and there now standeth the divine virtue [or power]: And the divine glance continually imagineth [or imprinteth] itself in the pure, from which the [sour] strong [property] is separated out from nature; and the divine glance maketh the pure sweet; for it mingleth itself [or infecteth] there.

30. But the sweetness is like oil or fire, wherein the flash continually kindleth itself, so that it shineth: But the oil being sweet, and mingled with the matrix of the water, therefore the shining light is steady [constant and fixed] and ²sweet: But being it cannot, in the nature of the water, continue to be an oil only (because of the infection of the water) therefore it becometh thick; and the [nature or] kind of the fire coloureth it red; and this is the blood and the tincture in a creature, wherein the noble life standeth.

² pleasant.

Of the Death and of the Dying.
The Gate of Affliction and of Misery.

31. Thus the noble life in the tincture standeth in great danger, and hath hourly to expect the [corruption, or destruction, breaking, or] dissolution; for as soon as the blood (wherein the spirit liveth) floweth out [or passeth away] the essence

[breaketh or] dissolveth, and the tincture flieth away like a glance or shadow; and then the source [or springing up] of the fire is out, and the body becometh stiff.

32. But alas! the life hath many greater and more powerful enemies; especially the four elements and the constellations [or stars]. As soon as [any] one element becometh too strong, the tincture flieth from it, and then the life hath its end: If it be overwhelmed with water, it groweth cold, and the fire goeth out, then the flash flieth away like a glance or shadow: If it be overwhelmed with earth, *viz.* with impure matter, then the flash groweth dark, and flieth away: If it be overwhelmed with air, that it be stopped, then the tincture is stifled, and the springing essences, and the flash breaketh into a glance, and goeth into its ether. But if it be overwhelmed with fire or heat, the flash is enflamed, and burneth up the tincture, from whence the blood becometh dark, and swarthy, or black, and the flash goeth out in the meekness.

33. O how many enemies hath the life among the constellations [or stars], which qualify [or mingle their influence] with the tincture and elements. When the planets and the stars have their conjunctions, and where they cast their poisonous rays into the tincture, there ariseth in the life of the meek tincture, stinging, tearing, and torturing. For the sweet [or pleasant] tincture (being a sweet and pleasing refreshment) cannot

endure any impure thing. And therefore when such poisonous rays are darted into it, then it resisteth and continually cleanseth itself; but as soon as it is overwhelmed, that it is darkened, then the flash goeth out, the life breaketh, and the body falleth away, and becometh a cadaver, carcase [or dead corpse]; for the spirit is the life.

34. This I have here shewn very briefly and summarily, and not according to all the circumstances, that it might thereby be somewhat understood [by the way, what] the life [is]. In its due place all shall be expounded at large, for herein is very much contained, and there might be great volumes written of it; but I have set down only this, that the overcoming and the sleep might be apprehended.

The Gate [or Exposition] of the heavenly Tincture, how it was in Adam before the Fall, and how it shall be in us after this Life.

35. Great and mighty are these secrets, and he that seeketh and findeth them, hath surpassing joy therein; for they are the true heavenly bread for the soul. If we consider and receive the knowledge of the heavenly tincture, then there riseth up the knowledge of the divine kingdom of joy, so that we wish to be loosed from the vanity, and to live in this birth; which yet cannot be, but we must finish our day's work.

36. Reason saith: Alas! If *Adam* had not

lusted, he had not fallen asleep : if I had been as he I would have stood firm, and have continued in paradise.   Yes, beloved reason, you have hit the matter well, in thinking so well of thyself!   I will shew thee thy strength, and the gate ; and do but thou consider how firm thou shouldst stand, if thou didst stand as *Adam* did before the tempting tree.

37. Behold, I give you a true similitude : Suppose that thou wast a young man, or young maid [or virgin] (as *Adam* was both of them in one [only] person), how dost thou think thou shouldst stand?   Suppose thus, set a young man of good complexion, beautiful, and virtuous ; and also a fair chaste modest virgin [or young maid], curiously featured, and put them together ; and let them not only come to speak together, and converse lovingly one with another, but so that they may also embrace one another ; and command them not to fall in love together, not so much as in the least thought, also not to have any inclination to it, much less any infection in the will ; and let these two be thus together forty days and forty nights, and converse with one another in mere joy ; and command them further, that they keep their will and mind stedfast and never [1] conceive one thought to desire one another and not to infect [themselves] with any essence or property at all, but that their will and inclination be most stedfast and firm to the command ; and

[1] Or propose in thought.

that the young man shall will [and purpose] never to copulate with this, nor any other maid [or virgin]; and in like manner the maid [or virgin] be enjoined the same. Now, thou reason, full of misery, defects, and infirmities, how do you think you should possibly stand here? Would you not promise fair with *Adam*? But you would not be able to perform it.

38. Thus, my beloved reason, I have set a gloss before you, and thus it was with *Adam*. God had created his work wisely and good, and extracted the one out of the other. The first ground was himself, out of which he created the world, and out of the world [he created] man, to whom he gave his spirit, and intimated to him, that without wavering or any other desire, he should live in him most perfectly.

39. But now man had also the spirit of this world, for he was [come] out of this world, and lived in the world: And *Adam* (understand the spirit which was breathed into him from God) was the chaste virgin; and the spirit which he had inherited out of nature, from the world, was the young man. These were now both together, and rested in one arm.

40. Now the chaste virgin ought to be bent into the Heart of God, and to have no imagination to lust after the beauty of the comely young man; but yet the young man was kindled with love towards the virgin, and he desired to copulate with

her; for he said, Thou art my dearest spouse [or bride], my paradise, and garland of roses, let me into thy paradise : I will be impregnated in thee, that I may get thy essence, and enjoy thy pleasant love; how willingly would I taste of the friendly sweetness of thy virtue [or power]! If I might but receive thy glorious light, how full of joy should I be!

41. And the chaste virgin said, Thou art indeed my bridegroom and my companion, but thou hast not my ornament; my pearl is more [1] precious than thou, my virtue [or power] is incorruptible [or unfadeable], and my mind is constant [or stedfast]; thou hast an inconstant mind, and thy virtue is corruptible [or brittle]. Dwell in my [2] court, and I will entertain thee friendly, and do thee much good : I will adorn thee with my ornaments, and I will put my garment on thee; but I will not give thee my pearl, for thou art dark, and that is shining and bright.

42. Then said the spirit of nature (*viz.* the young man), My fair pearl and chastity, I pray thee let me enjoy thy comfort, if thou wilt not copulate with me, that I may impregnate in thee, yet do but enclose thy pearl in my heart, that I may have it for my own. Art thou not my golden crown? How fain would I taste of thy fruit.

43. Then the [3] chaste spirit out of God in *Adam* (*viz.* the virgin) said, My dear love, and my companion; I plainly see thy lust, thou wouldst fain

[1] costly.

[2] As in the outward court of the temple.

[3] Or modest.

copulate with me; but I am a virgin, and thou a man; thou wouldst defile my pearl, and destroy my crown; and besides, thou wouldst mingle thy sourness with my sweetness, and darken my bright light; therefore I will not [do so]. I will lend thee my pearl, and adorn thee with my garment, ¹into thy own but I will not give it to be ¹ thy own.

¹ into thy own disposing.

44. And the companion (*viz.* the spirit of the world in *Adam*) said, I will not leave thee, and if thou wilt not let me copulate with thee, then I will ² Or might. take my innermost and strongest ² force, and use thee according to my will, according to the innermost ² power; I will clothe thee with the power of the sun, stars, and elements; wherein none will know thee, [and so] thou must be mine eternally: And although (as thou sayest) I am inconstant, and that my virtue is not like to thine, and my light not like thine, yet I will keep thee well enough in ³ at my my treasure, and thou must be ³ my own.

³ at my disposal.

45. Then said the virgin, Why wilt thou use ⁴ Or force. ⁴ violence? Am I not thy ornament, and thy crown? I am bright, and thou art dark; behold, if thou coverest me, then thou hast no glance [or lustre]; and [then] thou art a dark [dusky or black] worm: And [then] how can I dwell with thee? Let me alone; I [will] not give myself to be thy own: I will give thee my ornament, and thou shalt live in my joy, thou shalt eat of my fruit, and taste ⁵ Or mingle. my sweetness; but thou canst not ⁵ qualify with me; for the divine virtue is my essence, therein is

my fair [or orient] pearl, and my bright [shining] light generated; my fountain is eternal: If thou darkenest my light, and defilest my garment, then thou wilt have no beauty [or lustre], and canst not subsist, but thy worm will [corrupt or] destroy thee, and so I shall lose my companion, which I had chosen for my bridegroom, with whom I meant to have rejoiced; and then my pearl and beauty would have no [1] company: Seeing I have given [1 recreation or delight.] myself to be thy companion for my joy's sake; if thou wilt not enjoy my beauty, yet pray continue in my ornament and excellency, and dwell with me in joy, I will adorn thee eternally.

46. And the young man said, Thy ornament is mine already, I [will] use thee according to my will; in that thou sayest I shall be broken (corrupted or destroyed), yet my worm is eternal, I will rule with that; and yet I will dwell in thee, and clothe thee with my garments.

47. And here the virgin turned her to the Heart of God, and said, My heart and my beloved, thou art my virtue, from thee I am clear and bright, from thy root I am generated from eternity; deliver me from the worm of darkness which infecteth [poisoneth] and tempteth my bridegroom, and let me not be darkened in the obscurity; I am thy ornament, and am come that thou shouldst have joy in me: Wherefore then shall I stand with my bridegroom in the dark? And the divine answer said, *The seed of the woman shall break*

the head of the serpent, or worm ; *and thou shalt*, etc.

48. Behold, dear soul, herein lieth the heavenly tincture, which we must set down in a similitude, and we cannot at all express it with words.   Indeed, if we had the [1]tongue of angels, we could then rightly express what the mind apprehendeth ; but the pearl is clothed [covered or veiled] with a dark [cloak or] garment : The virgin calleth stedfastly to the [2]Heart of God, that he would deliver her companion from the dark worm ; but the divine answer [3]still is, *The seed of the woman shall break the serpent's head* ; that is, the darkness of the serpent shall be separated from thy bridegroom ; the dark garment wherewith the serpent clotheth thy bridegroom, and darkeneth thy pearl and beauteous crown, shall be broken [corrupted or destroyed], and turn to earth ; and thou shalt rejoice with thy bridegroom in me ; this was my eternal [4]will, it must stand.

49. Now then when we consider the high mysteries, the spirit openeth to us the understanding, that this [afore-mentioned] is the true ground concerning *Adam* : For his original spirit (*viz.* the soul) that was the worm, which was generated out of the eternal will of God the Father, and in the time of the creation was by the *Fiat* (after the manner of a spirit) created out of that place where the Father from eternity generateth his Heart, between the fourth and the fifth forms in the centre

[1] angelical tongues.

[2] the Son of God.

[3] standeth.

[4] Or purpose.

of God, where the light of God from eternity discovereth itself, and taketh its beginning, and therefore the light of God came thus to help him, as a fair virgin, and took the soul to be her bridegroom, and would adorn the soul with her fair heavenly crown, with the noble virtue of the pearl, and beautify it with her garment.

50. Then the fourth form in the centre of the soul brake forth, there where the spirit of the soul was created, [*viz.*] between the fourth and the fifth forms in the centre, [1] near the Heart of God; and [1] next to. so the fourth form was in the glance in the darkness, out of which the world was created, which in its form parteth itself in its centre into five parts in its rising, till [it attain] to the light of the sun. For the stars also in their centre are generated betwixt the fourth and the fifth forms, and the sun is the [2] spring of the fifth form in the centre; as in [2] Or fountain. the eternal centre, the Heart and light of God [is], which hath no ground; but this [centre] of the stars and elements hath its ground in the fourth form in the dark mind, in the rising up of the awakened [or kindled] flash of the fire.

51. Thus the soul is generated between both the centres, between the centre of God (understand [between the centre] of the Heart or light of God, where it is generated out of an eternal place), and also between the [propagated or] out-sprung centre of this world; and it [the soul] hath its beginning from both, and qualifieth with both; and therefore

thus it hath all three Principles, and can live in all three.

52. But it was the law and will of the virgin, that as God ruleth over all things, and [1]imprinteth himself everywhere, and giveth virtue and life to all, and yet the thing comprehendeth him not, although he be certainly there; so also should the soul [2]stand still, and the form of the virgin should govern in the soul, and crown it with the divine light; the soul should be the comely young man which was created, and the virtue [or power] of God [should be] the fair virgin; and the light of God [should be] the fair [orient] pearl and crown, wherewith the virgin would adorn the young man.

53. But the young man desired to have the virgin to be his own, which could not be, because she was a degree higher in the birth than he; for the virgin was from eternity, and the bridegroom was given to her, that she should have joy and delight with him in God.

54. But now when the young man could not obtain this of the virgin, then he reached back after the worm in his own centre. For the form of this world pressed very powerfully upon him, which also was in the soul, and [this form] would fain have had the virgin to be its own, that he might make her his [3]wife (as was done in the fall; yet the wife was not from the pearl, but out of the spirit of this world); for it (viz. the nature of this world) continually groaneth [or longeth] after the virgin,

[1] mouldeth, or imageth.

[2] Or have continued in true resignation.

[3] Or woman.

that it might be delivered from vanity; and it meaneth to qualify [or mingle] with the virgin; but that cannot be, for the virgin is of a higher [1] birth.

[1] Or descent.

55. And yet when this world shall break in pieces, and be delivered from the vanity of the worm, it shall not obtain the virgin; but [2] it must continue without spirit and [3] worm, under its own shadow, in a fair and sweet rest, without any wrestling [struggling] or desiring: For thereby it cometh into its highest degree and beauty, and ceaseth [or resteth] eternally from its labour. For the worm which here tormenteth it, goeth into its own Principle, and no more toucheth the shadow nor the figure of this world to eternity, and then the virgin governeth with her bridegroom.

[2] this world.

[3] Or soul.

56. My beloved Reader, I will set it you down more plainly; for every one hath not the [4] Pearl, to apprehend the virgin; and yet every one would fain know how the fall of *Adam* was. Behold, as I mentioned just now, the soul hath all the three Principles in it; *viz.* the most inward, [which is] the worm or brimstone-spirit and the source according to which it is a spirit; and then [it hath] the divine virtue, which maketh the worm meek, bright, and joyful, according to which the worm or spirit is an angel, like God the Father himself (understand, in such a manner and birth); and then also it hath the Principle of this world; wholly undivided in one another, and yet none [of

[4] Or the light of the wisdom.

the three Principles] comprehendeth the other, for they are three Principles, or three births.

57. Behold, the worm is the eternal, and in itself peculiarly [a Principle], the other two [Principles] are given to it, each by a birth; the one to the right, the other to the left. Now it is possible for it to lose both the forms and births that are given to it; for if it reach back into the strong [or tart power, or] might of the fire, and become false to the virgin, then she departeth from it, and [she] continueth as a figure in the centre, and then the door of the [1] virgin is shut.

[1] Or Wisdom of God.

58. Now if thou wilt [turn] to the virgin again, then thou must be born anew through the water in the centre, and [through] the Holy Ghost; and then thou shalt receive her again with greater honour and joy; of which Christ said, *There will be more joy in heaven for one sinner that repenteth, than for ninety and nine righteous, who need no repentance*; so very gloriously is the poor sinner received again of the virgin, that [2] it must no more be a shadow, but a living and understanding creature, and [an] angel of God. This joy none can express, only a regenerate soul knoweth it; which the body understandeth not; but it trembleth, and knoweth not what is done to it.

[2] the converted soul.

59. These two forms, or Principles, the worm loseth at the departing of the body; although indeed it continueth in the figure, which yet is but of a serpent, and it is a [3] torment to it, that it was

[3] Or gnawing.

an angel, and is now a horrible fierce poisonous worm and spirit; of which the Scripture saith, *That the worm of the wicked dieth not, and their plague* [torment or source] *continueth eternally.* If the worm had had no angelical and human form, then its source [torment or plague] would not have been so great; but that causeth it to have an eternal anxious desire, and yet it can attain nothing; it knoweth the shadow of the glory [it had], and can never more live therein.

60. This therefore in brief is the ground of what can be spoken of the fall of *Adam*, in the highest depth. *Adam* hath lost the [1]virgin by his lust, and hath received the [2]woman in his lust, which is a [3]cagastrish person, and the virgin waiteth still continually for him [to see] whether he will step again into the new birth, and then she will receive him again with great glory. Therefore, thou child of man, consider thyself; I write here what I certainly know, and he that hath seen it witnesseth it; or else I also should not have known it.

[1] Divine Wisdom.
[2] Or wife.
[3] Subject to corruption, and mingled with it.

THE THIRTEENTH CHAPTER

Of the Creating of the Woman out of Adam.

The fleshly, miserable, and dark Gate.

1. I CAN scarce write for grief, but seeing it cannot be otherwise, therefore we will for a while wear the garment of the woman, but yet live in the virgin; and although we receive [or suffer] much affliction in the [garment of the] woman, yet the virgin will recompense it well enough. And thus we must be [1] bound with the [2] woman till we send her to the grave, and then she shall be a shadow and a figure; and the virgin shall be our bride and precious crown. She will give us her [3] pearl and crown, and clothe us with her ornaments, for which we will give the venture for the lily's sake. And though we shall raise a great storm, and though Antichrist tear away the woman from us, yet the virgin must continue with us, because we are married to her; let every one take its own, and then I shall have that which is mine.

[1] *Schleppen,* begirt, surrounded.

[2] With fragility, or with the earthly tabernacle.

[3] The divine brightness.

2. Now when *Adam* was thus in the Garden of *Eden,* and the three Principles having produced such a strife in him, his tincture was quite wearied,

and the virgin departed. For the lust - spirit in *Adam* had overcome, and therefore he sank down into a sleep. The same hour his heavenly body became flesh and blood, and his strong virtue [or power] became bones ; and then the virgin went into her ether and shadow, yet into the heavenly ether, into the principle of the virtue [or power], and there waiteth upon all the children of *Adam*, [expecting] whether any will receive her for their bride again, by the [1] new birth.   [1] regeneration.

3. But what now was God to do? He had created *Adam* out of his eternal will ; and because it could not now be, that *Adam* should generate out of himself the virgin in a paradisical manner, therefore God put the *Fiat* of the great world into the midst. For *Adam* was now fallen [2] home again [2] Or into the bosom of the *Fiat*. to the *Fiat* as a half broken person. Now therefore seeing he was half killed by his own lust and imagination, that he might live, God must help him again ; and if he be now to generate a kingdom, then there must be a woman, as all other beasts [have a female] for propagation : The angelical kingdom in *Adam* was gone ; therefore now there must be [3] a kingdom of this world.   [3] Or a propagated generation.

4. Then what was it that God now did with *Adam*? *Moses* saith, *When Adam slept, he took one of his ribs and* [made or] *built a woman of it,* (viz. of the rib which he took from man), *and closed up the place with flesh.* Now *Moses* hath written very rightly : But who is it that can understand

15

him here? If I did not know the first *Adam* in his virgin-like form in paradise, then I had been at a stand, and should have known no other than that *Adam* had been made flesh and blood of a lump of earth, and his wife *Eve* of his rib and hard bones; which before the time [of my knowledge] hath oft seemed very strange and wonderful to my thoughts, when I have read the [1]glosses upon *Moses*, that so [high or] deep learned men should write so of it: [2]Some of them will dare to tell of a pit in the [orient or] east country, out of which *Adam* should be taken and made as a potter maketh a vessel or pot.

[1] expositions, and marginal notes.

[2] *Damascenus.*

5. If I had not considered the Scripture, which plainly saith, *Whatsoever is born of flesh is flesh*; also, *Flesh and blood shall not inherit the kingdom of heaven*; also, *None goeth into heaven but the Son of Man* (viz. the pure virgin) *which came from heaven, and which is in heaven*; which was very helpful to me [to think] that the child of the virgin was the angel, which has restored again all that which was lost in *Adam*, for God brought again in the woman (in her virgin-like body) the virgin child, which *Adam* should generate. And now if I had not considered the text in *Moses*, (where God saith, *It is not good that man should be alone, we will make a help for him*), I should yet have stuck in the [3]will of the woman.

[3] Or in the earthly thoughts.

6. But that text saith, *God looked upon all that he had made, and behold, it was all very good*:

Now if it were good in the creation, then it must needs have become evil when God said [afterwards], *It is not good for man to be alone.* If God would have had them like all beasts to have a bestial propagation, he would at one and the same instant [at first] have made a man and a woman. But that God did abominate [the bestial propagation] it appeared plainly in the first child of the woman, *Cain,* the murderer of his brother, also the fruit [or the curse] of the earth sheweth it plainly enough. But what shall I spend the time for, with these testimonies? The proof of it will clearly follow. And it is to be proved, not only in the Scripture, which yet maketh a cover [over it], but in all things, if we would take time to do it, and not spend our labour about vain and unprofitable things.

7. Now thus saith reason: What are then the words of *Moses* concerning the woman? To which I say: *Moses* hath written rightly, but I (living thus [1] in the woman) understand it not rightly. *Moses* indeed had a brightened [or glorified face or] countenance, but he must hang a veil before it, so that none could see his face. But when the [2] Son of the Virgin, *viz.* the virgin [wisdom] came, he looked him in the face, and put the veil away.

[1] In the divided transitoriness.

[2] the eternal Wisdom of the Father.

8. Then reason asketh: What was the rib [taken] out of *Adam* to be [made] a woman? The gate of the depth: Behold, the virgin sheweth us this, that when *Adam* was overcome, and the virgin passed

into her ether, then the tincture (wherein the fair virgin had dwelt) became earthy, weary, feeble and weak; for the powerful root of the tincture, from whence it had its potency without any sleep or rest (*viz.* the heavenly matrix, which [1] containeth paradise and the kingdom of heaven) withdrew in *Adam*, and went into its [2] ether.

[1] Or is the foundation of.

[2] air or receptacle.

9. Reader, understand [and consider] it aright: the Deity (*viz.* the fair virgin) is not [3] destroyed and come to nothing; that cannot be; only, she is remaining in the divine Principle; and the spirit, or the soul of *Adam*, is, with its own proper worm, remaining in the third Principle of this world: But the virgin, *viz.* the divine virtue [or power] standeth in heaven, and in paradise, and beholdeth herself in the earthly quality of the soul, *viz.* [4] in the sun, and not in the moon; understand, in the highest point of the spirit of this world, where the tincture is noblest and most clear, from whence the mind of man doth exist.

[3] broken.

[4] In the heavenly, and not in the earthly part thereof.

10. And she would fain return again into her place to her bridegroom, if the earthly flesh, with the earthly mind and senses [or thoughts did not hinder, or] were not in the way, for the virgin doth not go into them, she will not be bound [to, or] in the earthly centre; she finisheth the whole time (while the woman liveth in her stead) of her speculation with longing and much calling, admonishing and hearty seeking: But [to] the regenerate she appeareth in a high triumphing

manner, in the centre of the mind ; [she] also often diveth into the tincture of the blood of the heart, whereby the body, with the mind and senses, cometh to tremble and triumph so highly, as if it were in paradise ; it also presently getteth a paradisical will.

11. And there the noble grain of mustard-seed is sown, of which Christ saith, *That it is at first small, and afterwards groweth to be like a great tree* ; so far [or so long] as the mind persevereth in the will. But the noble virgin stayeth not continually, for her birth is [of a] higher [descent] ; and therefore she dwelleth not in earthly vessels ; but she sometimes visiteth her bridegroom at a time when he is desirous of her ; although she always with observancy preventeth and calleth him, before he [calleth] her : which is only understood in the lily. This the spirit speaketh in a high and worthy seriousness, therefore observe it, ye children of God, the angel of the Great Council cometh in the valley of *Jehosaphat* with a golden charter, which he selleth for oil without money ; whosoever cometh shall have it.

12. Now when the tincture was become thus earthy and feeble, by the overcoming of the spirit of the great world, then it could not generate [in a] heavenly [manner], and was also possessed with inability ; and then the counsel of God stood there, and said : Seeing he is become earthly, and is not able [to propagate], we will make a help for him ;

and the *Fiat* stood in the centre, and severed the matrix from the *limbus*: And the *Fiat* took a rib in the midst of *Adam*, out of his right side, and created a woman out of it.

13. But you must clearly understand [or conceive], that when the *Fiat* to the creating [of the woman] was in *Adam*, in his sleep, his body had not then such hard gristles and bones : O no; that came to pass first when mother *Eve* did bite the apple, and also gave to *Adam*; only the infection and the earthly death, with the fainting and mortal sickness, stuck in them ; the bones and ribs were yet strength and virtue, from which the ribs should come to be.

14. But you must highly and worthily understand [and consider] how it was taken out [of his side], not as a spirit, but wholly in substance : Thus it may be said, that *Adam* did get a rent ; and the woman beareth *Adam's* spirit, flesh and bones. Yet there is some difference in the spirit ; for the woman beareth the matrix, and *Adam* the *limbus* or man ; and they two are one flesh, undivided in nature, for now they two together must generate one man again, which one alone could do before.

A pleasant Gate.

15. We being here in describing the corruptibility of *Adam*, the spirit frameth in our thoughts a heavenly mystery, concerning *Adam's* rib, which

the *Fiat* took from him, and made a woman of it; which [rib] *Adam* afterwards must want; for the text in *Moses* rightly saith, *God closed up the place with flesh.*

16. But now the [1] wrath of the serpent hath so brought it to pass, that *Adam* is fallen in the lust, and yet the purpose of God must stand; for [2] *Adam* must rise again at the day of the resurrection wholly and unbroken in the first image, as he was created. So likewise the serpent and the devil have brought it about, that so terrible a rent is made in him.

17. Wherefore the spirit sheweth us, that as little as the worm or spirit of the soul could be helped, except that the virgin came, and did go into death in the worm in the abyss of the spirit of the soul (which in its own abyss reacheth the gate of hell and the fierce anger of God) and regenerate [3] him anew, and make him a new creature in the first image, which is done in the Son of the Virgin, in Christ; so little also could *Adam's* rib, and his hollow side, where it stood, be helped [healed] or brought to perfection, except that the second *Adam* (Christ) suffer himself in the virgin to be wounded [pierced or cut] in the same place, that his precious blood might come to help the first *Adam*, and repair his broken side again; this, of high and precious worth, we speak according to our knowledge; which when we shall write of the suffering and death of Christ the Son of the virgin,

[1] the malice or fierce rage.

[2] mankind.

[3] *Adam.*

we will so clear it, that thou, O thirsty soul, shalt find a living fountain, which shall be little beneficial to the devil.

Further concerning the Woman.

18. Reason asketh: Is *Eve* merely created out of the rib [taken] out of *Adam*? Then she should be far inferior to *Adam*. No, beloved reason, it is not so; the *Fiat* (being a sharp attracting) took from *Adam* of all essences and properties of every virtue, but it took from him no more members in substance; for the image should be a man, after a masculine kind in the *limbus*, yet not at all with this deformity. Understand it rightly in the ground, he should be (and he was also) a man, and he had a virgin-like heart, wholly chaste in the matrix.

19. Therefore *Eve* was for certain created out of all *Adam's* essences, and so *Adam* thereupon had a great rent, and so likewise the woman might come to her perfection to [be] the image of God; and this again sheweth a great mystery, whereby the virgin very preciously witnesseth again, that the Son of the Virgin hath not only suffered his side to be pierced through, and shed his blood out of the hole of his side, but he hath also suffered his hands and feet to be struck through, and a crown of thorns to be pressed upon his head, so that the blood gushed out from thence; and in his body he endured to be whipped, so that his blood ran

down all over. So very lowly hath the Son of the Virgin debased himself, to [1]help the sick and broken *Adam*, and his weak and imperfect *Eve*, to repair them and bring them again into the first glory.

[1 to heal.]

20. Therefore you must know for certain, that *Eve* was created out of all *Adam's* essences. But there were no more ribs nor members broken from *Adam* ; which appeareth by the feebleness and weakness of the woman, and also by the command of God, who said, *Thy will shall be in subjection under thy man* [or husband], *and he shall be thy lord* [or ruler]. Because the man is whole and perfect, except a rib, therefore the woman is a help for him, and must help him to do his work in humility and subjection ; and the man must know that she is very weak, being out of his essences ; he must help her in her weakness, and love her as his own essences : In like manner the woman must put her essences and will into [the essences and will of] the man, and be friendly towards her man [or husband] ; that the man may take delight in his own essences in the woman ; and that they two might be but one only will. For they are one flesh, one bone, one heart, and generate children in one [only] will, which are neither the man's nor the woman's alone, but of both together, as if they were from one only body. And therefore the severe commandment of God is set before the children, that they should with earnestness and

subjection honour their father and mother, upon pain of temporary and eternal punishment: [1] Of which I will write concerning the Tables of *Moses*.

[1] *Note, the Author lived not so long to perform his purpose upon the Book of Exodus.*

Concerning the Propagating of the Soul.
The Noble Gate.

21. The mind hath from the beginning of the world had so very much to do about this gate, and hath continually so searched therein, that I cannot reckon the wearisome heap of writers [about it]. But in the time of the lily this gate shall flourish as a bay-tree [or laurel-tree]; for its branches will get sap from the virgin, and therefore will be greener than [2] grass, and whiter than the [whitest] roses, and the virgin will bear the pleasant smell thereof upon her pearly garland, and it will reach into the paradise of God.

[2] *Klee. Trifolium.*

22. Seeing then the mystery presenteth itself to us, therefore we will open the blossom of the sprout: Yet we would not have our labour given to the wolves, dogs, or swine, which root in our garden of delight, like [wild] boars, but to those that seek, that the sick *Adam* may be comforted.

23. Now if we will search after the tincture, what it is in its highest degree, we shall find the [3] spirit: For we cannot say, that the fire is the tincture, nor the air either. For the fire is wholly contrary to the tincture; and the air doth stifle it; it is a very pleasant [4] refreshment; its root, out of which it is generated, is indeed the fire: But if

[3] *spiritum.*

[4] *Or habitation.*

I may rightly mention the seat where it sitteth, I cannot say otherwise, but that it is between the three Principles, *viz.* [between] the kingdom of God, the kingdom of hell, and the kingdom of this world, in the midst, and [it] hath none [of the three] for its own, and yet it is generated from all three : And it hath as it were a several Principle, which yet is no Principle, but a bright pleasant habitation. Neither is itself the spirit, but the spirit dwelleth in it, and it so reneweth the spirit, that [1] it becometh clear and visible. Its true name is Wonderful, and none can name [that name], but he to whom it is given, he nameth it only in himself, and not without [or outwardly], it hath no place of its rest in the substance, and yet resteth continually in itself, and giveth virtue and beauty to all things, as the [2] glance of the sun giveth light, virtue and beauty to all things in this world ; and it is not the thing itself, though indeed it worketh in the thing, and maketh the thing grow and blossom, and yet it is found really [to be] in all things, and it is the life and heart of all things, but it is not the spirit which is generated out of the essences.

[1] the spirit.

[2] Or sunshine.

24. The tincture is the pleasant sweetness and softness in a fragrant herb and flower, and the spirit thereof is bitter and harsh, and if the tincture were not, the herb would get neither blossom nor smell ; it giveth to all essences virtue to grow. It is also in metals and stones ; it maketh that the

silver and gold do grow, and without it [the tincture] there is nothing in this world could grow. Among all the children in nature, [it only] is a virgin, and hath never generated any thing out of itself; neither can it generate, and yet it maketh that all things impregnate.   It is the most hidden thing, and also the most manifest; it is [1] a friend of God, and a play-fellow of virtue; it suffereth itself to be detained by nothing, and yet it is in all things; but if anything be done to it against the right of nature, then it flieth [away], and that very easily: It standeth not fast, and yet it continueth immovable; it continueth in no kind of decaying of any thing; all the while that it standeth in the root of nature, not altered nor destroyed, so long it continueth.   It layeth no burthen upon anything, but it easeth the burthen in all things; it maketh that all things rejoice, and yet it generateth no shouting [2] noise; but the voice cometh out of the essences, and becometh loud in the spirit.

25. The way to it is very near; whosoever findeth that [way] dareth not to reveal it, neither can he, for there is no language that can express it: And although any seek long after [3] it, if the tincture will not, he cannot find it; nevertheless it meeteth them that seek after it aright, in its own way [or manner], as its nature is, with a virgin-like mind, not being [prone] to covetousness and [wantonness or] voluptuousness; it suffereth itself

[1] *Amica Dei.* Friendess, or she-friend of God.

[2] laughter, or out-cry.

[3] the tincture.

to be imprinted [represented or imagined] in a thing (where it was not before) by [1] faith, if it be right in a virgin-like manner: It is powerful, and yet doth nothing; when it goeth out of a thing, it cometh not into it again, but it stayeth in its [2] ether, it never breaketh [or corrupteth] more, and yet doth grow.

[1] Or belief.

[2] air, or receptacle.

26. Now you will say, this must be God! No, it is not God, but it is God's [3] friend. Christ said, *My Father worketh, and I work also*; but it worketh not; it is in a thing imperceptibly, and yet it may well be overpowered and used; especially in metals, there it can (if itself be pure) make pure gold of iron, and of copper; it can make a little grow to be a great deal, and yet it puts forth nothing. Its way is as subtle as the thoughts of a man, and the thoughts do even arise from thence.

[3] She-friend.

27. And therefore when a man sleepeth, so that the tincture resteth, then there are no thoughts in the spirit; but the constellation rumbleth in the elements, and beateth into the brains what shall (through their operation) come to pass, which yet is often broken again by another [4] conjunction, so that it cometh not to effect; besides, it can shew nothing exactly, except it cometh by a conjunction of planets and fixed stars, and that only goeth forward, but it representeth all [in an] earthly [manner], according to the spirit of this world; so that where the [5] sidereal spirit should speak of men, it often speaketh of beasts, and continually repre-

[4] aspect of the planets.

[5] Or starry spirit.

sents the contrary; as the earthly spirit fancieth from the starry spirit, so he dreameth.

28. Seeing now we have spoken of the tincture, as of the house of the soul, so we will speak also of the soul, what it is, and how it can be propagated, wherein we can the better bring the tincture to [1] light. The soul is not so subtle as the tincture; but it is powerful and hath great might [or ability]. It can by the tincture (if it rideth upon the virgin's bride-chariot [2] in the tincture) turn mountains upside-down, as Christ said; which is done in the pure faith, in the place where the tincture is master, which doth it, and the soul giveth the thrust; whereas yet no power can be discerned. Even as the earth [3] moveth upon the heavenly tincture, whereas there is not more than one only tincture in the heaven, and in this world, yet [it is] of many sorts, according to the essence of every thing. In the beasts it is not as in men, also not in fishes as in beasts; also in stones and gems otherwise; also otherwise in angels, and in the spirit of this world.

29. But in God, angels, and in the virgin-like souls (understand pure souls) it is alike; where yet it is only [4] for God. The devil hath also a tincture, but a false one (and it standeth not in the fire) wherewith he can gripe that man in the heart that letteth him in, as a [sly soothing] flattering false thief, that insinuateth himself, desiring to steal, concerning whom Christ warneth us, that we should watch.

[1] Or to be understood.

[2] That is, upon true resignation.

[3] Schwebet.

[4] on God's side.

30. And now if we will speak of the soul, and of its substance and essences, we must say that it is the [1]roughest [thing] in man; for it is the originality of the other substances [or things]. It is fiery, harsh, bitter, and strong, and it resembleth a great [and] mighty power, its essences are like brimstone: Its gate or seat out of the eternal originality is between the fourth and the fifth forms in the eternal birth, and in the [2]unbeginning band, of the strong might of God the Father, where the eternal light of his Heart (which maketh the second Principle) generateth itself, and if [3]it wholly lose the bestowed virgin of the divine virtue [or power] (out of which the light of God generateth itself, which is given to the soul to be its pearl, as is mentioned above) then it becometh, and is, a devil, like all other [devils] in essences, form, and in [4]quality also.

31. But if it put its will [5]forward into meekness (*viz.* into the obedience of God) then it is in the source [or of the quality and property] of the Heart of God, and receiveth divine virtue, and then all its rough essences become angelical and joyful; and then its rough essences are very serviceable to it, and are better and more profitable to it, than that it were altogether sweet in the originality; in which [being sweet] there would be no strength, nor such mighty power as in the harsh, bitter, and fiery [essences].

32. For the fire in the essence cometh to be a

[1] Or crudest, most undigested, or raw.

[2] Or indissoluble band.

[3] the soul.

[4] active property.

[5] into true resignation.

¹ pleasant or delightful.

¹soft meek light, and is nothing else but a zealous [or eager] kindling of the tincture, and the harsh essence causeth that the divine virtue can draw it to itself, and taste it, for in the [sour or] harsh essence the taste doth consist, in nature: In like manner the bitter essence serveth to [make] the moving rising joy, fragrancy and growing; and out of these forms the tincture goeth forth, and it is the house of the soul; as the Holy Ghost [goeth forth] from the Father and the Son, so also the tincture goeth forth from the light of the fiery soul, and then also from its virtuous [or powerful] essences, and so it ²resembleth the Holy Ghost, but yet the Holy Ghost of God is a degree higher; for he goeth forth from the centre of the light wholly in the fifth form, from the Heart of God, at the end of nature.

² is like.

33. Therefore there is a difference between the tincture in man, and the Holy Ghost; and the bestowed virgin of the divine virtue [or power] dwelleth in the tincture of the soul, [that is] if it be true and faithful; but if [the soul be] not [faithful] then ³she departeth into her centre, which is not wholly shut up; for there is but half a birth between, except the soul pass into the ⁴stock of harshness and malice [evil or wickedness], and then there is a whole birth between. For the harshness standeth in the fourth form of the darkness, and the bitterness in the fire, between the fourth and fifth forms, as is mentioned before.

³ the virgin.

⁴ Stock of a tree which is grafted upon.

34. Now [reason's] question is, How hath *Eve* received the soul from *Adam?*   Behold, when God's [1]harsh *Fiat* took the rib [2]out of *Adam,* then it attracted out of all essences also to it, and the *Fiat* imaged [formed, imagined, or impressed][2] itself together therein, [that it might] continually and eternally stay therein.   But now the tincture in *Adam* was not yet extinguished, but the soul of Adam sat yet wholly with might and virtue [or power] in the tincture ; only the virgin was departed : And therefore now the *Fiat* [3]took the tincture, and the [sour] harsh essences mingled [or qualified] with the [sour] harsh *Fiat* ; for it, (*viz.* the *Fiat*) and the [sourness or] harshness in the essences, are one kind of essence.

> [1] sour, astrin-gent, or at-tractive.
>
> [2] Or in.
>
> [3] received.

35. Thus the *Fiat* inclined itself now to the Heart of God, and the essences received the divine virtue [or power], and there sprang up the blossom in the fire ; and out of the blossom [sprang] again the own [proper] tincture, and thus *Eve* was a living soul : And the tincture filled itself in the growth (even as it is a cause of all growing), so that [4]instantly there was a whole body in the tincture.   For that was possible, they were not yet fallen into sin, neither were there yet any hard gristles and bones.

> [4] suddenly.

36. You must understand [or conceive] it a-right : *Eve* gat not *Adam's* soul, nor *Adam's* body, but one only rib ; but she was extracted from the essences, and gat her soul in her essences

16

[that were] given her, in the tincture, and the body grew for [or to] her in her own sprung-up tincture, yet in virtue [or power]; but the *Fiat* had already formed [or made] her a woman. Indeed she was not deformed, but altogether lovely; for she was [1] Of distinction of sex. of a heavenly kind, in paradise, yet the [1] marks were already also set upon her by the *Fiat* of the [2] macrocosm. [2] great world; and it could not otherwise be, she must be a woman for *Adam*; indeed they were in paradise. And if they had not eaten of the tree, and if they had returned to God, then they would have continued in paradise; but the propagation must now needs have been after a womanly manner, and would not have stood [eternally]. For Satan had brought it too far, although he had not yet suffered himself to be seen, only he strewed sugar abroad in the spirit of this world, till at length the lovely beast did lay itself forth upon the tree as a flatterer and liar.

The Gate of our Propagation in the Flesh.

37. As I have mentioned above, the noble tincture is now henceforth generated thus in a manly [or masculine] and womanly [or feminine] kind [or sex] out of the soul; the tincture is so subtle and mighty, powerful, that it [can go, or] goeth into the heart of another, into his tincture; which the devilish bewitching whores well know; yet they understand not the noble art, but they [3] Or poison. use the [false] tincture of the devils, and [3] infect

many in [their] marrow and bones, by their
[1]incantation, for which they shall receive their [1] exorcisms, conjuration, adjuration.
wages, with Lucifer, who would fain have raised
his tincture to be above God.

38. But know that the tincture is in menkind
somewhat diverse from that in womenkind; for
the tincture in menkind goeth out of the *limbus*,
or man, and the tincture in womenkind goeth
out of the matrix. For the virtue of the soul
frameth [imprinteth, fashioneth or imageth] itself
not only in the tincture, but in the whole body;
for the body groweth in the tincture.

39. But thus the tincture is the longing, the
great desire after the virgin, which belongeth to
the tincture; for it is subtle, without understanding; but it is the divine inclination, and continually seeketh the virgin, [which is] its play-
fellow; the [2]masculine seeketh her in the [2] manly.
[3]feminine, and the feminine in the masculine; [3] womanly.
especially in the delicate complexion, where the
tincture is most noble, clear, and vigorous; from
whence cometh the great desire of the masculine
and feminine sex, so that they always desire to
copulate, and the great burning love, so that the
tinctures mingle together, and [try, prove, or]
taste one another with their pleasant taste; whereas one [sex] continually supposeth that the other
hath the virgin.

40. And the spirit of the great world now
supposeth that he hath gotten the virgin; he

graspeth with his clutches, and will mingle his infection with the virgin, and he supposeth that he hath the prize ; it shall not now run away from him, he supposeth now he will find the Pearl well enough. But it is with him as with a thief, driven out of a fair garden of delight, where he had eaten pleasant fruit, who cometh, and goeth round about the enclosed garden, and would fain eat some more of the good fruit, and yet cannot get in, but must reach in with his hand, and yet cannot come at the fruit for all that ; for the gardener cometh, and taketh away the fruit ; and thus he must go away empty, and his lust is changed into discontent. Thus also it is with him [*viz.* with the spirit of this world], he soweth thus in his fiery [or burning] lust the [1] seed into the matrix, and the tincture receiveth it with great joy, and supposeth that to be the virgin ; but the [sour] harsh *Fiat* cometh thereupon, and attracteth the same to it, while the tincture is so well pleased.

[1] grain, or corn.

41. Now then the feminine tincture cometh in to aid, and striveth for the child, and supposeth that it hath the virgin : And the two tinctures wrestle both of them for the virgin, and yet neither of them both hath her, and which of the two overcometh, according to that the fruit getteth the mark of distinction of sex. But because that the feminine [tincture] is weak, therefore it taketh the blood also to it in the matrix, whereby it supposeth it shall retain the virgin.

The Secret Gate of Women.

42. Hence I must shew the ground to them that seek; for the doctor cannot shew it him with his anatomy, and though he should kill a thousand men, yet he shall not find that [ground]. They only know that [ground] that have [1] been upon it.

[1] Or attained it.

43. Therefore I will write from the virgin, which knoweth well what is in the woman. She is as subtle as the tincture. But she hath a life, and the tincture hath none: The tincture is nothing else but an exulting joyful mighty will, and a house [or habitation] of the soul, and a pleasant paradise of the soul, which is the soul's propriety [or own portion] so long as the soul with its imagination [2] dependeth on God.

[2] sticketh to God and goodness.

44. But when it becometh false, so that its essences flatter with the spirit of the great world, and desire the [3] fulness of the world, *viz.* 1. [In] the [sour] harshness [desire] much wealth [or riches], to eat and drink much, and to fill themselves continually. 2. In the bitterness [desire] great power, authority, and might, to rise high, to rule powerfully, and extol themselves above all, and put themselves forth to be seen like a proud bride. And 3. in the [4] source of the fire [desire] a fierce cruel power, and by kindling of the fire [of anger], supposing in the lustre thereof to be brave, and so are much delighted in themselves;

[3] Or its fill.

[4] in the active stirring of wrath.

then cometh the flatterer and liar, and ¹formeth or figureth himself also in the spirit of the great world, as [he did] in the Garden of *Eden*, and leadeth the soul : 1. In covetousness, to eating and drinking [too much], and saith continually, thou shalt [want and] not have enough, get more for thyself how thou canst, by hook or by crook, that thou mayest always have enough [to serve thy turn]. And 2. in the bitter form he saith, Thou art rich, and hast much, aspire and lift up thyself, thou art greater than other people, the inferior is not like thee [or so good a man as thou]. And 3. in the might or power of the fire, he saith, Kindle [or stir up] thy mind, make it implacable and stout, yield to none, terrify the simple, and so thou shalt be dreadful, and make thy authority continue, and then thou mayest do what thou listest, and all whatsoever thou desirest will be at thy service : And is not this a fine brave glory ? Art thou not indeed a lord on earth ?

45. And as soon as this is ²brought to pass, then the tincture becometh wholly false : For as the spirit in a thing is, so is also the tincture ; for the tincture goeth forth from the spirit, and is the habitation thereof. Therefore, O man ! whatsoever you sow here, that you shall reap, for your soul in the tincture remaineth eternally : And all your fruits stand in the tincture, manifested in the clear light, and follow after you ; this the virgin saith in sincerity [for a warning], with great longing after the lily.

46. And now if we consider of the tincture, [and search] how various it is, and [that it is] many times so wholly false; then we may [be able] fundamentally to demonstrate the falsehood of the many various spirits, [and] how they are generated. Therefore we will make a short entrance, concerning the propagation of the soul, which we will enlarge [when we speak] about the fall of *Adam*, and the birth of *Cain*. For the seed (as is above-mentioned) is sown in the lust of the tinctures, where the sour [or] harsh *Fiat* receiveth it, and supposeth that it hath received the virgin; there both the tinctures (the masculine and the feminine) then strive together about it, and there the spirit of the great world, *viz.* the spirit of the stars and elements, figureth [imageth or imprinteth] itself also in it, and he filleth the tinctures with his elements, which the tinctures in the *Fiat* receive with great joy, and suppose they have the virgin.

47. But being the *Fiat* is the mightiest among them all, (for it is as it were a spirit, and although it be no spirit, yet it is the sharp essence), therefore it attracteth the seed to it, and desireth the *limbus* of God in paradise, out of which *Adam's* body was created by the *Fiat*, and [1] would create an *Adam* [1 will.] out of a heavenly *limbus*; and then the spirit of the great world insinuates himself and supposeth, [and saith], The child is mine, I will rule in the virgin; and he always filleth it with the elements, from whence the tincture becometh full and very

thick [gross, swelled, or impregnated]; and there then the tincture getteth a loathing against the fulness; for the tincture itself is clear, and the *Fiat* with the elements is thick [gross and] swelled; from whence women (when they [1]grow big [with child]) know well enough, that many of them loathe some meats and drinks, and long still after some strange thing [to eat], for the tincture cometh to have a loathing of all that the spirit of this world with his elements filleth in, and willeth to have somewhat else; for this virgin doth not relish them, but becometh [discontented and] sorry, and forsaketh them, and goeth into her [2]ether, and cometh not again.

48. And then the spirit of the sun, stars, and elements of this world, supposeth with itself [saying], Now thou art in the right, the child is thine, the foundation is laid, thou wilt bring it up, the virgin must be thine, thou wilt live therein, and have thy joy [delight, and habitation] in her, her ornament must be thine; and thus [he] attracteth always to himself in his great lust, by the *Fiat*, which in eternity goeth not away; and [he] supposeth that he hath the virgin.

♄ *Saturnus :* This is done in the first month.

49. And there the blood of the mother (wherein the tincture of the mother is) is drawn into the seed. And when the [sour] harsh *Fiat* hath tried, [and perceiveth] that to be sweeter than its own essence,

then it frameth [imageth or representeth] itself with great earnestness [or longing] therein, and becometh sharp in the tincture, and will create *Adam*, and so severeth the *materia* [or matter]; and then the spirit of the stars and elements is in the midst, and ruleth mightily in the *Fiat*.

♃ *Jupiter :* This is done in the second month.

50. And then the *materia* [or matter] is severed according to the wheel of the stars, as they (*viz.* the planets) stand in order at this time, and which of them [all] is predominant, that (by the *Fiat*) figureth the matter most, and the child getteth a form, after the kind of that [planet].

♂ *Mars :* All this which followeth is done in the third month.

51. Thus the matter (by the *Fiat*) is severed into members. And now when the *Fiat* thus attracteth the blood of the mother into the matter, then [1] it is stifled [or choked]; and then the tincture [1 the blood.] of the blood becometh false, and full of anguish; for the [sour] harsh essence (*viz.* the *Fiat*) is terrified, and all the joy (which the sour [harsh] *Fiat* gat in the tincture of the blood) withdraweth; and the *Fiat* beginneth to tremble in the terror, in the sour [harsh] essence; and the terror goeth away like a flash, and would fain depart and fly away out of the essence, and yet is withheld by the *Fiat*, which [terror] is now turned hard, and made

tough by the essence, which now closeth the child about; this is the skin of the child. And the tincture flieth suddenly, flashing upwards in the terror, and would be gone; yet it cannot either (for it standeth in the out-birth [or procreation] of the essences) but [1] riseth up suddenly in the terror, and taketh the virtue [or power] of all the essences with it. And there the spirit of the stars and elements [2] figureth itself also therein, and filleth itself also therein, in the flight, and supposeth that it hath the virgin, and will go along with it; and the *Fiat* gripeth it all, and holdeth it [fast], and supposeth that the *Verbum Domini* [the Word of the Lord] is there in the [3] uproar, that will create the *Adam*; and it strengtheneth itself in the strong might of the terror, and createth again the uppermost [part] of the body, *viz.* the head: And from the hard terror (which is continually departing and yet cannot) cometh the skull, which encloseth the uppermost centre: And from the departing out of the essences of the tincture with the terror into the uppermost centre, come the veins and the neck to be, going thus from the body into the head, into the uppermost centre.

52. So also all the veins in the whole body come from the terror of the [4] stifling, where the terror goeth forth from all the essences, and would be gone; and the *Fiat* withholdeth it with his great strong might. And therefore one vein hath always

[1] stretcheth forth.

[2] representeth.

[3] hurlyburly, or flying up.

[4] choking, or stopping.

a diverse essence from another, caused by the first departing, where then the essences of the stars and elements do also mingle [or figure themselves] therein, and the *Fiat* holdeth it all, and createth it, and it supposeth that the *Verbum Domini* [the Word of the Lord] with the strong mighty power of God is there, where the *Fiat* must create heaven and earth.

The Gate of the great Necessity and Misery.

O man, consider thyself, how hardly thou art beset here, and how thou gettest thy misery in thy mother's body :

Observe it O ye [1] lawyers, from what spirit you [2] [come to] [3] know [what is] right; consider this well, for it is deep.

[1] jurists.
[2] can go to law.
[3] judge.

53. The spirit of the virgin sheweth us the mystery again, and the great secrecy; for the stifling [or stopping] of the blood in the matrix (especially in the fruit) is the first dying of the essences, where they are severed from the heaven, so that the virgin cannot be generated there, which should [have been] generated in *Adam*, from the heavenly virtue [or power] without woman, also without rending of his body. And here the kingdom [or dominion] of the stars and elements beginneth in man, where they take hold of man and mingle [or qualify] with him, make and fit him, also nourish and nurture him, of which you may read more about *Cain*.

Further in the Incarnation.

54. And so when the *Fiat* thus holdeth the terror in itself, so that the elements fill it, then that filling becometh hard bones; and there the *Fiat* figureth the whole man with his bodily form, all according to the first wrestling of the two tinctures, when they wrestle [or strive] together in the sport of love, when the seed is sown; and that tincture which there getteth the upperhand (whether the masculine or the feminine) according to that sex the man is figured. And the figuring [or shaping] is done very suddenly in the storm of the anguishing terror, where the blood is stifled [or stopped]; and there the elementary man getteth up, and the heavenly [man] goeth down. For in the terror, the bitter ¹ sting is generated, which rageth and raveth in the hard terrified [sourness or] harshness in the great anxiety of the stifled [or stopped] blood.

¹ Or pricking.

55. Women have sufficient experience of this, in the third month, (when this is done in the fruit), [and feel] how the raging and pricking cometh into their teeth, loins, back, and the like. This cometh upon them from the stifled [choked, or stopped] tincture in the fruit, and from their stifled [or stopped] blood in the matrix, because the evil tincture qualifieth [or mingleth] with the good [tincture] of their bodies. Therefore in the same manner as the tincture in the matrix suffereth pain, after the same manner also the good [tincture]

suffereth in the members [limbs or parts] of the mother, as in the hard bones, teeth, and ribs, as such people know very well.

56. So now when the bitter sting [or prickle] (which is generated in the anxious terror in the stifling [or stopping] and in the entering in of death), doth thus rage and rave, and shew forth itself in the terror, and flieth upwards, then it is caught and withheld by the [sour] harshness, so that it cannot get up aloft. For the [sour] harshness draweth it continually the more eagerly and vehemently, because of [1] its raging, and cannot endure it, from whence the pricking often becometh more terrible, and this is after no other manner, than as when a man is dying, and soul and body part asunder; for in the stifling [or stopping] of the blood by the [sour] harshness, the bitter death is also there; and therefore [2] it is like a furious whirling wheel, or swift horrible thought, which worrieth and vexeth itself: And here is a brimstone-spirit, a venomous [poisonous] horrible aching substance in the death; for it is the worm to the springing up of life.

[1] the raging of the prickle.

[2] the bitter sting or prickle.

57. And now when the spirit of the stars and elements hath mingled [or figured] itself together in the incarnation, then the virtue [or power] of the stars and elements is together wheeled in this raging, where then (in this anguish) the spirit of the stars attracteth the virtue of the sun to it, and [3] manifesteth itself in the virtue of the sun, from whence there ariseth a twinkling flash in this

[3] Or discovereth.

raging, from whence the hard [sour] harsh anxiety is terrified, and sinketh down, and there the terrible tincture goeth into its [1] ether; for the essence of the [sour] harshness in the *Fiat* is so mightily terrified at the flash, that it becometh [faint] impotent [or feeble], and sinketh back, [2] expandeth itself, and groweth thin.

58. And the terror [shriek], or flash of fire, is done in the bitter prickle; and when it reflecteth itself back in the dark [sour or] harsh anxiety in the mother, and findeth her so very soft [gentle] and overcome, then it is much more terrified than the mother: But this terror happening thus in the soft mother, she becometh white and clear in the twinkling of an eye, and the flash remaineth in the anguish, in the root of the fire, and now therefore it is a shriek [or terror] of great joy, and it is as when water is thrown into the fire, where the [sour] harsh [3] quality is then quenched, and the [sourness or] harshness is then so mightily over-joyed with the light, and the light with the mother, the [sourness or] harshness, wherein it is generated, that there is no similitude to [compare] it [with], for it is the birth and the beginning of the life.

⊙ *Sol:* All this which followeth is done in the entrance of the fourth month.

59. And as soon as the light of life appeareth in the [sour] harshness and soft mother, so that the [sourness or] harshness cometh to taste the light of

[1] Or receptacle.

[2] openeth itself outwards.

[3] source or property.

life, [and findeth] that it is so meek, pleasant
[lovely], and full of joy, then it exulteth with great
delight [desire and longing] after the light, to [1] mix [1] infect.
itself therewith, and apprehend it, so that its lust
[or longing delight] and virtue goeth forth from it
after the light; which lust [or longing delight] is
the virtue of the light; and this out-going [2] lust in [2] delight.
the love is the noble tincture, which is there new
generated to be the child's own; and the spirit
which is generated out of the anguish in the flash
of the fire, is the true [and real] soul which is
generated in man.

60. Now here it is especially to be observed,
where [3] it dwelleth, and whence heart, lungs, and [3] the soul.
liver come, especially the bladder and [4] guts, and [4] Or entrails.
the brain in the head; also the understanding and
senses; these I will here set down one after
another: It cannot [well or] sufficiently be expressed by a human tongue, especially the order
which is [5] observed in the twinkling of an eye in [5] done or per-
formed.
nature; it would require a great volume to describe
it in.   And as the world accounteth us too [6] weak [6] simple, or
silly, and void
to [be able to] describe it, so we account ourselves of understanding, and
much weaker [and more unable].   And it is with unable.
us as *Isaiah* saith, *I am found of them that*
sought me not, and known of them that were
ignorant of me, and of such as inquired not
after me.

61. I say, [7] this hath not been sought, but we [7] high knowledge.
sought the Heart of God, that we might hide us

therein from the ¹ tempest of tꞁ
we came there, then the loving
paradise met us, and offered us her love,
be kind [and friendly] to us, and be betro
us for a compauion, and shew us the way to
dise, where we shall be safe from the stor
tempest, and she carried a branch in her hand, aꞁ
said, We will plant this, and a lily shall grow, aꞁ
I will come to thee again; from whence we gᵉ
this longing to write of the amiable virgin, whic
did shew us the way into paradise, where we muꞁ
go through the kingdom of this world, and als
through the kingdom of hell, and no hurt done us
and according to that [direction of her's] we writ

THE FOURTEENTH CHAPTER

the Birth and Propagation of Man.

The very Secret Gate.

we consider now the springing up of the
life, and in what place of the body it is
the life is generated, then we shall rightly
..e whole ground of man, and there is nothing
..et in man [1] but that it may be found.   For [1] that may
not be found.
..ust needs say, that the heart is the place
..n the noble life is generated, and the life
..generateth the heart.

..s it is mentioned above, so the life in the
..h, with the kindling of the light, taketh its
..ing from the glance of the sunshine, from
..irit of the stars and elements in the great
.., where death and life wrestle one with the .

For when man departed from paradise into
..er birth (*viz.* into the spirit of this world,
..the quality of the sun, stars, and elements)
the paradisical [vision or] seeing ceased [or
..xtinguished], where man seeth from the divine
.., without [need of] the sun and stars ; where

¹ Or there the life in the Holy Ghost buddeth forth in the place of the four elements.

² man.
the ¹springing up of the life is in the Holy Ghost and the light of God is the glance of the spirit, from whence ²he seeth; which went out; for the spirit of the soul went into the Principle of this world.

3. You must not so understand it, as if it were extinguished in itself: No; but the soul of *Adam* went out from the Principle of God, into the Principle of this world; and therein now the spirit of every soul is thus generated again by human propagation, as is mentioned before, and it cannot be otherwise. And therefore if we would be fit for the kingdom of heaven, we must be regenerated anew in the spirit of God, or else none can inherit the kingdom of God, as Christ taught us faithfully; of which I will write hereafter, that it may be a fountain for the thirsty, and a light to the noble way, in the blossom of the lily.

4. And we must here know, that our life, which we get in our mother's body [or womb,] standeth merely and only in the power of the sun, stars, and elements; so that they not only figure [or fashion] a child in the mother's body, and give it life, but also bring it into this world, and nourish it the whole time of its life, and bring it up, also cause fortune and misfortune to it, and, at last, death and corruption; and if our essences (out of which our life is generated) were not higher, in their first degree out of *Adam*, [than the beasts], then we should be wholly like the beasts.

5. But our [1] essences are generated much higher [1] active, essential virtues, or faculties. in the beginning of the life in *Adam* than the beasts, which have their essences but merely from the spirit of this world, and it must also, with the spirit of this world in a corruptible substance, go into its eternal ether: Whereas, on the contrary, the essences of man are proceeded out of the unchangeable eternal mind of God, which cannot in eternity corrupt.

6. For we have a certain ground of this, in that our mind can find and conceive all whatsoever is in the spirit of this world, which no beast can do: For no creature can [2] conceive [further or] higher [2] think or imagine. than [what is] in its own Principle, out of which its own essences are proceeded in the beginning: But we (that are men) can certainly [3] conceive [of that [3] meditate, consider, or think of. which is] in the Principle of God, and also [of that which is] in the anguishing kingdom of hell, where the worm of our soul in the beginning in *Adam* originally is, and this no other creature can do.

7. But they think [consider or imagine] only how to fill themselves and multiply, that their life may subsist; and we also receive [4] no more from [4] than the beasts do. the spirit of the stars and elements. And [5] therefore [5] because our essences have a higher beginning than the beasts. also our children are naked and bare, with great inability, and without understanding; and now if the spirit of this world had full [perfect and absolute] power over the essences of the child, then he would easily put his rough garment upon it also (*viz.* a rough hide), but he must let that alone: And he

must leave the essences in the first and second Principles to man's own choosing, to bind and yield himself to which [Principle] he will; which man hath (undeniably) in his full power, which I will expound in its own place according to its worth, and deeply demonstrate it, in spite of all the gates of the devil, and this world, which strive much against it.

8. Our life in the mother's body hath its beginning wholly, as is above mentioned, and standeth there now in the quality of the sun and stars, where then, with the kindling of the light, a centre springeth up again, where instantly the noble tincture thus generateth itself (out of the light, out of the joyful essences of the [sour] harsh, bitter, and fiery kind [or quality]) and setteth the spirit of the soul in a great pleasant habitation: And the three [1]essences (*viz.* harshness, bitterness, and fire) are in the kindling of the life so very fast bound one to another, that they cannot (in eternity) be separated one from another, and the tincture is their eternal house, wherein they dwell, which [house] they themselves generate from the beginning unto eternity, which again giveth them life, joy, and lust [or delight].

[1] beings or substances.

The strong Gate of the indissoluble Band of the Soul.

9. Behold, the three essences, (*viz.* [sourness or] harshness, bitterness and fire) are the worm or

spirit [that dieth not]. ¹Harshness is one essence, ¹ Or sourness.
and it is in the *Fiat* of God, out of God's eternal
will; and the attracting of the [sour] harshness is
the sting [or prickle] of the bitterness, which the
[sour] harshness cannot endure, but attracteth
continually the more forcibly to it, from whence
the prickle continually groweth greater, which yet
the [sour] harshness holdeth ²prisoner; and this ² captive.
together is the great anxiety, which was there in
the dark mind of God the Father, when the darkness was anxious [or longed] after the light; from
whence in the anxiety (from the glance of the
light) it attained the twinkling flash: Out of which
the angels were created, which afterward were
enlightened from the light of God (³by their ³ by their
imagination into the Heart of God); and the other or imprinting
(like Lucifer) for their haughtiness [or pride's] sake, God in their
remained in the flash of fire and anxiety. thoughts.

10. This birth [or active property] with the
indissoluble band, is generated in every soul; and
there is no soul before the kindling of the light in
the child in the mother's body. For with the
kindling the eternal band is knit [or tied], so that
it standeth eternally, and this worm of the three
essences doth not die, nor sever itself; for it is not
possible, [because] they are all three generated out
of one [only] fountain, and have three qualities,
and yet are but one being [or substance]; as the
Holy Trinity is but in one only essence [or sub-
stance]; and yet they have three originalities in

one mother, and they are one [only] being [or substance] in one another. Thus also (and not a whit less) is the soul of man, but only one degree in the first going forth; for it is generated out of the father's eternal will (and not out of the heart of God), yet the heart is the nearest to it of all.

11. And now it may very exactly be understood by the essences and property of the soul, that in this house of flesh (where it is as it were generated) it is not at home; and its horrible fall may be also understood [thereby]. For it hath no light in itself of its own, it must borrow its light from the sun; which indeed springeth up along with it in its birth, but that is corruptible, and the worm of the soul is not so; and it is seen that when a man dieth [1] it goeth out. And if then the divine light be not again generated in the centre, then the soul remaineth in the eternal darkness, in the eternal anguishing [source or] quality of the birth, where nothing is to be found in the kindled fire, but a horrible flash of fire, in which [source, property, or] quality, also the devils dwell; for it is the first Principle.

[1] the light of the sun, or a man's faculty of beholding that light ceaseth.

12. And the soul here in this world useth the light of the third Principle, after which the soul of *Adam* lusted, and thereupon was captivated by the spirit of the great world. But if the soul be regenerated in the Holy Ghost, so that its centre to the regeneration springeth [2] forth, then it seeth with two lights, and liveth in two Principles. And

[2] In true resignation.

the most inward [Principle] (*viz.* the first) is shut up fast, and hangeth but to it, in which the soul is tempted and afflicted by the devil; and on the contrary, the [1] virgin (which belongeth to [and is in] the tincture of the regeneration, and in the departure of the body from the soul, shall dwell [in the same tincture]) is in continual strife and combat with the devil, and trampleth upon his head in the virtue [and power] of the [soul's] Prince and [2] Champion (*viz.* the Son of the Virgin), when a new body (out of the virtue [or power] of the soul) shall [3] spring forth in the tincture of the soul.

13. And that (when the soul is [4] departed from the body) it might no more possibly be tempted by the devil and the spirit of this world; there is a quiet rest for the soul included in its centre in its own tincture, which standeth in paradise, betwixt the kingdom of this world and the kingdom of hell, to continue until God shall put this world into its [5] ether, when the number of men, and figures (according to the depth of the eternal mind of God) shall be finished.

14. And now when we consider how the temporary and transitory life is generated, we find that the soul is a cause of all the [6] members [or faculties] of [or to] the life of man, and without it there would not be one member [to, or] of the life of man generated. For when we search [into] the beginning and kindling of life, we find strongly with clear evidences all manner of [faculties or]

[1] the virtue or power of God.

[2] Saviour or Conqueror.

[3] Or be generated.

[4] Or separated.

[5] Or receptacle.

[6] organs or instruments.

members; so that when the clear light of the soul kindleth, then the *Fiat* standeth in very great joy, and in the twinkling of an eye doth in the matrix sever the pure from the impure, of which the tincture of the soul in the light is the [1] worker, which there reneweth it, but the *Fiat* createth it.

[1] Or work-master.

15. And now when the [sour] harsh matrix is [made] so very humble, thin, and sweet, by the light, the [stern or] strong horror (which was so very poisonous before the light [kindled]) flieth upward; for it is terrified at the meekness of the matrix; and it is a terror of great joy, yet it retaineth its strong [or stern] right [or property], and cannot be changed; neither can it get far from thence (for it is withheld by the *Fiat*) but it raiseth itself suddenly aloft, and the terror maketh it a film from the [sour or] harsh *Fiat* which holdeth the terror fast, and that is now the gall [2] of the heart.

[2] about, or near the heart.

16. But when the matrix (from which the terror was gone forth) was thus loosed from the terror of the anxiety, and became so very sweet, like sweet water, then the spirit of the great world figured [or imprinted itself] instantly, in the matrix, and filleth the four elements also within it, and thinketh with itself, now I have the sweet virgin; and the *Fiat* createth [3] it, and severeth the elements, which also are in strife: And each of them would have the virgin, and are in a wrestling, till they overcome one another, and that the fire (being the mightiest and most strong) stayeth above, and the

[3] that which was brought in.

water sinketh down; and the earth, being a hard gross thing, must stay below: But the fire will have a [1] region of its own.

[1] kingdom or dominion.

17. For it saith, I am the spirit, and the life, I will dwell in the virgin; and the [sour] harsh *Fiat* attracteth all to it, and maketh it a Mesch [*massa*, [2] concretion], and moreover [it maketh it] flesh; [2] and the fire keepeth the uppermost region, *viz.* the heart: For the four elements sever themselves by their strife, and every one of them maketh itself a several [3] region; and the *Fiat* maketh all to be [3] flesh: Only the air would have no flesh; for it said, I dwell in no house; and the *Fiat* said, I have created thee, thou art mine, and closed it in with an enclosure, that is, the bladder.

[2] Or substance.

[3] Or dominion.

18. Now the other regions set themselves in order; first the stern flash, that is, the gall; and beneath the flash, the fire, whose region is the heart; and beneath the fire, the water, whose region is the liver; and beneath the water, the earth, whose region is [in] the lungs.

19. And so every element qualifieth [or acteth] in its own source [or manner of operation], and one could do nothing without the other, neither could one have any mobility without the other. For one generateth the other, and they go all four out of one original, and it is in its birth but one only [thing or] substance, as I have mentioned before at large about the creation, concerning the [4] birth of the four elements.

[4] Or generating.

20. The [sour, strong, or] bitter gall (*viz.* the terrible poisonous flash of fire) kindleth the warmth in the heart, or the fire, and is itself the cause, from whence all else take their original.

21. Here we find again, in our consideration, the lamentable and horrible fall in the incarnation, because when the light of life riseth up, and when the *Fiat* in the tincture of the spirit of the soul reneweth the matrix, then the *Fiat* thrusteth the death of the stifling [choking, checking, or stopping] and perishing, in the sternness (*viz.* the impurity of the stifled [or checked] blood) from itself, out of its essences, and casteth it away, and will not endure it in the ¹body, but as a ²superfluity; the *Fiat* itself driveth it out, and of its tough [glutinous] sourness maketh an inclosure round about it, *viz.* a film, or gut, that it may touch neither the flesh nor the spirit, and leaveth the nethermost port open for it, and ³banisheth it eternally, because that impurity doth not belong to this kingdom; as it happened also to the earth, when the ⁴*Fiat* thrust it out of the matrix in the midst in the centre, upon a heap [as a lump], being it was unfit for heaven, so also ⁵here.

¹ *corpus.*
² excrement.

³ condemneth.

⁴ At the creation.

⁵ In the incarnation.

⁶ testimony.

22. And we find greater mysteries yet in ⁶evidence of the horrible fall; for after that the four elements had thus set themselves every one in a several region, then they made themselves lords over the spirit of the soul, which was generated out of the essences, and they have taken it into their

power, and qualify with it. The fire, *viz.* the mightiest of them, hath taken it into its [1]region [or jurisdiction] in the heart; and there it must [2]keep, and the blossom and light thereof goeth out of the heart, and moveth upon the heart, as the kindled light of a candle, where the candle resembleth the fleshly heart, with the essences out of which the light shineth. And the fire hath set itself over the essences, and continually reacheth after the light, and it supposeth that it hath the virgin, *viz.* the divine virtue [or power].

[1] Or dominion.

[2] The spirit must there be kept in obedience.

23. And there the holy tincture is generated out of the essences, which regardeth not the fire, but setteth the essences (*viz.* the soul) in its pleasant [3]joy. Then come the other three elements out of their regions, and fill themselves also by force therein, each of them would taste of the virgin, receive her and qualify [or mingle] with her: *viz.* the water, that filleth itself by force also therein, and it tasteth the sweet tincture of the soul. And the fire saith, I would willingly keep the water, for I can quench my thirst therewith, and refresh myself therein. And the air saith, I am indeed the spirit, I will blow up thy heat and fire, that the water do not choke thee. And the fire saith to the air, I will keep thee, for thou upholdest my quality for me, that I also go not out. And then cometh the element [of] (earth) and saith, What will you three do alone? You will starve and consume one another; for you depend all

[3] refreshment, or habitation.

three on one another, and devour yourselves, and when you shall have consumed the water, then you extinguish; for the air cannot move, unless it have some water; for the water is the mother of the air, which generateth the air: Moreover, the fire becometh much too fierce [violent and eager] if the water be consumed, and consumeth the body, and then our ¹region is out, and none of us can subsist.

¹ dominion or rule.

24. Then thus say the three elements (the fire, the air, and the water) to the earth, Thou art indeed too dark, too rough, and too cold, and thou art rejected by the *Fiat*: We cannot take thee in; thou destroyest our dwelling, and makest it dark and stinking, and thou afflictest our virgin, which is our only delight and treasure wherein we live. And the earth saith, Yet pray take my ²children in; they are lovely, and of good esteem; they afford you meat and drink, and cherish you, that you never suffer want.

² Its fruits.

25. Hereupon thus say the three elements: But so they may afterwards get a dwelling in us, and may come to be strong and great, and then we must depart, or be in subjection to them, and therefore we will not take them in either, for they may come to be as rough and cold as thou art: Yet this we will do, thou mayest let thy children dwell ³in our courts and porches, and we will come and be their guest, and eat of ⁴their fruit, and drink of their drink, else the water which

³ in the stomach and guts.
⁴ the virtue of their fruit.

is contained in the element would be too little for us.

26. Now thus say the three elements (fire, water, and air) to the spirit, Fetch us children of the earth, that they may dwell in our courts, we will eat of their [1] essences, and make thee strong. [1] Or substance. Here the spirit of the soul (like a captive) must be obedient, and must reach with his essences, and fetch them forth. And then cometh the *Fiat*, and saith, No: thou [2] mightest [so] outrun me; [2] Or mayest escape me. and [the *Fiat*] created the reaching forth, and there came forth from thence, hands, and all other essences and forms, as it is before our eyes, and the *astronomicus* [astronomer] knoweth it well, yet he knoweth not the secrecy of it, although he can explain the [3] signs according to the constellation [3] marks or tokens. and elements, which qualify [and mingle] together in the essences of the spirit of the soul.

27. And now when the hands (in the will) reach after the children of the earth (which [reaching forth] yet is no other than a will in the spirit of the child in the mother's body) then the *Fiat* is there, and maketh a great room in the courts of the three elements, and a tough firm enclosure round about it, that they may not touch the flesh: For the flesh is afraid of the children of the earth, because the earth is thrown away (for its rough stinking darkness) and it trembleth for great fear; and it looketh still about after the best [means] (lest the children of the earth should be too rough

for it, and might cause a stink) that so it might have an [1] opening, and might cast away the stink and the filth, and [so] it maketh out of the court (which is the maw [or stomach]) an outlet and gate, and environeth the same with its tough [sour] harshness, and so there is a gut.

[1] outlet.

28. But because the [2] enemy is not yet in substance, but only in the will of the spirit, therefore it goeth away very slowly downwards, and seeketh for the port, where it will make an outlet and gate, that it may cast away the stink and filth, from whence the guts are so very long and [3] crooked.

[2] the stink.

29. Now when this conference (which is spiritual, between the three elements, fire, air, and water) was perceived by the spirit of the earth (*viz.* the essences in the region of the lungs) then [4] it cometh at last (when the habitation or the court was already built for the children of the earth) and saith to the three elements, Wherefore will you take the body for the spirit? Will you take the children of the earth, and feed upon them? I am their spirit, and am pure; I can strengthen the essences of the soul with my virtue and essences, and uphold them well, take me in.

[3] winding and doubling like folds.

[4] the spirit of the earth.

30. And they say, Yes, we will take thee in, for thou art a member of our spirit; thou shalt dwell in us, and strengthen the essences of our spirit, that it may not faint; yet we must also have the children of the earth (for they have our

quality also in them) that we may rejoice.   And
the spirit of the lungs saith, Then I will live in
you wholly, and rejoice myself with you.

The Gate of the Sidereal, or [1] *Starry Spirit.*   [1] Astral spirit.

31. Thus now when the light of the sun, which
had discovered and imprinted itself in the fire-flash
of the essences of the spirit, and was shining in
the fire-flash (as in a strange virtue, and not in the
sun's own virtue), [when he] seeth that he hath
gotten the [2] region, and that the [3] essences of the
soul (which are the worm or the spirit) as also the
elements will rejoice in his virtue and splendour,
and that the elements have made their four regions
[or dominions] and habitations, for an everlasting
possession, and that [4] he should be a king, and that
[5] they should serve at court (in the spirit of the
essences) in the heart, and so exceedingly love him,
and rejoice in their service, and have besides
brought the [6] children of the earth, that the spirit
might present them (where then they will first
be frolic and potent, and eat and drink of the
[7] essences of the children of the earth), then [8] he
thinketh with himself, it is good to dwell here,
thou art a king, thou wilt bring [9] thy kindred
[offspring, or generation] hither, and raise them
up above the elements, and make thyself a region
[or dominion].   Art not thou the king?   Here is the
gate where the children of this world are wiser than
the children of light.   'O man! consider thyself!

[2] rule, government, or predominancy.

[3] *Note*, the essences of the soul are the worm or spirit that never dieth.

[4] the sun.

[5] the elements.

[6] the fruits of the earth.

[7] Or virtues.

[8] the sun.

[9] the worldly-wise, or the children of the sun.

And he draweth the constellations to him, and bringeth them into the essences, and sets them over the elements, with their wonderful and unsearchable various essences, (whose number is infinite), and maketh himself a region and kingdom of his generation in a strange country.

32. For the essences of the soul are not this king's own, he hath not generated them, nor they him; but he hath, by lust, imprinted himself also in its essences, and kindled himself in its fire-flash, on purpose to find its virgin, and live in her; which is the amiable divine virtue [or power]: Because the spirit of the soul is out of the eternal and had the virgin, before the fall, and therefore now the spirit of the great world continually seeketh the virgin in the spirit of the soul, and supposeth that she is there still, as before the fall, where the spirit of the great world appeared in *Adam's* virgin with very great joy, and desired also to live in the virgin, and to be eternal. Because he felt his corruptibility, and that he was so rough in himself, therefore he would fain partake of the loving kindness and sweetness of the virgin, and live in her, that so he might live eternally, and not break [corrupt or perish] again.

33. For by the great longing of the darkness after the light and virtue of God, this world hath been generated out of the darkness, where the holy virtue of God [shone, or] beheld itself in the darkness; and therefore this great desiring and longing

after the divine virtue, continueth in the spirit of the sun, stars, and elements, and in all things.   All groan and pant after the divine virtue, and would fain be delivered from the vanity of the devil : But seeing that cannot be, therefore all creatures must wait till their [1] dissolution, when they [shall go] [1] corruption. into their ether, and get a place in paradise, yet only in the figure and shadow, and the spirit [must] be dissolved, which here hath had such lust [or longing].

34. But now this lust [or longing] must be thus, or else no good creature could be, and this world would be a mere hell and wrathfulness.   And now seeing the virgin standeth in the second Principle, so that the spirit of this world cannot possibly reach to her, and yet that the virgin doth continually behold herself [or appear] in the spirit of this world, to [satisfy] the lust and longing in the fruit and growing of every thing, therefore [2] he is [2] the spirit of so very longing, and seeketh the virgin continually. the great world. He exalteth many a creature in great skill and cunning subtlety, and he bringeth it into the highest degree that he can ; and continually supposeth that so the virgin shall again be generated for him, which he saw in *Adam* before his fall; which also brought *Adam* to fall, in that [2] he would dwell in his virgin, and with his great lust so [3] pressed *Adam*, that he fell asleep; that is, he set [3] See more of himself by force in *Adam's* tincture close to the this strife in Chap. 12 v. virgin, and would fain have qualified in her, and 39-47.

18

[mingled] with her, and so live eternally, whereby the tincture grew weary, and the virgin withdrew.

35. And then *Adam* fell, and was feeble, which is called sleep: This was the [1] Tree of Temptation, [to try] whether it were possible for *Adam* to live eternally in the virgin, and to generate the virgin again out of himself, and so generate an angelical kingdom.

[1] Adam's inward Tree of Temptation.

36. But seeing it could not so be (because of the spirit of this world) therefore was the outward temptation first taken in hand by the tree of the fruit of this world. And there *Adam* became [2] perfectly a man of this world, and did eat and drink of the earthly essences, and infected [or mingled] himself with the spirit of this world, and became that [spirit's] own; as we now see by woeful experience, how that [spirit] possesseth a child in the mother's body in the incarnation: For he knoweth not any where else to seek the virgin, but in man, where he first of all espied her.

[2] Or at length.

37. Therefore he doth wrestle in many a man (that is of a strong complexion, in whom the virgin doth often behold herself) so very hard, continually supposing he shall get the virgin, and that she shall be generated for him: And the more the soul resisteth him, and draweth near to the Heart of God, and panteth to yield itself over thereto (where the amiable virgin not only freely looketh upon it, but dareth even for a long time even to sit in its nest [*viz.* in] the tincture of the soul), the more

strong and [eager or] desirous doth the spirit of this world come to be.

38. Where then the king (*viz.* the light of the sun) is so very joyful in the spirit, and doth so highly triumph, exult, and rejoice, that he moveth all the essences of the stars, and bringeth them into their highest degree, to generate her; where then all centres of the stars fly open, and the loving virgin beholdeth herself in them. Where then the essences of the soul (in the light of the virgin) can see in the centres of the stars, what is [1] in its original and source.

39. Of which my soul knoweth full well, and hath also received its knowledge thus, which [2] the learned master in the [3] hood of his degree cannot believe, because he cannot apprehend it; therefore he holdeth it to be impossible, and ascribeth it to the devil (as the *Jews* did by the Son of the Virgin, when he in [the virtue of] the virgin shewed signs and wrought miracles) which my soul regardeth not, neither esteemeth their pride, it hath enough in the Pearl; and it hath a longing to shew the thirsty [where] the Pearl [lieth]: The crowned hood [or cornered cap] may play merrily behind the curtain of Antichrist, [4] till the lily groweth, and then the smell of the lily will [cause some to] throw away the hood [or cap], saith the virgin; and the thirsty shall drink of the water of life; and [at that time] the Son of the Virgin will rule in the valley of *Jehosaphat*.

[1] in the original and well-spring of the soul.

[2] the great learned men in the universities, not taught by the Holy Ghost.
[3] crowned.

[4] They that are not blind shall see it.

40. Therefore seeing the mystery in the light of the virgin thus wonderfully meeteth us, we will here, for the seeking mind (which in earnest hope seeketh that it might find the Pearl) open yet one gate, as the same is opened to us in the virgin. For the mind asketh, Seeing that the sun, stars, and elements were never yet in the second Principle (where the virgin generateth herself out of the light) therefore how could they be able to know the virgin in *Adam*, so that they labour thus eagerly with longing after the virgin?

The Depth in the Centre.

41. Behold, thou seeking mind, that which thou seest before thy eyes, that is not the [1]element, neither in the fire, air, water, nor earth; neither are there four, but one only, and that is fixed and invisible, also imperceptible: For the fire which burneth is no element, but [it is] the fierce [stern wrath], which cometh to be such in the kindling of the anger, when the devils fell out of the [1]element: The element is neither hot nor cold, but it is the inclination [to be] in God, for the Heart of God is *Barm* [that is, warmth] and its [2]ascension is attractive and always finding; and then the *hertz* [that is, the heart] is the holding the thing before itself, and not in itself; and then the *ig* [the last syllable of the German word *Barm-hertz-ig* (that is, warm-hearted, or merciful) expounded according to the language of nature] is the continual dis-

[1] That one pure, holy, eternal element.

[2] rising up.

covering of the thing, and this is altogether *ewig* [eternal]; and that is the ground of the inward element, which maketh the anger substantial, so that it was visible and palpable, which [anger] Lucifer with his legions did awaken; and thereupon he now remaineth to be prince in the anger [or wrath] (in the kindled element) as Christ (according to this form) calleth him a prince of this world.

42. And the element remaineth hidden to the anger and [1]fierceness [or wrath], and standeth in [1]grimness. paradise; and the [1]fierce wrath goeth still out from the element; and therefore God hath captivated the devils with the element in the [1]fierce wrath, and he keepeth them [in] with the element; and the [1]fierce wrath cannot [touch or] comprehend [2]it, like the fire and the light; for the [2]the element. light is neither hot nor cold, but the [1]fierce wrath is hot; and the one holdeth the other, and the one generateth the other.

43. Here observe; *Adam* was created out of the element, out of the attracting of the heart of God, which is the will of the Father, and therein is the virgin of the divine virtue [or power], and the outward regimen (which in the kindling parted itself into four parts) would fain have had the same [virgin] in itself; that is, the fierceness of the devil would fain have dwelt in the Heart of God, and have domineered over it, and have opened a centre there, which the fierceness without the light cannot do; for every centre was generated

and opened with the kindling of the light. Thus the fierceness would fain be over the meekness, and therefore hath God caused the sun to come forth, so that it hath thus opened four centres, *viz.* the going forth out of the element.

44. And when the light of the sun appeared in the fierce [sourness or] harshness, then the harshness became thin and [1]sweet, even water, and the fierceness in the fire-flash was extinguished by the water, so that the anger stood still, yet the will could not rest, but went forth in the mother, out of the water, and moved itself, which is the air: And that which the fierce sourness had [2]attracted to it, that was thrust out of the element, in the water, as you see that earth swimmeth in the water.

[1] pleasant.

[2] coagulated.

45. Thus the evil child panteth after the mother, and would get to be in the mother in the element, and yet cannot reach her. But in *Adam* that [child] did perceive the element; and thereupon the four elements have drawn *Adam* to them, and supposed then that they had the mother; because the virgin there shewed herself in the living spirit of *Adam*.

46. Hereupon now the spirit of the stars and elements would continually [get] again into the element; for in the element there is meekness and rest; and in the [3]kindling thereof there is mere enmity and contrary will, and the devil ruleth also therein; and they would fain be released from that abominable and naughty guest, and they seek with

[3] *Viz.* in the four elements.

great anxiety after [1] deliverance, as *Paul* saith, *All creatures groan together with us, to be freed from vanity.*

[1] the dissolution.

47. Then saith the mind, Wherefore doth God let it move so long in the anxiety? Alas! when will it be that I shall see the virgin? Hearken, thou noble and highly worthy mind, it must all enter in, [and serve] to the glory of God, and praise God; as it is written, *All tongues shall praise God*; let it pass till the number to the praise of God be full, according to the eternal mind.

48. Thou wilt say, How great is that [number] then? Behold, tell the stars in the firmament; tell the trees, the herbs, and every [spire of] grass, if thou canst; so great is the number that shall enter in, to the glory and honour of God. For in the end all stars pass again into the element, into the mother; and there it shall appear, how much good they have brought forth here by their working. For the shadow and the image of every [thing or] substance shall appear before God, in the element, and stand eternally; in the same thou shalt have great joy, thou shalt see all thy works therein; also all the afflictions thou hast suffered, they shall be altogether changed into great joy, and shall refresh thee indeed; wait but upon the *LORD*; the spirit intimateth, that when the time of the lily is [2] expired, then this shall be done.

[2] Or come about.

49. Therefore it is that God keepeth it hidden so long (as to our sight) that the number of the glory

of his kingdom may be great; but before him it is but as the twinkling of an eye. Have but patience, this world will most certainly be dissolved, together with the fierceness which must abide in the first Principle; therefore do thou beware of that.

¹ figures or parables.

50. My beloved Reader, I bring in my ¹types of the essences of the incarnation in the mother's body, in a [colloquy or] conference of the spirit with the

² *Note.*

essences and elements. ²I cannot bring it to be understood in any easier way: Only you must know, that there is no conference, but it is done most certainly so in the essences, and in the spirit. Here you will say to me, thou dost not dwell in the

³ Wast incarnate in thy mother's womb.

incarnation, and see it; thou ³didst once indeed become man, but thou knewest not how, nor what [was done then]; neither canst thou go again into thy mother's body [or womb] and see how it came to pass there. Such a doctor was I also; and in my own reason I should be able to judge no otherwise, if I should stick still in my blindness. But thanks be to God, who hath regenerated me, by water and the Holy Ghost, to [be] a living creature, so that I can (in this light) see my great in-bred [native] vices, which are in my flesh.

51. Thus now I live in the spirit of this world in my flesh, and my flesh serveth the spirit of this world, and my mind [serveth] God: My flesh

⁴ kingdom or dominion.

is generated in this world, and hath its ⁴region [or government] from the stars and elements, which dwell in it, and are the master of the [outward]

[1]life; and my mind is [2]regenerated in God, and
loveth God.   And although I cannot comprehend
and hold the virgin (because my mind falleth into
sins) yet the spirit of this world shall not always
hold the mind captive.

[1] Or body.

[2] Or generated of God.

52. For the virgin hath given me her promise,
not to leave me in any misery, she will come to help
me in the Son of the Virgin.   I must but hold to
him again, and he will bring me well enough again
to her into paradise; I will give the venture,
and go through the thistles and thorns, as well as
I can, till I find my native country again, out of
which my soul is wandered, where my dearest virgin
dwelleth.   I rely upon her faithful promise, when
she appeared to me, that she would turn all my
mournings into great joy; and when I laid upon
the mountain towards the [3]north, so that all the
trees fell upon me, and all the storms and winds
beat upon me, and Antichrist gaped at me with his
open jaws to devour me, then she came and comforted
me, and married herself to me.

[3] Or midnight.

53. Therefore I am but the more cheerful, and care
not for him; he ruleth [and domineereth] over me no
further than over the [4]house of sin, whose patron he
himself is; he may take that quite away, and so I shall
come into my native country.   But yet he is not absolutely lord over it, he is but God's ape; for as an ape
(when its belly is full) imitateth all manner of tricks
and pranks to make itself sport, and would fain seem
to be the finest and the nimblest beast [it can], so also

[4] transitory house of flesh.

¹ *Note*, I desire
not to write
the exposition
of this yet.
doth he.   ¹ His power hangeth on the great tree of
this world, and a storm of wind can blow it away.

54. Now seeing I have shewn the Reader, how
the true element sticketh wholly hidden in the
outward kindled [elements], for a comfort to him,
that he may know what he [himself] is, and that
he may not despair in such an earnest manifestation
[or revelation as this is], therefore now I will go on
with my conference between the elements, sun, and
stars, where there is a continual wrestling and overcoming, in which the child in the mother's body [or
womb] is figured; and I freely give the Reader to
know, that indeed the true element lieth hidden in
the outward man, which is the chest of the treasure
[or cabinet of the precious gem and jewel] of the
² in.   soul, if it be faithful, and yield itself up ² to God.

55. So now when the heart, liver, lungs, bladder,
stomach, and spirit, together with the other parts
[or members] of the child, are figured in the mother's
body, by the constellation and elements, then the
region or regimen riseth up, which at length figureth
[fashioneth or formeth] all whatsoever was wanting:
And now it exceedingly concerneth us to consider
³ Or senses,   of the originality of speech, mind, and ³ thoughts,
inward senses.   wherein man is an image and similitude of God,
and wherein the noble knowledge of all the three
Principles doth consist.

56. For every beast also standeth in the springing
up of the life (formerly mentioned) in the mother's
body, and taketh its beginning after the same

manner in the [dam's or] mother's body, and its spirit liveth also in the stars and elements, and they have their [faculty of] seeing from the glance of the sun : And in the same [beginning of the life] there is no difference between man and beast.   For a beast eateth and drinketh, smelleth, heareth, seeth, and feeleth, as well as man ; and yet they have no understanding in them, but only to feed and multiply.   We must go higher, and see what the image of God is, which God so dearly loved, that he spent his Heart and Son upon it, and gave him to [1] become man, so that he came to help man again after the fall, and freed and redeemed him again from the bestial birth, and brought him again into paradise, into the heavenly [2] region.

[1] be incarnate.

[2] kingdom or dominion.

57. Therefore we must look after the ground [of it], how not only a bestial man, with bestial qualifications [or condition] is figured [or formed], but also a heavenly, and an image of God, to the honour of God and [the magnifying of] his deeds of wonder ; to which end he so very highly graduated man, that he had an eternal similitude and image of his own substance.   For to that end he hath manifested himself by heaven and earth, and created some creatures to [be] eternal, understanding, and rational spirits, to live in his virtue and glory, and some to [be] figures ; so that (when their spirit goeth into the ether and dissolveth) the spirits which are eternal might have their joy and recreation [3] with them.

[3] in.

58. Therefore we must search and see, what kind of image that is, and how it taketh its beginning so, that man beareth an earthly, elementary, and also an heavenly image. And not only so, but he beareth also a hellish [image] on him, which is inclined [or prone] to all sins and wickedness; and all this taketh beginning together with the beginning of the life.

59. And further, we must look, where then the own will sticketh, [whereby] man can in [his] own power yield up himself how he will, [either] to the kingdom of heaven, or to the kingdom of hell. To this looking-glass we will invite them that hunger and thirst after the noble knowledge, and shew them the ground, whereby they may in their minds be freed from the errors and contentious controversies in the antichristian kingdom. Whosoever now shall rightly apprehend this gate, ¹ being of all beings, or substance of all substances. he shall understand the ¹essence of all essences; and if he rightly consider it, [he shall so] learn to understand what *Moses*, and all the Prophets, and also what the holy Apostles have written, and in [or from] what kind of spirit every one hath spoken; also what hath ever been, and what shall or can be afterwards.

The most precious Gate in the Root of the Lily.

60. Now if we consider the three Principles, and how they are in their original, and how they generate themselves thus, then we [shall] find the essence of

all essences, how the one goeth out of the other thus, and how the one is higher graduated than the other, how the one is eternal, and the other corruptible, and how the one is fairer and better than the other : Also thus we [shall] find wherefore the one willeth [to go] [1] forward, and the other [2] backward : [1] in resignation. Also, [thus we shall] find the love and desire, and [2] in self. the hate [and enmity] of every thing.

61. But now we cannot say of the originalness of the essence of all essences otherwise, than that in the original there is but one only essence, out of which now goeth forth the essence of all essences ; and that one essence is the eternal mind of God, that standeth [hidden] in the darkness, and that same essence hath longed from eternity, and had it in the will to generate the light : And that longing is the source [or eternal working property], and that will is the springing up.   Now the springing up maketh the stirring and the mobility, and the mobility maketh the attracting in the will, and the will maketh again the longingness, so that the will always longeth after light : And this is an eternal band, that is without beginning and without end ; for where there is a willing, there is also desiring, and where there is a desiring, there is also, in the will's desiring, an attracting of that which the will desireth.   Now the desiring is sour, hard, and cold, for it draweth to it, and holdeth it ; for where there is nothing, there the desiring can hold nothing ; and therefore if the will desireth to

hold anything, the desiring must be hard, that the will may comprehend it; and being there was nothing from eternity, therefore the will also could comprehend and hold nothing.

62. Thus we find now that the three from eternity are an unbeginning and indissoluble band; *viz.* [1]longing, willing, and desiring; and the one always generateth the other, and if one were not, then the other also would not be, of which none know what it is; for it is in itself nothing but a spirit, which is in itself in the darkness; and yet there is no darkness, but a nothing, neither darkness nor light. Now then the [1]longing is an hunger [seeking], or an infecting of the desiring, and the will is a retention in the desiring; and now if the [desiring] must retain the will, then it must be comprehensible, and there must not be one [only] thing alone in the will, but two; now then seeing they are the two, therefore the attracting must be the third, which draweth that [which is] comprehensible into the will. Now this being thus from eternity, therefore it is found of itself, that from eternity there is a springing and moving; for that [which is] comprehended must spring and be somewhat, that the will may comprehend somewhat; and seeing that it is somewhat, therefore it must be sour and attractive, that it [may] come to be somewhat. And then seeing it is sour and attractive, therefore the attracting maketh the comprehensibility, that so the will [may] have

[1] attracting.

somewhat to comprehend and to hold; and then it being thus comprehensible, therefore it is thicker [grosser or darker] than the will, and it shadoweth the will, and covereth [1] that [which is attracted] and the will is in [1] that, and the longing maketh them both; and seeing now that the will is in that [which is] comprehensible, therefore that [which is] comprehensible is the darkness of the will; for it hath with its comprehensibility enclosed the will; now the will not being [2] out of that [which is] comprehensible, it longeth continually after the light, that it might be delivered from the darkness, which yet itself maketh with the longing and attracting.

[1] Which is comprehensible.

[2] gotten out.

63. From whence now cometh the anxiety, because the will is shut up in the darkness; and the attracting of the will maketh the mobility; and that [which is] movable maketh the will's rising up out of the darkness. Now therefore the rising up is the first [3] essence; for it generateth itself in the attracting, and is itself the attracting. And yet now the will cannot endure the attracting either, for it maketh that dark with the attracted essence [being or substance], which the will comprehendeth, and resisteth it, and the resisting is the stirring, and the stirring maketh a parting or breaking in that [which is] attracted, for it severeth [it]; and this also the sourness in the attracting cannot endure, and the anguish in the will is [thereby] the greater, and the attracting to hold

[3] *essentia*, proceeding, virtue.

the stirring [is] also the greater. So when the stirring is thus very hard knit together, and held by the sour attracting, then it eateth [gnaweth, presseth, or nippeth] itself, and becometh prickly, and stingeth in the sour anguish. And when the sourness attracteth the more vehemently [or strongly] to it, then the prickle becometh so very great in anxiety, that the will springeth up horribly, and setteth its purpose to fly away out of the darkness.

64. And here the eternal mind hath its original, in that the will will [go] out of that [1]source, into another [2]source of meekness, and from thence the eternal [1]source in the anguish hath also its original, and it is the eternal worm which generateth and eateth itself, and in its own fierceness in itself liveth in the darkness which itself maketh; and there also the eternal infection [or mixture] hath its original, back from which there is no further to be searched into, for there is nothing deeper, or [3]sooner; the same always maketh itself from eternity, and hath no maker or creator. And it is not God, but God's original [4]fierceness [or wrath], an anxiety, [or aching anguish], generating in itself, and gnawing [eating or devouring] in it, and yet consuming nothing, neither multiplying nor lessening.

65. Seeing then the eternal will, which is thus generated, getteth in the anxiety a mind after somewhat else, that it might escape the sourness

[1] property, or activity.
[2] flowing or working.
[3] Than the eternal property of hell.
[4] grim sternness.

[or fierceness], and exult in the meekness, and yet
it cannot otherwise be done than out of itself,
therefore the mind generateth again a will to live
in the meekness; and the originality of this will
ariseth out of the first will, out of the anguishing mind, out of the dark sourness, which in the
stirring maketh a breaking wheel; where the re-
comprehended will discovereth itself in the breaking
wheel in the great anxiety, in the eternal mind,
where somewhat [must] be which stood in the
meekness.   And this appearing [or discovery] in
the anxious breaking wheel, is a flash of a great
swiftness, which the anguish sharpeneth thus in
the sourness, so that the sharpness of the flash is
consuming, and that is the fire-flash, as it is to be
seen in nature, when one [1] hard substance striketh
against another, how it [grindeth or] sharpeneth
itself, and generateth a flash of fire, which was not
before.   And the re-comprehended mind [2] comprehendeth the flash, and discovereth itself now in the
sourness; and the flash with its strong [or
fierce] sharpness consumeth the comprehended
sourness, which holdeth it [*viz.* the will in the
mind] captive in the darkness; and now it is free
from the darkness.

66. Thus the sourness receiveth the flash, and
goeth in the terror [shriek or crack] backwards, as
it were overcome, and from the terror [shriek or
crack] becometh soft; in which meekness the flash
discovereth itself, as in its own mother.   And from

[1] A flint and steel.

[2] Or conceiveth.

the meekness it becometh ¹white and clear: And in the flash there is great joy, that the will therein is delivered from the darkness.

67. Thus now the eternal mind ²uniteth itself in the re-comprehended [or re-conceived] will, in [or unto] the meekness of the deliverance out of the darkness of the anxiety; and the sharpness of the consuming of the eternal darkness stayeth in

the flash of the meekness; and the flash ³discovereth itself in the anxious mind in many thousand

thousands, yea, ⁴without end and number. And in that discovery the will and the inclination [or yielding up itself] discover themselves always again in a great desire to go forth out of the darkness; where then in every will the flash standeth again to [make an] opening, which I call the *centrum* [the centre] in my writings all over in this book.

68. Thus then the first longing and desiring (*viz.* the fierce [or stern] generating in the first

will) with the dark mind, continueth ⁵in itself, and [hath] therein the discovering of the always enduring fire-flash in the dark mind; and the same dark mind standeth eternally in anguish, and in the flash, in the breaking, attracting, rising up, and desiring without intermission [to be] over the meekness, when as in the breaking, with the fire-flash, (in the sharpness of the flash), in the essence,

the attracting springeth up like a ⁶*centrum* or *Principium*.

The Gate of God the Father.

69. And thus now in the sharpness of the fire-flash, the light in the eternal mind springeth up out of the re-comprehended will to meekness and light, that it might be freed from the darkness; and so this freedom from the darkness is a meekness and [1]satisfaction of the mind, in that it is free from the anxiety, and standeth in the sharpness of the fire-flash, which breaketh the sour darkness, and maketh it clear and light in its [first glimpse, shining, or] appearing.

[1] well-doing.

70. And in this [shining or] appearing of the sharpness, standeth the all-mightiness [or omni-potency]; for [2]it breaketh the darkness in itself, and maketh the joy and great meekness, like that when a man is come out of an anguishing [or scorching] fire to sit in a temperate place of refreshment; and thus the flash in itself is so fierce and sudden, yea fiercer and more sudden than a thought, and out of the darkness in itself (in its kindling) seeth into the light; and then is so very much terrified, that it lets its power (which it had in the fire) sink down. And this terror [or shriek or crack] is made in the sharpness of the flash; and this now is the terror [shriek or crack] of great joy; and there the re-comprehended will desireth the crack or joy in the meekness; and the desiring is the attracting of the joy, and the attracting is the infecting [or mingling] in the will; and that

[2] the appearing or flash.

[which is] attracted maketh the will swell [or be impregnated], for it is therein, and the will holdeth it [fast].

71. Now here is nothing which the will with the sharpness or essence could draw to it, but the meekness, the deliverance from the darkness; this is the desire of the willing, and therein then standeth the pleasant joy, which the will draweth to itself; and the attracting in the will impregnateth the will, that it becometh full.

72. And thus the comprehended will is swelled [or impregnated] by the joy in the meekness, which it desireth (without intermission) to generate out of itself, for its own joy again, and for its sweet taste [or relish] in the joy. And the same will to generate, comprehendeth the meekness in the joy (which standeth in the swelled [or impregnated] will) and it bringeth the essences (or the attracting) of the willing again out of the will, before the will; for the desiring draweth forth the swelling [or impregnation] out of the swelled [or impregnated] will, before the will; and that [which is] drawn forth is the pleasant virtue, [1]joy, and meekness. And this now is the desiring of the eternal will (and no more) but to eat and to draw again this virtue into it, and to be satiated therewith, and [it can] desire nothing higher or more [1]refreshing: for therein is the perfection [or fulness] of the highest [1]joy and meekness.

[1] habitation.

73. And so in this virtue (which is in God the Father, as is before mentioned) standeth the omniscience [or all knowledge] of what is in the originality in the eternity; where the flash then [1] discovereth itself in many thousand thousands [2] without number. For this virtue of joy in the [refreshment or] habitation, is proceeded from the sharpness of the flash, and (in the sharpness of the all-mightiness over the darkness) seeth [or looketh] again in the eternal sharpness in the dark mind; and that mind inclineth itself to the virtue and desireth the virtue, and the virtue goeth not back again in the darkness, but [3] beholdeth itself therein, from whence [it is] that the eternal mind is continually longing [panting or lusting] after the virtue [or power]; and the virtue is the sharpness, and the sharpness is the attracting. This is called the [4] eternal *Fiat*, which there createth and corporizeth what the eternal will in the almighty meekness (which there is the might and the breaking [or destroyer] of the darkness, and the building of the Principle), and what the will in the eternal [skill or] knowledge discovereth, and in itself conceiveth [apprehendeth, or purposeth], to do. And whatsoever giveth itself up to the meekness, that will the will create by the sharp *Fiat* which is the eternal essence. And this now is the will of God, whatsoever inclineth itself to him, and desireth him, that same he will create in the meekness; even all whatsoever (out of the many thousand

[1] Or sparkleth into.
[2] infinitely.

[3] As the sun doth in the water.

[4] Note.

thousands, out of the infiniteness) inclineth itself

¹ Or his.   in ¹ its virtue to him.

74. Now thus the infiniteness hath the possibility, while it is yet in the first essence [or substance],

² enter into resignation.   that it can ² incline itself to him; but here you must not understand it any more concerning the whole, for God only is the whole [*totum universale*], the great deep all over; but this [which is] in the infiniteness is divided; and it is in the appearing [flash or sparkling] of the plurality [or multiplicity], where the whole, in and through himself in the eternal impregnated darkness, [sparkleth, or] dis-covereth itself *in infinitum* [or infinitely]. This

³ Or these in-finite sparks.   discovery, [or ³ these sparklings], stand altogether in the originality of the fire-flash, and may again,

⁴ Or bitterness of the frost.   in the impregnated darkness (*viz.* in the ⁴ cold sourness, and in the flash of the fire), discover

⁵ Or unite themselves.   [flash or sparkle] and ⁵ give up themselves, or again conceive a will out of the darkness, to go out of the anxiety of the mind (through the sharpness in

⁶ In true resignation.   the flash) ⁶ in the meekness, to God.

75. For the sharpness in the flash is always the *centrum* [or *centre*] to the regeneration in the second Principle; to which now the worm in the spark inclineth [or uniteth] to generate itself [in], whether it be in the eternal cold out of the sharp essence through the flash in the fierceness [or sternness] of the fire, or out of the sharpness in the regeneration of the meekness to God; therein it

⁷ Or recalling.   standeth, and there is no ⁷ recovery [back from

thence].   For, the meekness goeth not back again
into the dark, fierce, and cold essence, in the first
attracting, which from eternity is before the re-
comprehended [or re-conceived] will; but it cometh
to help that [darkness], and enlighteneth whatsoever cometh to it out of the strong might of God,
and this liveth in the virtue, and in the light
eternity with God.

76. And the deep of the darkness is as great as
the habitation of the light; and they stand not
one distant from the other, but together in one
another, and neither of them hath beginning or
end; there is no limit or place, but the sharp
regeneration is the mark [stroke, bounds] or
limitation between these two Principles.

77. Neither of them is above or beneath, only the
regeneration out of the darkness in the meekness is
said to be above; and there is such a [bar or] [1] firmament between them, that neither of them both doth
comprehend the one the other; for the [bar or]
mark of limitation is a whole birth or Principle,
and a firm centre, so that none of them both can
go into the other, but [only] the sharp fire-flash,
the strong might of God, that standeth in the
midst in the centre of the regeneration, and that
only looketh into the worm of the darkness; and
with its terror in the darkness maketh the eternal
anguishing source, the rising-up in the fire, which
yet can reach nothing but only the anguish, and in
the anguish the fierce [stern] flash.   And so now

[1] clift, door, or gulf.

whatsoever becometh corporized there, in the stern [fierce or strong] mind, in the sparkling [or shining] of the infiniteness, and doth not put its will (in the corporizing) [1] forward, into the centre of the regeneration, in the meekness of God, that remaineth in the dark mind, in the fire-flash.

78. And so that creature hath no other will in itself, neither can it ever make any other will from anything; for there is no more in it, but [a will] to fly up in its own un-regenerated might above the centre, and to rule [or domineer] in the might of the fire over the meekness of God, and yet it cannot reach it.

79. And here is the original [cause] that the creature of the darkness willeth to be above the Deity, as the devil did; and here is the original of self-pride; for such as the [2] source in the creature is, such also is the creature. For the creature is [proceeded] out of the essence; and on the other side, the [2] source (*viz.* its worm) is [proceeded] out of the eternal will of the dark mind.

[2] Or fountain.

80. And this will is not the will of God, neither is it God; but the [3] re-conceived will [4] to meekness in the mind, is God's regenerated will, which standeth there in the centre of the birth in the sharpness of the breaking [or destroying] of the darkness, and in the pleasant [5] loving kindness of the fulness of the joy and springing up of the light in the re-impregnating of the will, and to generate the virtue of the eternal omniscience and

[3] re-purposed.

[4] in resignation.

[5] Or well-doing.

wisdom in the love, that is God; and the out-
going from him is his willing [or desiring], which
the essence (*viz.* the sharp *Fiat*) createth; and God
dwelleth in the second Principle, which is eternally
generated out of the eternal centre out of the
eternal will, [and this] is the kingdom of God
without number and end, as it further followeth.

The Gate of the Son of God, the pleasant Lily in the Wonders.

81. Therefore as the will doth thus impregnate
itself from eternity, so also it hath an eternal
willing [or desiring] to [1] bring forth the child with [1] generate.
which it is big [impregnated, or conceived]. And
that eternal will to [1] bring forth, doth bring forth
eternally the child which the will is conceived
withal; and this child is the eternal virtue [or
power] of meekness, which the will conceiveth
again in itself, and expresseth [or speaketh forth]
the depth of the Deity, with the eternal wonders
of the wisdom of God.

82. For the will [is it] that expresseth; and
the child of the [eternal] virtue, and the eternal
meekness, is the Word which the will speaketh;
and the going forth out of the spoken Word, is
the spirit, which in the sharp might of God, in
the centre of the regeneration, out of the eternal
mind, out of the anxiety in the fire-flash in the
sharpness of the [destroying or] breaking of the

darkness, and ¹breaking forth of the light in the meekness, out of the eternal will from eternity, goeth forth out of the Word of God, with the sharp *Fiat* of the great might of God; and it is the Holy Ghost [or Spirit] of God, which is in the virtue [or power] of the Father, and goeth eternally forth from the Father through the Word, out of the mouth of God.

The Gate of God's Wonders in the Rose of the Lily.

83. Now reason asketh, Whither goeth the Holy Ghost, when he goeth forth out of the Father and Son, through the Word of God? Behold, thou sick *Adam*, here the gate of heaven standeth open, and very well to be understood, by those that will [or have a mind to it]. For the bride saith, *Come, and whosoever thirsteth, let him come*, and whosoever cometh, drinketh of the fountain of the knowledge of the eternal life in the smell and virtue of the lily of God in paradise.

84. As is mentioned above, so the ground of the Holy Trinity is in one only divine and undivided essence [being, or substance], God the Father, Son, and Holy Ghost; from eternity arising from nothing, always generated from and out of itself from eternity; not beginning nor ending, but dwelling in itself; comprehended by nothing, having neither beginning nor end; subject to no locality, nor limit [number], nor place. It hath no place of its

rest, but the deep is greater than we [can perceive or] think, and yet it is no deep, but it is the unsearchable eternity; and if any here will think [to find] an end or limit, they will be confounded [or disturbed] by the Deity, for there is none; it is the end of nature. And whosoever [goeth about to] think [or dive with his thoughts] [1] deeper, doth [1] Or further. like Lucifer, who in [high-mindedness or] pride, would fly out above the Deity, and yet there was no place, but he went on himself, into the fiery fierceness, and so he perished [withered, or became dry as] to the fountain of the kingdom of God.

85. Now see the lily, thou noble mind, full of anguish and afflictions of this world; behold, the Holy Trinity hath an eternal will in itself, and the will is the desiring, and the desiring is the eternal essences, wherein then standeth the sharpness (viz. the *Fiat*) which goeth forth out of the heart, and out of the mouth of God by the Holy Ghost [or Spirit] of God. And the will [that is] gone forth out of the spirit, [that] is the divine virtue, which conceiveth [or comprehendeth] the will, and holdeth it, and the *Fiat* createth it [viz. that virtue], so that in it, as in God himself, all essences are, and [so that] the blossom of the light in it may spring up [and blossom] out of the Heart of God; and yet this is not God, but [it is] the chaste virgin of the eternal wisdom and understanding, of which I treat often in this book.

86. Now the virgin is [present] before God, and

¹ uniteth.

² hovereth.

³ Or God's fruit.

¹inclineth herself to the spirit from which the virtue proceedeth, out of which she (*viz.* the chaste virgin) is; this is now God's companion to the honour and joy of God; the same appeareth or discovereth herself in the eternal wonders of God. In the discovery, she becometh longing after the wonders in the eternal wisdom, which yet is herself, and thus she longeth in herself, and her longing is the eternal essences, which attract the holy virtue to her, and the *Fiat* createth them, so that they stand in [or become] a substance; and she is a virgin, and never generateth any thing, neither taketh any thing into her; her inclination standeth in the Holy Ghost, who goeth forth from God, and attracteth nothing to him, but ²moveth before God, and is the ³blossom [or branch] of the growth.

87. And so the virgin hath no will to conceive [or be impregnated with] anything; her will is [only] to open the wonders of God; and therefore she is in the will in the wonders, to discover [or make] the wonders [appear] in the eternal essences; and that virgin-like will createth the sour *Fiat* in the essences, so that it is [become] a substance, and standeth eternally before God, wherein the eternal wonders of the virgin of the wisdom of God are revealed.

88. And this substance is the eternal element, wherein all essences in the divine virtue stand open, and are visible: and wherein the fair and

chaste virgin of the divine wisdom always discovereth herself according to the number of the infiniteness, out of the many thousand thousands without end and number. And in this discovering there go forth out of the eternal element, colours, arts, and virtues, and the [1] sprouts of the lily of [1] fruits. God; at which the Deity continually rejoiceth itself in the virgin of the wisdom; and that joy goeth forth out of the eternal essences, and is called paradise, in regard of the sharpness of the generating [or bringing forth] of the pleasant fruit of the lily [*in infinitum* or] infinitely; where then the essences of the lily spring up in wonders in many thousand thousands without number, of which you have a similitude in the [springing or blossoming earth.

89. Beloved mind, behold, consider this, this now is God and his heavenly kingdom, even the eternal element and paradise, and it standeth thus in the eternal original from eternity to eternity. Now what joy, delight, and pleasantness is therein, I have no pen that can describe it, neither can I express it; for the earthly tongue is too much insufficient to do it; [all that men can say of it] is like dross compared with gold, and much more inferior; yea, although the virgin [2] bringeth it into [2] discovereth it in the mind. the mind, yet all is too dark and too cold in the whole man, so that he cannot express so much as one spark [or glimpse] thereof sufficiently. We will defer it till [we come] into the bosom of the

virgin; we have here only given a short hint of it, that the author of this book may be understood; for we are but a very little drop out of the fountain of the wisdom of God; and we speak as a little sparkle [or glimpse], but [high] enough for our ¹ Or in respect. earthly [understanding], and ¹ for our weak knowledge here upon earth; for in this life we have no need of any higher knowledge of the eternal substance [being or essence]; if we do but barely and nakedly speak of what hath been from eternity, it is enough.

THE FIFTEENTH CHAPTER

Of the [1]Knowledge of the Eternity in the Corruptibility of the Essence of all Essences.

1. NOW if we consider of the eternal will of God, [and] of the [2]essence of all essences; then we find in the originalness but one [only being, substance or] essence, as is mentioned above. Out of this [only] essence is generated from eternity the other [being, substance, or] essence, *viz.* the divine essence, and we find that both the [beings, substances or] essences stand in divine omnipotence, but not in one [3]source, neither do they mix together, nor can either of them both be [destroyed, dissolved, corrupted, or] broken.

2. But yet they have two sorts of inclinations [or desires], each in itself for its own. Yet because the divine [being or] essence from eternity is generated out of itself, therefore it is inclined to help the weak, and is rightly called *Barmhertzig-keit* [mercifulness].

3. And now seeing the virgin of the eternal wisdom hath [4]discovered herself in the eternal

original, and in the eternal mind in the sharp
essence of the breaking of the darkness in the fire-
flash [hath found] the depth of the [¹very] image
of God, and that the similitude of God is there
in the eternal original, therefore she hath longed
after the similitude, and that longing maketh the
attracting in the will, and the will stood [²right]
against the similitude; and the *Fiat* in the
attracting of the willing, created the will in the
similitude, out of which came the angels all together.
But now the eternal essences were in the similitude,
and the wisdom discovered [or manifested] herself
in the essences in many thousand thousands, that
the eternal wonders might be revealed [or made
manifest]; and thereupon there went forth (according to every essence, as out of a fountain) many
thousand thousands.

4. And from thence came the names of the
thrones and principalities, as according to the
essences of the first and great ³source, which in
the discovering of the eternal wisdom of God goeth
forth again into many thousand thousands, yet
there is a certain number [of them], and in the
centre of God none [or no number, but infiniteness];
and thus out of the fountain of every essence are
gone forth, first the ⁴thrones, and in the throne
many thousand thousands.

5. These the *Fiat* created to a similitude and
image of God, and overshadowed the same in the
Fiat with the overflowing virtue of God; and the

¹ *Ebenbild.*

² Or presented
before.

³ Or fountain.

⁴ Or throne-
angels.

will of God [1] set itself [right] against the image and
similitude, and they now which received the will,
they became angels, for they set their imagination,
in the will, in the heart of God, and they did eat
of the *Verbum Domini* [of the Word of the Lord];
but they that set their imagination in the dark
mind, as Lucifer [did, that he might] fly out above
the Deity and meekness in the might of the fire in
the flash, in the sharp might of God, and be lord
alone, they became devils, and they have that
name from their being thrust [or driven] out of
the light; for they were in the light when the
Fiat created them, for the *Fiat* which created
them stood in the light.

6. Thus the devil is the fault, and guilty of his
own fall, for he suffered himself to be moved by
the matrix of the [2] sternness [fierceness, sourness, or
wrath], whereas he yet had his own will to take
hold of light or darkness. And Lucifer was a
throne (that is, a [3] source [or fountain] of a great
essence) from whence went forth all his servants
[or ministers], and they did like him; and so they
were thrust back into the darkness, for the light
of God goeth not into the [grimness, wrath or]
fierceness.

7. And there the *Fiat* (which created the fierce
[wrathful or grim] devils, in hope that they would
of devils become angels, who set their imagination
therein, that thereby they might domineer over
God and the kingdom of heaven) was infected in

[1] Or presented itself before.

[2] Or grimness.

[3] a fountain with a great many veins, or as a stock with many branches.

the figuring of the similitudes; and so instantly kindled the element in the similitude, *viz.* in the out-birth [or procreation], in the speculating [or beholding], so that the essence hath generated to the highest essences, from whence go forth the four elements of this world, of the third Principle; and the sharp *Fiat* of God (which stood in the out-birth [or procreation]) hath created the out-birth, out of which the earth and stones are proceeded.

8. For when the *Fiat* kindled the element in the out-birth, then the kindled *materia* [or matter] became palpable [or comprehensible], this was not now fit for paradise, but it was ex-created, [or made external]. Yet that the element with its out-birth might no more generate thus, therefore God created the heaven out of the [1] element, and [caused or] suffered out of the element (which is the heavenly *limbus*), the third Principle to spring up; where the spirit of God again discovered [or revealed] itself in the virgin, *viz.* in the eternal wisdom, and found out, in the out-birth, in the corruptible substance, the similitude again. And the discovering stood in the sharp attraction of the *Fiat*, and the *Fiat* created it so that it became essential [or substantial]; and the same are the stars, a mere *quinta essentia*, an extract of the *Fiat's*, out of the *limbus* of God, wherein the hidden element standeth.

[1] the one pure element.

9. But that the sharp and severe essence with the attraction might cease, therefore God generated

a similitude according to the fountain of the Heart of God, *viz.* the sun ; and herewith sprang up the third Principle of this world, and that [*viz.* the sun] put all things into meekness and [1] well-fare.

[1] well-doing, or kindness.

10. Seeing then that the eternal wisdom of God (*viz.* in the chaste virgin of the divine virtue) had discovered itself in the Principle of this world, in which place the great prince Lucifer stood in the heaven, in the second Principle, therefore the same discovering was eternal, and God desired to shed forth the similitude out of the essences, which the *Fiat* created according to the kind of every essence, that they should (after the breaking [or dissolution] of the outward substance) be a figure and image in paradise, and a shadow of this substance.

11. And that there should go nothing in vain out of the substances of God, therefore God created beasts, fowls, fishes, worms, trees and herbs out of all essences ; and besides [created] also figured spirits out of the *quinta essentia*, in the elements, that so, after the fulfilling of the time (when the out-birth [shall] go into the ether) they should appear before him, and that his eternal wisdom in his works of wonder might be known.

12. But seeing it was his will also in this throne, in the eternal element, to have creatures that should be instead of the fallen devils, and possess the place [of them] in the heaven in paradise, therefore he created man out of the [2] element.

[2] the eternal one element.

13. And as this place was now twofold, and

¹with the eternal originality threefold (*viz.* [having] the first principle in the great anxiety, and the second Principle in the divine habitation in paradise, and then the third Principle in the light of the sun, in the quality of the stars and elements), so must man also be created out of all three, if he must be an angel in this place, and receive all knowledge and understanding, whereby he might have eternal joy also with [or in] the figures and images, which stand not in the eternal spirit, but in the eternal figure, as all things in this world are [or do].

14. And there God manifesteth himself according to his eternal will, in his eternal wisdom of the noble virgin, in the element, which in paradise standeth in the sharpness of the divine virtue [or power]. And the *Fiat* created man out of the element in paradise, for it attracted to it out of the quintessence of the sun, stars, and elements in paradise, in the element of the originality (from whence the four elements proceed) and created man to the image of God (that is, to the similitude of God) and breathed into him into the element of the body (which yet was nothing else but paradisical virtue) the spirit of the eternal essences out of the eternal originality ; and there man became a living soul, and an image of God in paradise.

15. And the wisdom of God, the pleasant virgin, did ²discover herself in him, and with the discovering opened *Adam's* centre, in [or to] many

thousand thousands, which should proceed out of this fountain of this image; and the noble virgin of the wisdom and virtue [or power] of God was espoused [or contracted] to him, that he should be modest and wholly chaste to his virgin, and set no desire in the first, nor in the third Principles, to qualify [mix with] or live therein, but his inclination or longing must be to get into the Heart of God, and to eat of the [1] *Verbum Domini* [of the Word of the Lord] in all the fruits of this world.

[1] The Word that proceedeth out of the mouth of God.

16. For the fruits were also good, and their inclination [or that which made them to be desired] proceeded out of the inward element, out of the [2] paradise.   Now *Adam* could eat of every fruit in the mouth, but not [3] in the corruptibility, that must not be, for his body must subsist eternally, and continue in paradise, and generate a chaste virgin out of himself, like himself, without rending of his body ; for this could be, seeing his body was [proceeded] out of the heavenly element, out of the virtue of God.

[2] the divine habitation.

[3] Or in the stomach or maw, where the meat turneth to corrupt dung.

17. But when the chaste virgin found herself thus in *Adam* with great wisdom, meekness, and humility, then the outward elements became lusting after the eternal, that they might [4] raise themselves up in the chaste virgin, and [5] qualify in her ; seeing that *Adam* was extracted out of them [*viz.* the four elements], out of the *quinta essentia*, therefore they desired their own, and would qualify therein, which yet God did forbid to *Adam*,

[4] discover or manifest.

[5] Or mix with her, or work in her.

[saying] that he should not eat of the knowledge of good and evil, but live in [the] one [only element], and be contented with paradise.

18. But the spirit of the great world overcame *Adam*, and put itself in with force, *in quintam essentiam* [into the quintessence], which there is the fifth form, the extract out of the four elements and stars; and there must God create a woman [or wife] for *Adam* out of his essences, if he must be to fill the kingdom, according to the appearing [discovering, shining, or sparkling] of the noble virgin, [with many thousand thousands], and build [or propagate] the same. And thus man ·became earthly, and the virgin departed from him in paradise; and there she warned [called and told] him that he should lay off the earthliness, and then she would be his bride and loving spouse. And now it cannot be otherwise in this world with man, he must be [1] generated in the virtue of the outward constellation and elements, and live therein till the earthliness falleth away.

[1] begotten, conceived, born, nourished, and preserved.

19. And thus he is in this life threefold, and the threefold spirit hangeth on him, and he is generated therein, neither can he be rid of it, except he [corrupt or] break to pieces; yet he can be rid of paradise, whensoever his spirit imagineth in the fierceness [or wrath] and falsehood, and giveth up himself thereto, that so he might be above meekness and righteousness in himself, as a lord, like Lucifer, [and] live in pride [and stateliness]; and

then paradise [1] falleth [away], and is shut up; [1] ceaseth, vanisheth, or
and he loseth his first image which standeth in the disappeareth.
hidden element in Paradise.

20. For the Adamical [2] however (according to the [2] though he
liveth in the
inward element which standeth open in the mind) four elements.
can live in paradise, if he striveth against evil, and
wholly with all his strength give himself up to the
Heart of God, then the virgin dwelleth with him,
(in the inward element in paradise), and enlighteneth
his mind, so that he can tame the Adamical body.

21. For these [3] three births are [inbred or] [3] Or these
three proper-
generated together with every one in the mother's ties, darkness,
[womb or] body, and none ought to say, *I am* light, and the
four elements.
not elected; for it is a lie, [and he] belieth the
element, (wherein man also liveth); and besides
[he] belieth the virgin of wisdom, which God
giveth to every one which seeketh her with earnestness and humility. So [likewise] the possibility of
seeking is also in every one, and it is inbred [or
generated] in him with the all-possible hidden
element [to which all things are possible]; and
there is no other cause of perdition in man, than
[was in or] with Lucifer, whose will stood free; he
must either reach into God in humility, chastity,
and meekness, or into the dark mind, in the climbing up of malice and fierceness [or grimness], which
yet ([4] in its flowing forth) desireth not to lift itself [4] the fierceness
in its working
up above God, but it inclineth itself only above the would not lift
up itself above
meekness, in the fire-flash, in the stern [or fierce] God.
regeneration: But the devils would (as creatures)

be above all, and be lords wholly [of themselves], and [1] so it is also with man here.

[1] *Note*, the evil of nature is not in fault, but the creature is in fault, and guilty.

22. The pride of nature indeed inclineth one man more strongly than another, but it forceth [or compelleth] none that they must be proud; and if there be a force [or strong compulsion upon any], then it is when man willingly, for temporal honour and pleasure sake, lets the devil into his eternal essences; and then he [the devil] seeth presently how that man is inclined [or led] by the spirit of this world, and in that way tempteth him accordingly; if man letteth him but in, he is then a guest very hardly to be driven out again; yet it is very possible, if that man entirely and sincerely purposeth to turn, and to live according to the will of God, then the virgin is always ready [before-hand] in the way to help him.

23. It goeth very hard, when the [grain of] mustard-seed is sown, (for the devil opposeth strongly), but whosoever persevereth, findeth by experience what is written in this book. And although he cannot be rid of the untowardness of the incitements of the four elements, yet nevertheless the

[2] in the pure eternal one element.

noble seed in the [2] *limbus* of God continueth with him, which seed springeth and groweth, and at last becometh a tree, which the devil favoureth [or relisheth] not; but he goeth about the tree like a fawning cur which pisseth against the tree; and then by his servants he casteth all mishaps upon him; and by his crew [of followers and con-

federates] he thrusteth many out of [1]his house, [1] out of this earthly rotten tabernacle.
that he may do him no more displeasure. But it
goeth well with him [that feareth God], and he
cometh into the land of the living.

24. Therefore we say now (according to our high
knowledge), that the source [or active desire] of all
the three Principles doth imprint itself together
[2]with the child's incarnation [or becoming man], in [2] Or in.
the mother's body. For after that man is figured
[or shaped] from the stars and elements, by the
Fiat, so that the elements have taken possession
of their regions [kingdoms, or dominions] (*viz.* the
heart, liver, lungs, bladder, and stomach, wherein
they have their regions), then must the [3]artificer [3] Or work-master, the *Fiat*.
in his twofold form rise up out of all essences;
for there standeth now the image of God, and
the image of this world, and there also is the image
of the devil. Now there must be wrestling and
overcoming, and there is need of the Treader
upon the Serpent, even in the mother's [womb
or] body.

25. Therefore, ye fathers and mothers, be honest
and live in the fear of God, that the Treader upon
the Serpent may also be in your fruit. For Christ
saith, *A good tree cannot bring forth evil fruit,
and an evil tree cannot bring forth good fruit.*
And although this indeed is meant of the mind
that is [4]brought up; which hath its own under- [4] Or cometh to act of itself.
standing [or meaning], thus, that no false mind
bringeth forth good fruit, nor any good mind evil

fruit; yet it is effectually necessary for the children [that the parents be honest and virtuous], because the child is generated from the essences of the parents.

26. And though it be clear that the stars in the outward birth [geniture or operation] do alter the essences in every one according to their [1] source [quality, influence, or property], yet the element is still there, and they cannot alter that with their power, except man himself do it; they have only the outward region; and besides, the devil dare not [2] image [or imprint] himself, before the time of the understanding, when man can incline himself to the evil or to the good. Yet none must presume upon this [impotency of the devil, and four elements], for if the parents be wicked, God can well forsake a wicked seed. For he willeth not that the Pearl should be cast before swine; although he is very inclined to help all men, yet it is [effectual] but for those that turn to him; and although the child is in innocency, yet the seed is not in innocency; and therefore it hath need of the Treader upon the Serpent [or Saviour]. Therefore, ye parents, consider what ye do; especially ye knaves and whores; ye have a hard lesson [to learn] here, consider it well, it is no jesting matter, it shall be shewn you [3] in its place, that the heaven thundereth [and passeth away with a noise]. Truly the time of the rose bringeth it forth, and it is high time to awake, for the sleep is at an end, there shall a great

[1] operation.

[2] Or give himself into the imagination.

[3] in the book of *Election and Predestination.*

[1]rent be before the lily; therefore let every one take heed to his ways.

[1] cleaving asunder, shaking and alteration, as by an earthquake.

27. If we now search into the life of man in the mother's [womb or] body, concerning his virtue [or power], speech, and [2] senses, and the noble and most precious mind; then we find the cause whereof we have made such a long [3] register concerning the eternal birth; for the speech, senses, and mind, have also such an original, as is abovementioned concerning the eternal birth of God, and it is a very precious gate [or exposition].

[2] Or thoughts.

[3] catalogue or relation.

28. For behold, when the gate of this world in the child is made ready, so that the child is [become] a living soul out of the essences, and now [henceforth] seeth only [by or] in the light of the sun, and not in the light of God, then cometh the true [4] artificer, instantly in the twinkling of an eye, (when the light of the life kindleth), and figureth [that which is] his; for the centre breaketh forth in all the three Principles. First, there are the four essences in the *Fiat* in the stern might of God, which there are the child's own, the worm of its soul, which standeth there in the house of the great anxiety, as in the originality. For the seed is sown in the will, and the will receiveth the *Fiat* in the tincture, and the *Fiat* draweth the will to it inwardly, and outwardly [draweth] the seed to a [5] mass; for the inward and outward [6] artificer is there.

[4] the master, the *Fiat*.

[5] concretion, substance, or body.

[6] Or master.

29. When the will thus draweth to it, then it becometh inwardly and outwardly impregnated,

and is darkened; the will cannot endure this, *viz.* to be set in the dark, and therefore falls into great anxiety for the light; for the outward *materia* [or matter] is filled with the elements, and the blood is choked [checked or stopped]; and there then the tincture withdraweth, and there is then the right abyss of death, and so the inward [*materia* or matter] is filled from the essences of the virtue [or power], and in the inward there riseth up another will, out of the stern virtue of the essences, [that it might] lift itself up into the light of the meekness; and in the outward standeth the desire to be severed, the impure from the pure, for that the outward *Fiat* doth.

30. We must consider, in the virtue [or power] of the virgin, that the will first is threefold, and each in its centre is fixed [stedfast or perfect] and pure, for it proceedeth out of the tincture. In the first centre there springeth up between the parents of the child the inclination [or lust], and the bestial desire to copulate; this is the outward elementary centre, and it is fixed in itself. Secondly, there springeth up, in the second centre, the inclinable love to the copulating; and although they were at the first sight angry and odious one to another, yet in the copulating the centre of love springeth up, and that only in the copulating; for the one pure tincture receiveth [or catcheth] the other, and in the copulating the [1]mass receiveth them both.

31. Now thus the love qualifieth [or mixeth]

[1] *massa*, or concretion.

with the inward [one] element, and the element
with the paradise, and the paradise is before [or in
the presence of] God. And the outward seed hath
its essences, which qualify first with the outward
elements, and the outward elements qualify with
the outward stars, and the outward stars qualify
with the outward sternness [grimness, fierceness,
frowardness], wrath and malice, and the wrath and
malice in the fierceness [severity, or austereness]
qualifieth with the original of the first fierceness of
the abyss of hell; and the abyss qualifieth with
the devils.

32. Therefore, O man! consider what thou hast
received with thy bestial body, to eat and to drink
of evil and good, which God did forbid. Look here
into the ground of the essences, and say not with
reason, It was merely for disobedience, which God
was so very angry at, that his anger could not
be quenched. Thou art deceived, for if the
clear Deity were angry, it would not have become
man for thy sake to help thee; look but upon
the [1] mark, in the eternity, and then thou wilt [1] Or aim.
find all.

33. Thus also the kingdom of darkness and of
the devil is sown together in the copulating, and
the third centre of the [2] great desire springeth up [2] Or hot zeal.
along with it, out of which the fierceness [grimness,
or wrath], and the house of flesh, are generated.
For the pure love, which reacheth the element, and
consequently the paradise, hath a wholly modest

¹ perfect or complete.

and chaste centre, and it is ¹ fixed in itself, of which I here give you a true example.

Diligently and deeply to be considered.

²Text, Menschen.
³ Or flower.

34. Behold two young ²people, who have attained unto the ³blossom of the noble tincture in the matrix and *limbus*, so that it be kindled, how very hearty, faithful, and pure love they bear one towards another, where one is ready to impart the very heart within them to the other, if it could be done without death ; this now is the true paradisical blossom, and this blossom ⁴qualifieth, with the [one] element and paradise. But as soon as ever they ⁵take one another, and copulate, they infect one another with their ⁶inflammation [or burning lust] which is generated out of the outward elements and stars, and that reacheth the abyss ; and so they are many times at deadly enmity [or have venomous spiteful hatred] one against another. And though it happen that their complexions were noble, so that still some love remaineth, yet it is not so pure and faithful as the first before copulation, which is ⁷fiery, and that in the burning [or burnt] lust, [is] earthly and cold, for that must indeed keep faithful while it cannot be otherwise ; as it is seen by experience in many, how afterward in wedlock they hunt after whoredom, and seek after the devil's ⁸sugar, which he stroweth in the noble tincture, if man will let him.

⁴ mixeth or uniteth.

⁵ Or marry.

⁶ Or brand, or lust burnt to ashes, as it were a firebrand.

⁷ Or warm.

⁸ wanton lust.

35. Whereby then you see here, that God hath

not willed the earthly copulation. Man should have continued in the fiery love which was in paradise, and generated out of himself. But the [1] woman was in this world in the outward elementary kingdom, in the inflammation of the forbidden fruit, of which *Adam* should not have eaten. And now he hath eaten and thus destroyed us; therefore it is now with him [the Adamical man] as with a thief that hath been in a pleasant garden, and went out of it to steal, and cometh again and would fain go into the garden, and the gardener will not let him in, he must reach into the garden with his hand for the fruit, and then cometh the gardener and snatcheth the fruit out of his hand, and he must go away in his burning lust and anger, and come no more into the garden, and instead of the fruit there remaineth his desirous burning lust with him; and that he hath gotten, instead of the paradisical fruit, of that we must now eat, and live in the [2] woman.

[1] the divided nature in lust and wantonness.

36. Thus I give you accurately to understand what man is, and what man soweth, and what groweth in the seed, *viz.* three kingdoms, as is above-mentioned; and seeing the three kingdoms are thus sown, so are they in like manner before the tree of temptation; and there beginneth the struggling and great strife; there stand the three kingdoms in one another. The element in paradise will keep the pure mind and will, which standeth in the love in the tincture of the seed; and the

[2] in the divided nature, and in the earthly tabernacle, and feed and multiply therein.

outward elements, (*viz.* that which went forth from the element), will have the element, and mix itself therewith; and then cometh the outward fierceness of the stars, and draweth it together [1] with the outward *Fiat,* and setteth itself [in the rule or dominion], whereby the inward will in the love together with the element and the paradise becometh darkened; and the love in the paradise goeth into its ether, and is extinguished in the tincture of the seed; and the heavenly centre goeth under, for it passeth into its Princip e.

[1] Or by.

37. And then cometh the woman with her stopped [or congealed] blood, with the stars and elements, and setteth herself in [the dominion]. And here is the paradisical death, where *Adam* in the living body died; that is, he died [as] to paradise and the element, and lived to the sun, stars, and the outward elements; concerning which, God said to him, *That day thou eatest of good and evil, thou shalt die the death*; and this is the gate of the first death in the paradise, in which now man liveth in the elementary woman of this world in the corruptibility.

38. And it highly concerneth us to know and apprehend, that when the seed is sown in the matrix, and that it is drawn together by the *Fiat* (when the stars and the outward elements set themselves in [the dominion], and that the love and meekness is extinguished; for there cometh to be a fierce substance in the stopping [or congeal-

ing] of the tincture) that before the kindling of the
light of life, in the child, there is no heavenly
creature.   And although [1] it be figured [or shaped] [1] the creature.
with all the forms [or parts] of the body, yet for
all that the heavenly image is not therein, but the
bestial.   And if that body perish [corrupt, or
break] before the kindling of the spirit of the
soul in the springing up of the life, then nothing
of this figure appeareth before God on the day of
the restitution, but its shadow and shape; for it
hath yet had no spirit.

39. This figure doth not (as many judge) go into
the [2] abyss, but as the parents were, so is also their [2] Or hell.
figure; for this figure is the parents', till the
kindling of its life, and then it is no more the
parents', but its own.   The mother affordeth but
a lodging, and the nutriment; and therefore if
she destroyeth it willingly in her body, she is a
murderess, and the divine law judgeth her to the
temporal death.

40. Thus now the stars and the elements (after
the withdrawing of the love in the tincture) take
the house into possession, and fill it in the first
[3] month.   And in the second, they sever the [3] Or moon.
members [or parts] by the sour *Fiat*, as is mentioned before.   And in the third, the strife
beginneth about the regions of the stars and
elements, where then they separate, and every
element maketh its own house and region for
itself; *viz.* the heart, liver, lungs, bladder, and

[1] a dwelling for the senses and thoughts.

stomach; as also the head to be the [1] house of the stars, where they have their region [or dominion], and their princely throne, as it followeth further:

41. And now after that the stars and elements (as is mentioned before) have gotten their region and the house to dwell in, then beginneth the mighty strife in great anxiety about the king of the life. For the chamber of the building [or fabric] standeth in very great anguish, and [here] we must consider the original of the essence of all essences, the eternal birth and the root of all things; as that there is in the house of the anguish, first one only essence [or being], and that [2] essence is the mixing of all [3] essences, and it hath first a will to [4] generate the light, and that will is attractive [astringent or sour].

[2] being.
[3] Or beings.
[4] Or bring forth.

42. For the desiring is the attracting of whatsoever the will desireth; and that will is first pure, neither darkness nor light, for it dwelleth in itself, and it is even the gate of the divine virtue that filleth all things. And thus the attracting filleth the will with the things which the will desireth; and although it be pure, and desireth nothing but the light, yet there is no light in the dark anxiety that it can attract, but it draweth the spirit of the essences of the stars and elements into itself, and therewith the will of the divine virtue is filled, and the same is all rough and dark. And thus the will

is set in the darkness, and this is done also in the heart.

43. The will now standing thus in the dark anxiety, it [1] getteth another will to fly out of the anxiety again, and to generate the light; and this other will is the mind, out of which proceed the senses [or thoughts] not to continue in the anxiety: And the will [appeareth] discovereth itself in the essences of the sourness, as in the fierce hardness of death; and the glimpse [or glance] breaketh through the essences of the sour hardness, as a swift [or sudden] flash, and sharpeneth itself in the sour hardness, that it becometh [pale, white, or] [2] glimmering, like a flash of fire, and in its sudden flight breaketh the sour darkness; and there standeth the hardness, and the harsh sourness of death like a broken turning wheel, which with the flash of the breaking flieth swiftly as a thought; as also then the re-conceived will (which is the mind) appeareth so very suddenly. And seeing it cannot fly forward out of the essences, it must go into the turning wheel, (for it cannot get from that place), and so it breaketh the darkness. And when the darkness is thus [3] broken, [then] the sharp glance discovereth itself in the pleasant joy without [or beyond] the darkness in the sharpness of the will, *viz.* in the mind, and findeth itself habitable therein, from whence the flash (or glance) is terrified, and flieth up with strong might through the broken essences out of the heart, and would out

[1] Or con-
ceiveth.

[2] Text,
Blanck.

[3] Or dispelled.

at the mouth, and raiseth itself far from the heart, and yet is held by the sour [or harsh] *Fiat*, and it then maketh itself a several region (*viz.* the tongue) wherein then standeth the shriek [or the crack] of the broken essences. And seeing then it reflecteth [or recoileth] back again into the heart, as into its first dwelling-house, and findeth itself so very habitable and pleasant (because the gates of the darkness are broken), then it kindleth itself so highly in the loving will, by reason of the meekness, and goeth no more like a stern [or fierce] flash through all essences, but [it] goeth trembling with great joy; and the might of the joy is now many hundred times stronger, than first the flash [or glance] was, which yielded [or discovered] itself through the sour harsh essences of the death, and goeth with strong might out of the heart into the head, in the will [or purpose] to possess the heavenly region.

[1] the will.

44. For [1] it is paradisical, and it hath its most inward root therein. When *Adam* in sin died the first death, then said God, *The seed of the woman shall* [2]*break the serpent's head.* The same word [3] imprinted itself in *Adam*, in the centre of the springing-up of his life, and so in like manner with the creation of *Eve* in the springing up of her life, and so in like manner in all men, so that we can, in our first mind, through the word and virtue of God in the Treader upon the Serpent, who in the time became man [or was incarnate], trample upon [or

[2] break with treading upon it.

[3] imagined, figured, or formed itself.

break] the head and will of the devil, and if this might [or power] were not [1] in this place, then we were in the eternal death. Thus the mind is its own, in the free will, and moveth in the virtue [or power] of God, and in his promise, in the free substance [or being].

[1] *Viz.* in the place of the springing-up of the life.

45. Seeing then that the shriek of joy in the virtue of God (which breaketh the doors of the deep darkness) thus springeth up in the heart, and flieth with its glimpse [or sparkling] into the head, then the virtue of the joy setteth itself above, as being the strongest, and the flash [or glance] beneath, as being the weakest; and so when the flash [or glance] cometh into the head into its seat, then it maketh itself two open gates. For it hath broken the doors of the deep darkness, and therefore it continueth no more in the darkness, but it must be free as a victorious prince [or conqueror], and will not be held captive. And this signifieth to us the resurrection of Christ from the dead, who is now free, and will not be held [therein], which in its due place shall be very deeply described. And those gates which the glance holdeth open, they are the eyes, and the spirit of joy is their root, which [spirit] springeth up at first in the kindling of the life.

46. Thus then the strong re-conceived will (to fly out from the darkness and to be in the light in the heart) generateth itself; and therefore we cannot know [or apprehend] it to be any other

than the noble virgin, the wisdom of God; which thus springeth up in joy, and in the beginning marrieth herself with the spirit of the soul, and helpeth it to the light, which after the springing up of the soul (*viz.* after the kindling of the virtue of the sun in the essences) putteth herself into its paradisical centre, and continually warneth the soul, [1] of the ungodly ways, which are held before it by the stars and elements, and brought into its essences.   Therefore the virgin keepeth her throne thus in the heart, and also in the head, that she may defend and keep them off from the soul, all over.

[1] of the ways of the ungodly.

47. And we must further [2] consider, that when the shriek [or crack] maketh its dwelling-house, in its strong breaking-through, out of the gate of the anxious darkness, *viz.* the tongue, that the shriek [or crack] hath not then yet seen the virgin; but when it reflected [or shone] back again into the heart, into the opened darkness, and found her so habitable, there then first sprang up its joy, habitableness, and pleasantness, and it became paradisical, and desired not [to go] into the tongue again, but into the head, and [desired] there to have its region out of the source of the heart.   Therefore the tongue ought not in all [or altogether] to be believed, for it sitteth not in the heavenly region, as the friendly pleasant virtue [doth]; but it hath its region in the crack and flash, and the flash is as near the hellish region as the crack is, for they are

[2] think, or conceive.

both generated in the [1] sharpness of the stars, in
the essences, and the tongue speaketh both lies and
truth ; in which of the two the spirit armeth itself,
according to that it speaketh : Also it many times
speaketh lies in [2] great men ; when it is armed
from the essences, then it speaketh in the crack,
like a rider in his [haughty, surly, vaunting state
or] high mindedness.

[1] Or stern grim sharpness.

[2] Such as have esteem, authority, and riches, or such as are high minded, and stout, and have the world at will.

The Life of the Soul. The Gate.

48. Thus now when the virtue of the life and
the spirit of the second Principle, [3] is generated in
the first originality of the first Principle (*viz.* in
the gate of the deep darkness, which the will of
the virtue of the virgin, in the fierce earnest
flash of the fierce might of God, did break, and set
itself in the pleasant habitation) then instantly
the essences of the stars and elements, in the flash
of the springing-up of the life, pressed in also, yet
after the building of the pleasant habitation first
[made].

[3] Or was.

49. For the habitation is the element, and the
virtue of the inward element is the paradisical love,
which the outward elements (being generated out
of the element) will have for their mother, and the
sharp *Fiat* bringeth them into the habitation.
And there the light of the life becometh rightly
kindled, and all essences live in the habitation.
For in the beginning of the life each Principle
[4] taketh its light.

[4] Or catcheth.

50. The first Principle (*viz.* the darkness) taketh the fierce and sudden fire-flash; and so when the [1] re-comprehended will, in the first will of the first attracted darkness of the harshness, discovereth itself, and breaketh the darkness in the flash, then the harsh dark fire-flash remaineth in the first will, and standeth over the heart, in the gall, and kindleth the fire in the essences of the heart.

[1] re-conceived, or re-purposed.

51. And the second Principle retaineth its light for itself, which is the pleasant [2] habitation, which shineth there, where the darkness is broken [or dispelled], wherein the courteous loving virtue, and the pleasantness ariseth, from whence the shriek [or crack] in the strong might becometh so very joyful, and [3] turneth its forcible rushing into a joyful trembling; where then the fire-flash of the first Principle sticketh to [4] it, which causeth its trembling. But its source [or active property] is pleasantness and joy, that cannot sufficiently be described; happy are they that find it [by experience].

[2] Or joy.

[3] Or allayeth it with trembling for joy.

[4] the shriek or crack.

52. And the third Principle retaineth its light wholly for itself, which (as soon as the light of life springeth up) presseth into the tincture of the soul, to the [5] element, and reacheth after the element; but it attaineth no more than to the light of the sun, which is proceeded out of the *quinta essentia*, out of the element. And thus the stars and elements rule in their light and virtue, which is the sun's, and qualify with the soul, and bring many distempers, and also diseases into the

[5] the inward one element.

essences, from whence come stitches, agues, swellings and [other] sicknesses, [as] the plague, etc. into those [essences], and at last their corruption and death.

53. And now when the light of all the three Principles shineth, then the tincture goeth forth from all the three Principles, and it is highly [worthy] to be observed, that the middlemost Principle receiveth no light from nature; but as soon as the darkness is broken up [or dispelled], it shineth in most joyful habitableness, and [hath] the noble virgin dwelling in the joy, *viz.* in that tincture; and the Deity appeareth so very highly and powerfully in man, that we cannot find it so in any other thing, let us take what else we will into our consideration.

54. In the first Principle is the fire-flash; and in the tincture thereof is the [1] terrible light of the sun, which hath its original very sharply out of the eternal originalness, out of the first Principle, with its root out of the fifth essence, through the element, which may be expounded in another place, it would be too long to do it here. And besides, it should be hidden; he that knoweth it, will conceal it, as he would also [conceal] the springing-up of the stars and planets. For the cornered cap will needs have it under the jurisdiction of his school-learning, though indeed he apprehendeth little or nothing at all in the light of nature. Let it remain [hidden] till the time of the lily, there it standeth

[1] the dazzling light of the sun.

all [1] open : And the tincture is [then] the light of
the world.

55. And it is here very exactly seen how the
third Principle [2] uniteth itself with the first, and
how they have one [only] will, for they proceed
from one another; and if the second Principle were
not in the midst [between them] then they were
but one [and the same] thing.   But speaking here
of the tincture in the life, we will therefore shew,
in the light of nature, the true ground of all the
three births.

56. The noble tincture is the dwelling-house of
the spirit, and hath three forms; one is eternal,
and incorruptible; the other is mutable [or
transitory], and yet with the holy [or saints]
continueth eternally; but with the wicked it is
mutable [or transitory], and flieth into the ether;
the third is corruptible [3] in death.

57. The first tincture of the first Principle is
properly the [4] habitation in the fire-flash, which is
the source [life, or active property] in the gall,
which maketh the brimstone-spirit (viz. the indissoluble worm of the soul, which ruleth powerfully
in the sharp essences, and moveth and carrieth the
body whithersoever the mind, in the second centre,
will) to be its dwelling-house; its tincture is like
the fierce [austere or grim] and sharp might of
God; it kindleth the whole body, so that it is
warm, and that it grow not [5] stiff [or congealed
with cold], and upholdeth the wheel in the crack

in the essences, out of which the hearing ariseth.
It is sharp, and proveth the smell of every thing
in the essences; it maketh the hearing, though
itself is neither the hearing nor smelling; but it
is the gate that letteth in good and evil, as the
tongue and also the ear [doth]. All which cometh
from hence, because that [1]its tincture hath its
ground in the first Principle; and the kindling of
the life happeneth in the sharpness, in the breaking
through the gate of the eternal darkness.

[1] the active life of the gall.

58. Therefore are the essences of the spirit of
the soul so very sharp and fiery, and [therefore]
the essences go forth out of such a sharp fiery
tincture, wherein now stand the five senses, *viz.*
seeing, hearing, smelling, tasting, and feeling; for
the fierce sharpness of the tincture of the first
Principle, proveth in its own essences [in or] of
the soul, or [in the essences] of the worm of the
soul, in this place rightly so called, [it proveth, I
say] the stars, and elements, *viz.* the out-birth out
of the first Principle, and whatsoever uniteth [or
yieldeth] itself to it, it taketh that into the essences
of the worm of the soul; *viz.* all whatsoever is
harsh [or sour,] bitter, stern, [or fierce,] and fiery,
all whatsoever generateth itself in the fierceness,
and all whatsoever is of the same property with
the essences; all that which riseth up along there
in the fiery source, and elevateth itself in the
breaking of the gate of the darkness, and boileth
[springeth, or floweth up] above the meekness;

and all whatsoever is like the sharp austere eternity, and qualifieth [or mixeth] with the sharpness of the fierce anger of the God of the eternity, wherein he holdeth the kingdom of the devils captive. O man! consider thyself here, it is the sure ground, known by the author, in the light of nature, in the will of God.

59. And in this tincture of the first Principle, the devil tempteth man; for it is his source [well-spring, or property], wherein he also liveth. Herein he reacheth into the heart of man, into his soul's essences, and leadeth him away from God, into the desire to live in the sharp (*viz.* in the fiery) essences, that it might be elevated above the humility and the meekness of the heart of God, and above the love and meekness of the creatures, [on purpose to seem] to be the only fair and glistering worm in the fire-flash, and to domineer over the second Principle. And [thus] he maketh the soul of man so extreme proud, as not to vouchsafe himself to be in the least like any meekness, but to be like all whatsoever liveth in a quality [or property] contrary to it.

¹ the devil.

60. And in the bitter essences ¹ he maketh the worm of the soul prickly, spiteful, envious, and malicious, grudging every thing to any; as the bitterness indeed is friends with nothing, but it stingeth and grindeth, raveth and rageth like the abyss of hell, and it is the true house of death as to the pleasant life.

61. And in the sour [or harsh] essence of the tincture of the worm of the soul, he infecteth the sour [1] harsh essence, whereby it becometh sharply attractive, and getteth a will to draw all to itself, and yet is not able to do it; for the conceived will is not easily filled, but is a dry hellish thirsty hunger to have all; and if it did get all, yet the hunger would not be the less, but it is the eternal hunger and thirst of the abyss, the will of hell-fire and of all devils, who continually hunger and thirst, and yet eat nothing; but it is their satiating that they [suck or] draw into themselves the strong source of the essences of the harsh, bitter might of the fire, wherein consisteth their life and satiating; and the abyss of the wrath and of hell is also such [a thing].

[1] or astringent substance.

62. And this is the source of the first Principle, which (without the light of God) cannot be otherwise, neither can it change or alter itself; for it hath been so from eternity.   And out of this source, the essences of the worm of the soul, in the time of its creating, were extracted by the *Fiat* of God, and created in paradise, [and set] [2] before the light of God, which enlightened the fire-flash, and put it into very high meekness and humility.

[2] Or for.

63. For because man was to be eternal, therefore he must also come to be out of the eternal; for nothing is created out of the fountain of the Heart of God. For that is the end of nature, and hath no such essences; no comprehensible

[or palpable] thing entereth therein; otherwise it would be a filling and darkness, and that cannot be: Also from eternity, there hath been nothing else but only the source [or working property] where the Deity continually riseth up, as is mentioned before.

64. And this source of the spirit of the soul is eternal, and its tincture is also eternal; and as the source is [in it] at all times [1] of this world, (while it sticketh in the elementary house of flesh), so is the tincture also, and the dwelling-house of the soul; and in which source the mind inclineth itself, whether it be in the divine, or hellish, in that [source] the worm liveth, and of that Principle it eateth, and is either an angel or a devil; although its judgment is not in this [life's] time, for it standeth in both the gates, so long as it liveth in the flesh, except it dive [or plunge itself] wholly into the abyss, whereof (when I write of the sin of man) I shall treat deeply and exactly. Read of it concerning *Cain.*

65. The mind (which knoweth [or understandeth] nothing in the light of nature) will marvel at such writings, and will suppose that it is not true, that God hath extracted and created man out of such an original. Behold, thou beloved reason and precious mind, bring thy five senses hither, and I will shew thee whether it be true [or not]. I will shew thee [plainly] that thou hast not the least spark [of cause] to allow any other ground [to build upon],

[1] Or in.

except that thou wilt let thy heart be embittered by the devil in bestial reason, and except that thou wilt wilfully contemn the light of nature, which standeth in the presence of God. And indeed, if thou art in such a bestial way, leave my writings, and read them not, they are not written for such swine, but for the children [of wisdom] that are to possess the kingdom of God. But I have written them for myself, and for those that seek, and not for the wise and prudent of this world.

66. Behold, what are thy five senses? In what virtue do they consist? Or how come they in the life of man? Whence cometh thy seeing, that thou canst see by the light of the sun, and not otherwise? Consider thyself deeply, if thou wilt be a searcher into nature, and wilt boast of the light of nature. Thou canst not say that thou seest only by the light of the sun, for there must be somewhat which can receive the light of the sun, and which doth mix with the light of the sun (as the star doth which is in thine eyes) which is not the sun, but consisteth of fire and water; and its glance, which receiveth the light of the sun, is a flash, that ariseth from the fiery, sour and bitter gall, and the water maketh it soft [or pleasant]. Here you take the meaning to be only concerning the outward, *viz.* the third Principle, wherein the sun, stars, and elements are; but the same is also true in every one of the creatures in this world.

67. Now what is it that maketh the hearing,

that you can hear that which stirreth and maketh a noise? Wilt thou say that it is caused by the noise of that outward thing which giveth the sound? No! there must also be somewhat that must receive the sound, and qualify or mix with the sound, and distinguish the sound of what is played or sung; the outward cannot do that alone, the inward must receive and distinguish the noise. Behold, here you find the beginning of the life, and the tincture wherein the life consisteth; for the tincture of the crack in the springing up of the life, in the breaking-open of the dark gate, standeth in the sounding, and hath its gate open (next the fire-flash near the eyes) and receiveth the noise of whatsoever soundeth.

68. For the outward sounding qualifieth with the inward, and is severed [or distinguished] by the essences; and the tincture receiveth all, be it evil or good, and thereby testifieth that itself, with its essences that generate it, is not generated out of the Deity, else the tincture would not let in the evil, and [that which is] false into the essences of the soul.

69. Therefore we must consider, that the noise in the tincture of man is [of a] higher [nature] than [that] in the beasts; for man searcheth and distinguisheth all things which give a sound, and knoweth from whence it cometh, and how it doth exist, which the beasts cannot do, but stare at it, and know not what it is; whereby it may be

understood, that the original of man is out of the
eternal, because he can distinguish all things that
in the out-birth came out of the eternal.   And
hence it is, that the body (being all things out of
the eternal nothing are caused to be something
which is comprehensible [or palpable], and yet
there, that nothing is not a mere nothing, but it is
a ¹ source) after the corrupting shall stand in the ¹ Or active
eternal figure, and not in the spirit, because it is property.
not out of the eternal spirit; for otherwise, if it
were out of the [eternal] spirit, then it should
also search out the beginning of every thing, as
[well as] man, who in his sound receiveth and
distinguisheth all things.

70. Thus now the habitation of man's sound,
wherein the understanding is, must be from eternity,
although indeed, in the fall of *Adam*, man hath set
himself in the corruptibility, and in great want
of understanding, as shall follow here.   In like
manner also we find concerning the smelling; for
if the spirit did not stand in the sound, then no
smell of any thing would press [or pierce] into the
essences; for the spirit would be whole and swelled.
But it standing thus in the gate of the ² broken ² disrupted.
darkness in the crack and in the sound, therefore all virtues of all things press in into that gate,
and try themselves by one another, and what the
essences of the spirit love, that it desireth, and
draweth the same into the tincture; and then hands
and mouth fall to it, and stuff it into the stomach,

22

[1] Or *atrium.* into the [1] outward court of the four elements, from whence the earthly essences of the stars and elements feed.

71. And the taste also is a trying and attracting of the tincture in the essences of the spirit. And so the feeling also, if the spirit of man with its essences did not stand in the sound, there would be no feeling; for when the sour essences draw to them, then they awaken the bitter prickle [or sting] in the fire-flash, which stirreth itself, either by gripping, thrusting, or striking, and thereupon in [2] Text, *An-rühren* [C. J. B.]. all [2] driving the bitter prickle in the fire-flash is awakened; and therein standeth the moving; [and] all in the tincture.

THE SIXTEENTH CHAPTER

*Of the noble Mind of the Understanding, Senses
and Thoughts. Of the threefold Spirit and
Will, and of the Tincture of the Inclination,
and what is inbred in a Child in the Mother's
Body [or Womb]. Of the Image of God, and
of the bestial Image, and of the Image of the
Abyss of Hell, and Similitude of the Devil,
to be searched for, and found out in* [any]
one Man.

[1] Or in every one.

*The noble Gate of the noble Virgin. And also the Gate of
the Woman of this World, highly to be considered.*

1. IF we consider ourselves in the noble knowledge, which is opened to us in the love of
God, in the noble virgin of the wisdom of God, (not
for our merit, honesty [virtue], or worthiness, but
merely of his own will, and original eternal purpose)
even in those things which appear to us in his love,
then we must needs acknowledge ourselves to be
unworthy of such a revelation; and being we are
sinners, we are deficient in the glory that we should
have before him.

2. But seeing it is his eternal will and purpose to

do us good, and to open his secrets to us according to his counsel, therefore we ought not to withstand, nor to bury the bestowed talent in the earth, for we must give account of it in the appearing of his coming. Therefore we will thus labour in our vineyard, and commend the fruit to him, and will set down in writing a Memorial for ourselves, and leave it to him. For we can search or conceive no further, than only what we apprehend in the light of nature; where [1] our gate standeth open; not according to the measure of our purpose, when and how we will, but according to his gift, when and how he will. We are not able to comprehend the least sparkle of him, unless the gates of the deep be opened to us in our mind; where then the zealous [earnest] and highly desirous kindled spirit [2] is as a fire, to which the earthly body ought to be subject, and will grudge no pains to serve the desirous fiery mind. And although it hath nothing to expect for its labour but scorn and contempt from the world, yet it must be obedient to its lord, for its lord is mighty, and itself is feeble, and its lord leadeth, [driveth], and preserveth it, and yet in its [ignorance, or want of] understanding, it knoweth nothing of what it doth, but it liveth like all the beasts. And yet its will is [not] to live thus, but it must follow the worthy mind, which searcheth after the wisdom of God; and the mind must follow the light of nature; for God manifesteth [or revealeth] himself in that light, or else we should know nothing of him.

[1] Or our comprehensibility.

[2] Or goeth.

3. And now when we consider our mind, in the light of nature, and what that is, which maketh us zealous [or earnest], which burneth there [in] as a light, and is desirous [thirsty or covetous] like fire, which desireth to receive from that place where it hath not sown, and would reap in that country where the body is not at home [or dwelleth not], then the precious virgin of the wisdom of God meeteth us, in the middlemost seat in the centre of the light of life, and saith, The light is mine, and the [power or] virtue and glory is mine, also the gate of knowledge is mine, I live in the light of nature, and without me you can neither see, know, nor understand anything of my virtue [or power]. I am thy bridegroom in the light; and thy desire [or longing] after my virtue [or power] is my attracting in myself; I sit in my throne, but thou knowest me not; I am in thee, and thy body is not in me. I distinguish [or separate], and thou seest it not. I am the light of the senses, and the root of the senses is not in me, but near me. I am the bridegroom of the root, but she hath put on a rough coat. I [will] not lay myself in her arms till she putteth that off, and then I will rest eternally in her arms, and adorn the root with my virtue [and power], and give her my beautiful form, and will espouse myself to her with my Pearl.

4. There are three things which the mind hath in it, and which rule it, yet the mind in itself is the desirous will. And those three things are three

kingdoms, or Principles; one is eternal, and the
second is eternal, but the third is corruptible; the
one hath no beginning; the second is without beginning, eternally generated; and the third hath
a beginning and end, and corrupteth again [or
perisheth].

5. And, as the eternal mind in the great unsearchable depth, is from eternity, so is the indissoluble band, and the spirit in the [1]source, which
continually generateth itself, never decayeth, and
therein, in the centre of the deep, is the re-
conceived will to the light; and the will is the
desiring, and the desiring attracteth to it, and that
which is attracted maketh the darkness in the will,
so that in the first will, the second will generateth
itself again, that it might fly out of the darkness; and
the second will is the mind, which discovereth itself
in the darkness, and the [discovery or]glance breaketh
[or dispelleth] the darkness, so that it standeth in
the sound and in the crack; where then the flash
sharpeneth itself, and so standeth eternally in the
broken darkness, so that the darkness thus standeth
in the sound of the stars.   And in the breaking of
the darkness, the re-conceived will is free, and dwelleth without the darkness, in itself; and the flash
which there is the separation and the sharpness,
and the noise [or sound] is the dwelling of the will,
or of the continually conceived mind; and the noise
and the sharpness of the flash are in the dwelling
of the will free from the darkness.   And the flash

[1] Or perpetual
working pro-
perty.

elevateth the will, and the will triumpheth in the sharpness of the flash, and the will discovereth itself in the sharpness of the sound in the flash of the light, [1] without the darkness in the breaking, in the infiniteness. And in that infiniteness of the flash, there is in every discovery of the whole [2] in the particular (in every reflection) again a centre of such a birth as is in the whole. And those particulars are the senses, and the whole is the mind out of which the senses proceed; and therefore the senses are mutable [or transitory], and not in the [3] substance; but the mind is whole, and in the substance.

6. My beloved Reader, just thus is our mind also. It is the indissoluble band, which God by the *Fiat* in the moving spirit breathed into *Adam* out of the eternal mind, [from whence] the essences are a particular, or a sparkle out of the eternal mind, which hath the centre of the breaking, and in the breaking hath the sharpness in itself; and that will driveth [forth] the flash [or glimpse] in the breaking, and the sharpness of the consuming of the darkness is in the glimpse [or flash] of the willing, and the will is our mind. The glimpse is the eyes in the fire-flash, which discovereth itself in our essences [4] in us, and without us, for it is free, and hath both the gates open, that [gate] in the darkness, and that gate in the light. For although it continueth in the darkness, yet it breaketh the darkness, and maketh all light in

[1] *extra.*

[2] Or into a particular.

[3] whole or fixed.

[4] The glance of our eyes can look upon the evil and good both within and without us.

itself; and where it is, there it seeth. As our thoughts, they can ¹speculate a thing that is many miles off, when the body is far from thence, and it may be never was in that place; the discovery or glimpse [or piercing sight of the eye of the mind] goeth through wood and stone, through bones and marrow, and there is nothing that can ²withhold it, for it pierceth and breaketh the darkness every where without rending the body of any thing, and the will is its horse whereon it rideth. Here many things must be concealed, because of the devilish enchantment, (or else we would reveal much more here), for the *nigromanticus* [necromancer] is generated here.

² obstruct or hinder it.

7. But now the first will in the mind is out of the sour anxiety, and its glimpse [or discovery] in the original, is the bitter, strong [or sour] fire-flash in the sharpness, which maketh the stirring and noise, and also the seeing in the glance of the sharpness of the fire-flash, that so the re-conceived glimpses [discoverings or glances] in the thoughts have a light in them from whence they see, when they run [along] like a flash.

³ Or earnest will.

8. Yet this ³first will in the mind ought not to stay behind in the abyss of the sour fierceness, (in which the fierce malice is), but ought to go forward in the centre of the breaking forth out of the darkness into the light, for in the light there is mere meekness, lowliness, humility, good-will, and friendly desires, that it might with its

re-conceived will go out of itself, and to open itself in its precious treasury. For in the re-conceived will to the birth of the light there is no source of anxiety, but only mere friendly desires; for the glimpse riseth up out of the darkness in itself, and desireth the light; and the desiring draweth the light into itself, and there the anguish becometh an exulting joy in itself, an humble cheerfulness, a pleasant habitation. For the re-conceived will in the light is impregnated, and its fruit in the body is virtue [or power], which the will desireth to generate, and to live therein; and this desiring bringeth the fruit out of the impregnated will, [and presenteth it] before the will, and the will discovereth itself [glimmereth or shineth] in the fruit in an infinite pleasant number; and there goeth forth, in the pleasant number, in the discovered [or manifested] will, the high benediction [or blessing], favour, loving kindness, pleasant inclination [or yielding pliableness], the taste of joy, the well-doing of meekness [or affability], and [further] what my pen cannot express. The mind would much rather be freed from vanity, and live therein without molestation or disturbance.

9. Now these two gates are in one another; the nethermost goeth into the abyss, and the uppermost goeth into paradise; and a third gate cometh to these two, out of the element with its four issues, and presseth in together with the fire, air, water, and earth; and their kingdom is the

¹ Or mingle. sun and stars, which ¹qualify with the first will; and their desire is to be filled, to swell, and to be great.   These draw into them, and fill the chamber of the deep, [viz.] the free and naked will in the mind; they bring the glimpse [or glance] of the stars into the gate of the mind, and qualify with the sharpness of the glimpse [or flash]; they fill the broken gates of the darkness with flesh, and wrestle continually with the first will (from whence they are gone forth) for the kingdom [or dominion], and yield themselves up to the first will, as to their father, which willingly receiveth their region [or dominion].   For he is obscure and dark, and they are rough and sour, also bitter and cold; and their life is a seething source of fire, wherewith they govern in the mind, in the gall, heart, lungs, and liver, and in all members [or parts] of the whole body, and man is ²their own; the spirit which standeth in the flash bringeth the constellation into the tincture of its property, and infecteth the thoughts, according to the dominion of the stars; they take the body and tame it, and bring their bitter roughness into it.

² the four
elements' own.

10. Now the gate of the light standeth between both these regions, as in one [only] centre enclosed with flesh, and it shineth in the darkness in itself, and it moveth towards the might of the darkness and fierceness, and sheddeth forth its rays, even unto the noise of the breaking through, from whence the gates of seeing, hearing, smelling,

tasting, and feeling, go forth; and when these gates apprehend the sweet, loving, and pleasant rays of the light, then they become most highly joyful, and run into their highest region into the heart (as into their right dwelling-house) into the essences of the spirit of the soul, which receiveth it with joy, and refresheth itself therein; and there its sun springeth up (*viz.* the pleasant tincture in the [1] element of water) and by the sweet joy becometh blood. For all regions rejoice therein, and suppose that they have gotten the noble virgin again, whereas it is but her rays, as the sun shineth upon the earth, from whence all essences of the earth rejoice, spring, grow, and blossom. Which is the cause that the tincture riseth up in all herbs and trees.

[1] element-water.

11. And here we must accurately consider wherein every region rejoiceth; for the sun and stars apprehend not the divine light, as the essences of the soul [do] (and yet only that soul which standeth in the new birth); but [2] they taste the sweetness which hath imprinted [or imaged] itself in the tincture; for the blood of the heart, wherein the soul moveth, is so very sweet, that there is nothing to be compared to it. Therefore hath God by *Moses* forbidden man to eat the flesh in its blood; for the life standeth in it. For the bestial life ought not to be in man, that his spirit be not infected therewith.

[2] the sun and stars.

12. The three regions receive every one of them

their light, with the springing up of the tincture in the blood; and each [region] keepeth its tincture. The region of the stars keepeth the light of the sun; and the first Principle [keepeth] the [1] fire-flash; and the essences of the holy souls receive the most dear and precious light of the virgin, yet in this body only her rays, wherewith she fighteth in the mind against the crafty assaults of the devil, as St *Peter* witnesseth. And although the dear light stayeth for a while in many in the new birth [or regeneration], yet it is not steady in the house of the stars and elements, in the outward birth, but it dwelleth in its [own] centre in the mind.

[1] That is, the tincture or kindling of the life of the abyss.

The Gate of [2] Speech.

[2] Or language.

13. Seeing now that the mind standeth in free will, therefore the will discovereth itself according to that which the regions have brought into the essences, whether it be evil or good; whether it be fitting for the kingdom of heaven, or for the kingdom of hell; and that which the glimpse [or flash] apprehendeth, it bringeth that into the will of the mind. And in the mind standeth the king, and the king is the light of the whole body; and he hath five counsellors, which sit [all together] in the [3] noise of the tincture; and each of them trieth that which the glimpse with its infection hath brought into the will, whether it be good or evil; and these counsellors are the five senses.

[3] Or sound of the kindling.

14. First the king [1] giveth it to the eyes, to see [1] Or sendeth.
whether it be good or evil; and the eyes give it
to the ears, to hear from whence it cometh, whether
out of a true, or out of a false region, and whether
it be a lie or truth; and the ears give it to the
nose (the smell), that must smell, whether that
which is brought in (and standeth before the king)
cometh out of a good or [2] evil essence; and the [2] Or false.
nose giveth it to the taste, which must try whether
it be pure or impure, and therefore the taste hath
the tongue, that it may [3] spit it out again if it be [3] Or spew.
[4] impure; but if it be a thought to [be expressed [4] Or false.
in] a word, then the lips are the door-keepers,
which must keep it shut, and not let the tongue
forth, but must bring it into the region of the air,
into the [5] nostrils, and not into the heart, and [5] Text. *Blasen*
stifle it, and then it is dead. or *Breath.*

15. And when the taste hath tried it, and if it
be good for the essences of the soul, then it giveth
it to the feeling, which must try what quality it
is of, whether hot or cold, hard or soft, thick or
thin, and then the feeling [6] sendeth it into the [6] Or giveth.
heart, [presenting it] before the flash of the life,
and before the king of the light of life; and the
will of the mind [7] pierceth further into that thing, [7] flasheth or
a great depth, and seeth what is therein, [consider- discovereth.
ing] how much it will receive and take in of that
thing, and when it is enough, then the will giveth
it to the spirit of the soul, *viz.* to the eternal
[8] emperor, who bringeth it (with his strong and [8] chief ruler.

austere might) out of the heart, in the sound upon the tongue under the roof of the mouth, and there the spirit [1]distinguisheth according to the senses, as the will hath discovered [or manifested] it, and the tongue [1]distinguisheth it in the noise.

[1] divideth, or separateth.

16. For the region of the air must here drive the work through the throat, where then all the veins in the whole body tend and concur, and bring the virtue of the noble tincture thitherwards, and mingle themselves with the word; and thither also all the three regions of the mind come, and mingle themselves with the distinguishing [framing, articulating, or separating] of words; and there is a very wonderful form [or manner of work]. For every region [or dominion] will distinguish [or separate] the word according to its essences, for the sound goeth out of the heart, out of all three Principles.

17. The first will fashion it according to its fierce might and pomp, and mingleth therein prickly [stinging] sourness, wrath and malice. And the second Principle with the virgin standeth in the midst, and sheddeth its rays of loving meekness therein, and resisteth the first [Principle]. And if the spirit be kindled in [2]that, then the word is wholly gentle, friendly, and humble, and inclineth itself to the love of our neighbour; it desireth not to seize upon any with the haughty sting [or prickle] of the first Principle, but it

[2] the second Principle.

[1] covereth the prickles of the thorns, and qualifieth [1] blunteth or mollifieth.
the word with clearness [and plainness], and armeth
the tongue with righteousness and truth, and it
sheddeth abroad its rays, even into the will
of the heart. And when the will receiveth the
pleasant friendly rays of love, then it kindleth
the whole mind, with the love, righteousness,
chastity of the virgin, and the truth of all those
things that are by all regions tried upon the
tongue.   And thus it together with the five senses
maketh the tongue shrill, and [thereby] the dear
image of God appeareth inwardly and outwardly,
so that it may be heard and seen in the whole
[2] abyss, what form it is of.   O man ! behold what [2] Or deep of the mind.
the light of nature discovereth to thee.

18. Thirdly, there cometh the [3] third regimen to [3] Or the third Principle.
the imaging [or forming] of the word, from the
spirit of the stars and elements, and it mingleth
itself in the house and senses of the mind, and
desireth to form the word from the might of its
own self, for it hath [4] great power, it holdeth the [4] greatest.
whole man captive, and it hath clothed him with
flesh and blood, and it infecteth the will of the
mind, and the will [5] discovereth itself in the spirit [5] looketh upon itself.
of this world, in lust and beauty, might and power,
riches and glory, pleasure and joy ; and on the
contrary, in sorrow and misery, cares and poverty,
pain and sickness : Also in art and wisdom ; and
on the contrary, in folly and ignorance.

19. All this, the glimpse [or discovery] of the

senses bringeth into the will of the mind [and setteth it] before the king, before the light of the life, and there it is tried.   And the king giveth it first to the eyes, which must see what good is among all these, and what pleaseth them.   And here now beginneth the wonderful form [or framing] of man, [1] out of the complexions, where the constellation hath formed the child in the mother's body [or womb] so variously in its regions.   For according to what the constellation, in the time of the [2] incarnation of the child, in the wheel that standeth therein, and hath its aspect, (when the dwelling of the four elements, and the [3] house of the stars in the head, in the brains, are built by the *Fiat*), according to that is the virtue also in the brains, and so in the heart, gall, lungs, and liver ; and according to that is the inclination of the region of the air ; and according to that also a tincture springeth up, to [be] a dwelling of the life, as may be seen in the wonderful [[4] variety in the] senses and forms [or shapes] of men.

20.   Although indeed we can say this with ground of truth, that the constellation imageth and formeth no man, as to [make him to be] the similitude and image of God; but [it formeth only] a beast in the will, manners, and senses ; and besides that, it hath no might nor understanding, to be able to figure [or form] a similitude of God: Though indeed it elevateth itself in the highest [it can], in the will after the similitude of God, yet it gener-

[1] Or according to the complexions.

[2] Or the child's becoming man.

[3] Or the dwelling of the senses and thoughts.

[4] different thoughts.

ateth only a pleasant, subtle, and lusty beast in man (as also in other creatures) and no more. Only the eternal essences, which are propagated from *Adam* in all men, they continue with the hidden element (wherein the image consisteth) standing in man, but yet altogether hidden, unless the new birth in the water, and the Holy Ghost [or spirit] of God [be attained].

21. And thereupon it comes, that man many times in the dwelling of the brains, and of the heart, as also in all the five senses, in the region [or dominion] of the stars, is in his mind [1] often like [1] Or suddenly. a wolf, a churlish dog, crafty, fierce, and greedy; and [1] often like a lion, stern, cruel, sturdy and active in devouring of his prey; [1] often like a dog, snappish, envious, malicious; often like an adder and serpent, subtle, venomous, stinging, poisonous, slanderous in his words, and mischievous in his deeds, ill-conditioned and lying, like the quality of the devil in the shape of a serpent at the Tree of Temptation; [1] often like a hare, timorous, or fearful, starting and running away; [1] often like a toad, whose mind is so very venomous, that it poisoneth a tender [or weak] mind to the temporal death by its imagination, (which many times maketh witches and sorcerers, for the first ground serveth enough to it); [1] often like a tame beast; and [1] often like a merry beast, etc. all according as the constellation stood, in [2] its incarnation in [2] the child's. the wrestling wheel, with its virtue of the *quinta*

23

¹ In the mind
of the child.
² Or nativity.
³ Or over-
powereth the
first com-
plexion of the
hour of the
incarnation
or becoming
man.

essentia, so is the starry mind on ¹its region figured; although the hour of man's ²birth altereth much, and doth ³hold in the first, whereof I will write hereafter in its place, concerning man's birth [or nativity].

22. And now if the glance out of this mind, out of this or any other form not here mentioned, glanceth [or darteth] through the eyes, then it catcheth up its own form out of everything, as its starry kingdom is most potent at all times of the heaven, in the good or in the bad, in falsehood or in truth. And this is brought before the king, and there must the five counsellors try it, which yet

⁴ Or poisoned.

are unrighteous knaves themselves, being ⁴infected from the stars and elements, and so set in their region [or dominion]. And now those [counsellors] desire nothing more than the kingdom of this world; and to which sort the starry house of the brains and of the heart is most of all inclined, for that the five counsellors also give their advice, and will have it, be it for pomp, pride, stateliness, riches, beauty, or voluptuous life, also for art and

⁵ Or virtue.
⁶ Or the sick
soul is not
regarded.

⁵excellency of earthly things, ⁶and for poor *Lazarus* there is no thought; there the five counsellors are very soon agreed, for in their own form they are all unrighteous before God; but according to the region of this world they are very firm. Thus they counsel the king, and the king giveth it to the spirit of the soul, which gathereth up the essences, and falleth to with hands and mouth.

But if they be words [that are to be expressed] then it bringeth them to the roof of the mouth, and there the five counsellors distinguish [or separate] them according to the will of the mind ; and further [the spirit bringeth them upon the tongue, and there the senses divide or] distinguish them in the flash [glance, or in a moment].

23. And there stand the three Principles in strife. The first Principle, *viz.* the kingdom of sternness [or wrathful fierceness] saith, Go forth in the midst of the strong might of the fire, it must be [so]; then saith the second [Principle] in the mind, stay and consider, God is here with the virgin, fear the abyss of hell; and the third [Principle], *viz.* the kingdom of this world, saith, Here we are at home, we must have it [so], that we may adorn and sustain the body, it must be [so]; and it taketh the region of the air, *viz.* its own spirit, and bringeth that [region] out at the mouth, and keepeth the [1] distinction according to the kingdom of this world.

[1] difference, or separation.

24. And thus there goeth forth out of the earthly [2] senses and mind, lies and folly, deceit and falsehood, [also] mere subtlety, [with lust and desire] to be elevated; many [to be elevated] in the might of the fire, as by force and anger; and many by human art and [3] policy of this world, [4] which is but a knave in the sight of God, yet wrestleth [or holdeth fast] till it hath prevailed; many in the form of a tame and gentle beast, very cunningly

[2] Or thoughts.

[3] Or virtue.

[4] world.

¹ Or colour of good.

alluring, and drawing to itself, under a ¹fair pretence; many in pride, and stateliness of body [in carriage] and manners, which is a right diabolical beast, who contemneth all that doth not please him, and elevateth himself above all meekness and humility, and over the image of God; yea, there is so very much of false untowardness, that I may not mention it; every one followeth the region [rule or dominion] of the stars, even that which serveth most to the voluptuousness of the earthly life.

² *In summa.*

³ Or genereateth no holy man.

25. ²In brief, the regimen of the stars [or starry region] ³maketh not a holy man; and although men may converse under a holy show, yet they are but hypocrites, and desire to get honour [and esteem] thereby, their mind sticketh nevertheless in covetousness and pride, and in fleshly pleasure, in mere base lechery and lust, and they are in the

⁴ will or lust.

sight of God (according to the ⁴ desire of this world) no other than mere knaves, proud, wilful, [self-conceited] thieves, robbers, and murderers. There is not one, who (as to the spirit of this world) is righteous, we are altogether children of deceit and falsehood; and according to this image (which we have received from the spirit of this world) we belong to eternal death, but not to paradise; except it be, that we become regenerated anew, out of the centre of the precious virgin, who with her rays averteth the mind from the ungodly ways of sin and wickedness.

26. And if the love of God (which so dearly

loved the image of man, that itself is become man)
did not stand in the centre of the mind in the
[midst or] [1] point of separation, then man had been
a living devil, and he is indeed such a one, when
he despiseth the regeneration, and [2] goeth on according to the inbred nature of the first and third
Principles.

[1] Or parting
limit or mark.

[2] Or departeth.

27. For there remain no more than two Principles eternally, the third [Principle] wherein he
liveth here, perisheth; and if he desireth not now
the second [Principle], then he must remain in the
first original eternally with the devils; for after
this time it will be no otherwise, there is no source
which can come to help him [hereafter]; for the
kingdom of God goeth not back into the abyss, but
it riseth up forward in the light of meekness; this
we speak seriously and in earnest, as it is highly
known in the light of nature, in the ray of the
[3] noble virgin.

[3] the wisdom
of God.

The Gate of the Difference between Man and Beast.

28. My dear and loving reason, bring thy five
senses hither, and consider thyself, according to
the things above-mentioned, what thou art, how
thou wast created the image of God, and how
thou in *Adam* (by the infection of the devil) didst
let thy spirit of this world take possession of thy
paradise, which now sitteth in the room of paradise.
Wilt thou say that thou wast created thus [as]

to this world in *Adam* at the beginning? Then behold and consider thyself; and thou shalt find another image in thy mind and speech.

¹ animal
or living
creature.
² of.

29. Every ¹beast hath a mind, ²having a will, and the five senses therein, so that it can distinguish therein what is good or ill for it. But where remain the senses in the will [that come] out of the gates of the deep, where the will discovereth itself [or glimmereth] in the first Principle *in infinitum* [infinitely], out of which the understanding proceedeth, so that man can see into all things into their essences, how high they are graduated, whereupon followeth the distinction [or different articulation] of the tongue? For if a beast had them, then it could also speak, and distinguish voices, and speak of the things that are in substance [or being], and search into the originality. But because it is not out of the eternal, therefore it hath no understanding in the light of nature, be it never so nimble and crafty; neither doth its strength and force avail to the lifting it up into understanding; no, it is all in vain.

30. Man only hath understanding, and his senses reach into the essences and qualities of the stars and elements, and search out the ground of all things in the region of the stars and elements: And this now hath its original in man, in the eternal element, he being created out of the [eternal] element, and not out of the out-births of the four elements. And therefore the eternity

seeth into the [1] beginning out-birth in the corrupti- [1] inceptive.
bility; and the [2] beginning in the out-birth cannot [2] Or inception.
see into the eternity, for the [2] beginning taketh its
original out of the eternity, out of the eternal mind.

31. But that man is so very blind and ignorant,
or void of understanding, is because he lieth
captive in the regimen [or dominion] of the stars
and elements, which many times figure [or fashion]
a wild beast in the mind of man, a lion, a wolf,
a dog, a fox, a serpent, and such like; though
indeed man getteth no such body, yet he hath
such a mind; of which Christ spake to the
Jews, and called some of them wolves, foxes,
and serpents. Also *John the Baptist* said so
of the Pharisees, and we see apparently, how
many men live wholly like beasts, according to
their bestial mind, and yet are so audacious, that
they judge and condemn those that live in the
image of God, and [3] subdue their bodies.   [3] tame, or bring under subjection.

32. But if he speaketh or judgeth anything well,
he speaketh not from the bestial image of the mind,
wherein he liveth, but he speaketh from the hidden
man, which is hidden in the bestial [man], and
judgeth against his own bestial life; for the hidden
law of the eternal nature standeth hidden in the
bestial man, and it is in a hard restraint, and judgeth
[or condemneth] the [malicious] wickedness of the
[4] carnal mind.   [4] fleshly.

33. Thus there are three in man that strive
against one another, *viz.* the eternal proud malicious

anger, [proceeding] out of the originality of the mind. And secondly, the eternal holy chaste humility, which is generated out of the originality. And thirdly, the corruptible animal, wholly bestial, generated from the stars and elements, which holdeth the whole house in possession.

34. And it is here with the image of man, as St *Paul* said, *To whom you give yourselves as servants in obedience, his servant you are, whether it be of sin unto death, or of the obedience of God unto righteousness*, that driving [or property] you have. If a man yield his mind up to malice, pride, self, power, and force, to the oppressing of the miserable, then he is like the proud, haughty devil, and he is his servant in obedience, and loseth the image of God; and out of the image cometh a wolf, dragon, or serpent to be, all according to his essences, as he standeth figured in the mind. But if he yield up himself to another swinish and bestial condition, as to a mere bestial voluptuous life, to gormandizing, gluttony, and drunkenness, and lechery, stealing, robbing, murdering, lying, cozening, and [cheating] deceit, then the eternal mind figureth him also in such an image as is like an unreasonable ugly beast and worm. And although he beareth the elementary image in this life, yet he hath indeed the image of an adder, serpent, and beast, hidden therein, which will be manifested at the breaking [or deceasing] of the body, and it belongeth not to the kingdom of God.

35. But if he give himself up to the obedience of God, and [1] yield his mind up into God, to strive against malice and wickedness, and the lusts and desires of the flesh, also against all unrighteousness of life and conversation, in humility under the cross, then the eternal mind figureth him in the image of an angel, who is pure, chaste, and virtuous, and he keepeth this image in the breaking of the body, and hereafter he will be married with the precious virgin, the eternal wisdom, chastity, and paradisical purity.

36. Here in this life he must stick between the door and the hinges, between the kingdom of hell, and the kingdom of this world, and the noble image must suffer much wrong [or be wounded], for he hath not only enemies outwardly, but also in himself; he beareth the bestial and also the hellish image of wrath in him, so long as this house of flesh [2] endureth.   Therefore that causeth strife and division against himself, and also without him, against the wickedness of the world, which the devil mightily [3] presseth against him, and tempteth him on every side, mis-leadeth, and wringeth him every where, and his own household in his body are his worst enemies; therefore the children of God are bearers of the cross in this world, in this evil earthly image.

37. Now behold, thou child of man, (seeing thou art an eternal spirit) thou hast this to expect after the breaking [or deceasing] of thy body; thou wilt

[1] Or unite.

[2] lasteth

[3] Or driveth.

be either an angel of God in paradise, or a hellish ugly diabolical worm, beast, or dragon; all according as thou hast [1] been inclined [or given to] here in this life; that image which thou hast borne here in thy mind, with that thou shalt appear; for there can no other image go forth out of thy body at the breaking [or deceasing of it], but even that which thou hast borne here, that shall appear in eternity.

[1] hast behaved thyself.

38. Hast thou been a proud vainglorious, selfishly potent, and one that hast for thy pleasure sake oppressed the needy, then such a spirit goeth forth from thee, and then so it is in the eternity, where it can neither keep nor get anything for [to feed] its covetousness, neither can it adorn its body with anything, but with that which is there, and yet it climbeth up eternally in its pride, for there is no other [2] source in it; and thus in its rising it reacheth unto nothing else but the stern might of the fire in its elevation; it inclineth itself in its will continually in such a purpose as it did in this world; as it was wont to do here, so all appeareth in its tincture, therein it climbeth up eternally in the abyss of hell.

[2] Or working rising property.

39. But hast thou been a base slanderer, liar, deceiver, false murderous man, then such a spirit proceedeth from thee, and that desireth in the eternity nothing else but mere falsehood; it spitteth out from its fiery jaws, fiery darts full of abomination and reproach; it is a continual stirrer and breaker in the fierce sternness, devouring in itself,

and consuming nothing; all its [things, beings, essences, works, or] [1] substances appear in its tincture: its image is figured according as its mind hath been here.

40. Therefore I say, a beast is better than such a man, who giveth himself up into the hellish images; for a beast hath no eternal spirit, its spirit is from the spirit of this world, out of the [2] corruptibility, and passeth away with the body, till [it cometh] to the figure without spirit, that [figure] remaineth standing; seeing that the eternal mind hath by the virgin of the eternal wisdom of God discovered itself in the out-birth, for the manifesting of the great wonders of God, therefore those [creaturely figures], and also the figured wonders, must stand before [3] him eternally; although no bestial figure or shadow suffereth or doth anything, but is as a shadow or painted figure [or limned picture].

41. Therefore in this world all things are given into man's power, because he is an eternal spirit, and all other creatures [are] no other than a figure in the wonders of God; and therefore man ought well to consider himself, what he speaketh, doth, and purposeth, in this world; for all his works follow after him, and he hath them eternally before his eyes, and liveth in them. Except it be, that he is again new regenerated out of evil and falsehood, through the blood and death of Christ, in the water and the Holy Ghost, and then he breaketh forth

[1] Or whatsoever he hath ever been.

[2] Or fragility.

[3] God or the eternal mind.

out of the hellish and earthly image, into an angelical [image], and cometh into another kingdom, into which its untowardness [or vices] cannot follow, and that [untowardness, waywardness, or vice] is drowned in the blood of Christ, and the image of God is renewed out of the earthly and hellish.

42. Thus we are to consider, and highly to know in the light of nature, the ground of the kingdom of heaven, and of hell, as also [the ground] of the kingdom of this world, and how man in the mother's body inheriteth three kingdoms, and how man in this life beareth a threefold image, which our first parents by the first sin [1] inherited for us; therefore we have need of the Treader upon the Serpent, to bring us again into the angelical image. And it is needful for man to tame his body and mind [or bring them under subjection], with great earnestness [and labour], and to submit himself under the cross, and not to hunt so eagerly after pleasure, riches, and the bravery of this world, for therein sticketh perdition.

43. Therefore said Christ, *A rich man shall hardly enter into the kingdom of heaven*; because they take such delight in pride, haughtiness, and fleshly voluptuousness, and the noble mind is dead to the kingdom of God, and continueth in the eternal darkness. For the image of the spirit of the soul sticketh in the mind; and to whatsoever the mind inclineth and giveth up itself, in that is

[1] Or purchased.

the spirit of the soul figured by the eternal
Fiat.

44. Now if the spirit of the soul remaineth
unregenerated in its first Principle (which it hath
inherited out of the eternity, with the beginning
of its life), then also (at the breaking [or deceasing]
of its body) there proceedeth out of its eternal
mind such a creature, as its continual will hath
been here in this life.

45. Now if thou hast had an envious [spiteful]
dogged mind, and hast grudged everything to
others, (as a dog doth with a bone which himself
cannot eat), then there appeareth such a doggish
mind, and according to that source [or property]
is its worm of the soul figured, and such a will
it keepeth in the eternity, in the first Principle.
And there is no revoking, all thy envious wicked
proud works appear in thy [1] source, in thy own [1] Or active property.
[2] tincture of the worm of the soul, and thou must [2] Or kindling.
live eternally therein ; nay, thou canst not conceive
or apprehend any desire [or will] to abstinence [or
forbearance of it], but thou art God's and the holy
souls' eternal enemy.

46. For the door of the deep to the light of
God appeareth to thee no more; for thou art
now a perfect creature in the first Principle.   And
now though thou dost elevate thyself, and wouldst
break open the door of the deep, yet that cannot
be [done]; for thou art a whole spirit, and not
merely in the will only, wherein the door of the

deep can be broken open; but thou fliest out aloft over the kingdom of God, and canst not enter in; and the higher thou fliest, the deeper thou art in the abyss, and thou seest not God yet, who is so near thee.

47. Therefore it can only be done here in this life (while thy soul sticketh in the will of the mind) so that thou breakest open the gate of the deep, and pressest in to God through a new birth; for here thou hast the highly worthy noble virgin of the divine love for thy assistance, who leadeth thee in through the gate of the noble bridegroom, who standeth in the centre in the parting [1] mark, between the kingdom of heaven, and the kingdom of hell, and generateth thee in the water and life of his blood and death, and therein drowneth and washeth away thy false [or evil] works, so that they follow thee not [in such a source and property], that thy soul be not [2] infected therein, but according to the first image in man before the fall, as a new, chaste, and pure noble virgin's image, without any knowledge of thy untowardness [or vices], which thou hadst here.

[1] Or limit of separation.

[2] Or figured therein.

48. Thou wilt ask, What is the New [3] Regeneration? Or how is that done in man? Hear and see, stop not thy mind, let not thy mind be filled by the spirit of this world, with its might and pomp. Take thy mind, and break through [the spirit of this world] entirely, [4] incline thy mind into the kind love of God; make thy purpose

[3] Or second birth.

[4] Or unite or give up thy mind.

earnest and strong, to break through the pleasure of this world with thy mind, and not to regard it; consider that thou art not at home in this world, but that thou art a strange guest, captivated in a close prison, cry and call to him, who hath the key of the prison; yield thyself up to him, in obedience, righteousness, modesty, chastity, and truth.   And seek not so eagerly after the kingdom of this world: it will stick close enough to thee without that; and then the chaste virgin will meet thee in thy mind, highly and deeply, and will lead thee to thy bridegroom, who hath the key to the gate of the deep; thou must stand before him, who will give thee to eat of the heavenly manna, which will [1] refresh thee, and thou wilt be strong, and struggle with the gate of the deep, and thou wilt break through as the [2] day-break; and though thou liest captive here in the night, yet the rays of the break of day will appear to thee in the paradise, in which place thy chaste virgin standeth, waiting for thee with the joy of the angels, who will very kindly receive thee in thy new-born mind and spirit.

[1] Or quicken.

[2] *Aurora,* morning-redness, or day-star.

49. And though indeed thou must [3] walk here with thy body in the dark [4] night among thorns and thistles (so that the devil and also this world doth rend and tear thee, and not only buffet, despise, deride, and vilify thee outwardly, but also many times stop thy dear mind, and lead it captive in the lust of this world into the bath [or

[3] swim or bathe.

[4] In contempt and disesteem.

lake] of swine), yet then the noble virgin will help thee still, and will call upon thee to desist from thy ungodly [1] ways.

[1] Or doings.

50. Look well to it, stop not thy mind and understanding; when thy mind saith Turn, do [2] it not, then know that thou art so called by the dear virgin; and turn instantly, and consider where thou art lodged, in how hard a house of bondage thy soul lieth imprisoned; seek thy native country, from whence thy soul is wandered, and whither it ought to return again.

[2] the evil.

51. And then if thou wilt follow [3] it, thou wilt find in thyself, not only after this life, but in this life also in thy regeneration, that she will very worthily meet thee, and out of what kind of spirit this author hath written.

[3] the counsel of the wisdom of God.

Printed in the United States
39434LVS00006B/11

9 780766 126022